Rich Boy Cries for Momma

Rich Boy Cries for Momma

Ethan H. Minsker

Copyright © 2012 by Ethan H. Minsker

Minsker & Lee Productions, LLC
126 East 12th Street, Suite 3C
New York, NY 10003

All rights reserved. No part of this book may be used or reproduced in any manner whatsoever, stored in a retrieval system, or transmitted, in and form or by any means, electronic, mechanical, photocopying, recording, or otherwise, without the written prior permission of Ethan H. Minsker except in the case of breif quotations embodied in critical articles of reviews.

While this book is based on real events, the names and other identifying characteristics of the persons appearing in this memoir have been changed and most are composite characters. Any resemblance between a person living or dead is purely coincidental. The sequence of events has been modified for dramatic effect.

Grateful acknowledgement is made to Kevin Cyr for the cover art, Ted Riederer for the inside and backcover art and Un Lee for the cover graphic art text. Back cover art is the property of Ted Riederer. All other artwork is the property of the author.

Manufactured in the United States of America

First Edition

ISBN: 978-0-615-72120-0

ANTAGONIST ART MOVEMENT
PROJECT # 1910

The Antagonists create venues that foster a community of artists. They push individuals who don't necessarily have a background in art to make art. They challenge the artists to antagonize others into creation. They believe that you do not have to be what others expect you to be. Any success of this book must be attributed to the Antagonists. They have provided me with editors, artists, and insight. They said I can, where others said I could not.

Rich Boy Cries for Momma is the first in a series of three books continuing with *Bar Stool Prophets* and ending with *The Antagonist*.

To learn more about the Antagonist Movement, please visit: www.youtube.com/watch?v=el3VSm71Ero and www.antagovision.com/

PREFACE

Maybe Father's sperm was bent; or maybe I got it from the lead pipes that delivered drinking water; or maybe my parents' highly intelligent genes canceled each other out. Whatever the reason, I was born dyslexic. Something was out of balance with the chemicals that made up my brain.

I was told that it was a gift, that many of the most brilliant, famous, and powerful had some form of dyslexia. But I also heard that ninety percent of the prison population had it too. I wasn't sure where I would fall in. When you're told your whole life that you're a retard, you either end up believing it or trying to prove them wrong.

But to know my story, you need to start at the root.

My parents were 60s radical, war-protesting hippies who happened to be lawyers. Mother had acted as a draft-evasion counselor during the Vietnam War, working the loopholes to help those who wanted out of the draft. Father graduated at the top of his class from Cornell. Later at Harvard, he served as Note Editor of the Harvard Law Review, graduating Magna Cum Laude.

In our family, Mother was the one who handed out the punishment, grounding or scolding. Stern when she needed to be, Mother was our father figure. Third generation Irish, with vivid blue eyes and blond hair, she embellished her stories. She was beautiful like the Northeast, and believed in following the law only when it benefited her.

After graduating from law school, my parents moved to Washington D.C., where Father became a clerk for Justice Harlan of the Supreme Court. He worked two consecutive years there, and then became a partner for a law firm where he continued to work for the next thirty years. Father was a handsome Jew with dark, wavy hair who was raised in Brooklyn, NY. Kind to a fault, gentle and forgiving, he would have given us everything he had just to make us happy, but the one thing we really wanted he didn't have: time. He never deviated from the law, even at the inconvenience of his family.

I was born on August 25th at 4:35 a.m. in Boston. They had to pull me out with forceps. The umbilical cord had been wrapped around my neck. Six pounds and deprived of oxygen, I was placed in an incubator for the first six days of my life--one more reason I may be dyslexic.

The next year my sister Anastasia was born. The day they brought her home, she was a tiny, white, doughy blob with piercing blue eyes. It seemed as though she already knew everything. It was like she had a moon in constant orbit around her head, that only I could see, that read: *what are you looking at dumbass*? She grew into a beautiful girl with fine straight blond hair and features that mirrored my own.

As a child I had no idea what politicians were, even though I was raised in Washington D.C., a city filled with them. Mother would point out that a certain father of a friend of mine was a senator of such-and-such a state, or that Father's law partners were advisors to Robert F. Kennedy. Growing up, I couldn't elaborate on the differences between the Left and the Right, but knew that Republicans were evil. Or at least that's what my parents would say.

Of all the statues and monuments, the Reflecting Pool best represents Washington as a city. The water is eternally stagnant. Garbage litters the pool bottom. A faint odor of swamp billows from the sludge that lines it. In the rest of the city, the bridges, lights and roads all need repair. The city is kept clean – the grass and hedges cut – but if you stop and really look, you see the decay.

The District was laid out in a spider web grid, organized and assembled into numerous streets and avenues: Nebraska Avenue, Wisconsin Avenue, Connecticut Avenue, New Mexico Drive. A city divided by a compass, four pieces of a square. Residents live in row houses, primarily having been built for returning troops of the Great War and working class families.

In the 80s, the city was changing but I barely noticed. It had become one of the most dangerous places a person could live, beating out Belfast, Beirut, New York, Detroit and Los Angeles. It held the title for Murder Per Capita, earning D.C. the nickname, "Dodge City." Nightly news reports depicted a rising murder rate, ending each broadcast with that day's body count added to the year's total.

The nation and the world perceived the Capital as the center of power and control, yet it was lawless and corrupt. Crack ruled supreme and even our mayor succumbed to the taste of the rock. Bribery was the city's standard operation. Underfunded and in search of Statehood, D.C. became a breeding ground for malcontents.

To be born and raised in three quarters of the city meant a life condemned to poverty or the lower-end of the middle-class. It was a distinction between public and private schools, between public transportation and owning your own car, between needing clothes to be given to you versus wearing what you wanted. For many of the kids who lived in three-fourths of the city, there were no choices, hope or future – just the Here and the Now.

I was told that my dyslexia was a gift, but I would learn that the true gift was being born to rich white parents who lived in Northwest.

It Starts

I was at a full sprint. My combat boots bashed against the sidewalk. My leather jacket was hot and the running wasn't helping me cool down. *Where are my friends?*, I remember thinking as I passed a girl who was lost in the music that piped in from her headphones. It was dark and I scanned the sides of the street for a place to hide. George Washington University campus was unfamiliar. We only went there for shows so I didn't have an escape route planned. Foot steps were coming up fast from behind me. *Fuck, just run! If I get caught again, my parents are going to kill me.*

"That's him!" I heard someone yell from the crowd. "The one with the red hair!"

Passing a window, I caught a glimpse of my hair, bright and spiked out like a match that had just been lit. I started laughing. Behind me were the three rent-a-cops, fat and having a hard time keeping up. I made a sharp turn and lost the first one. Her hat fell off and she went back to get it. The other two picked up the pace. With every step, the chain and padlock around my neck bounced, slapping my chest and knocking my chin. I was drunk and, at full speed, felt myself tiring out soon. I couldn't take in enough air and my muscles were giving up on me.

Years earlier...

"That lying bastard!" Father yelled at the top of his lungs towards the TV during the Watergate hearings. I hadn't seen my father angry before. He paced the living room like the lions I'd seen at the National Zoo. I sat there and watched. I didn't care what was happening on the TV. Father was more entertaining with his red face and hair in disarray. Docile by nature, Father was the most peaceful man I would ever know and seeing him angry was something new to me.

He had wavy dark brown, shoulder-length hair and a thick scrub-brush for a mustache with black-rimmed glasses, making him resemble something between a Beatnik and Groucho Marx.

"Send him to jail, that lying bastard!" he continued as Nixon's face flashed across the TV. Not too long after, Nixon hired father's firm to represent him personally. Eventually, Father would spend 20 years working on the Nixon tapes lawsuit.

"I can't raise the children by myself," said Mother, her eyes fixed on Father.

He barely looked up from the TV.

"Let's get some help. Maybe my mother could move in," he suggested.

Mother raised an eyebrow. "That's not going to happen."

We were at our home on Tennyson Street in Chevy Chase D.C. The house was basic: two floors with a basement and a front and back yard. It looked like every other home on the block except for the white wash paint on the bricks out front. Mother did it herself, but never stripped off the old paint so now it was peeling. Our front lawn was covered with flecks of white paint.

Sister was 4. I was 5. For the moment I was happy. I didn't want anything to change. I liked having Mother around. But Mother didn't like working only part time.

My parents raised Sister and me on Dr. Spock, television, and Coca-Cola. They worked even on the weekends. Sister and I spent more time together than our parents did.

"Children, here is your new nanny, Patsy," said Mother one day. A young black woman was standing next to her. Patsy had full round lips, a round head, round breasts, and a small round belly hovering over her round hips. She was circles stacked on top of circles. Thinking back on it later, I realized she was attractive. Sister stood behind me, peering over my shoulder at the new nanny.

Patsy kneeled down to our height and smiled, "It's nice to meet you," she said in a Caribbean accent. She held her hand out and I shook it.

"I'm off to work," said Mother and she was out the door.

"When you're hungry, let me know," Patsy said as she stood up. "I'm going to do some cleaning." She looked around the room. "Maybe you two could show me where the vacuum is?" She made the beds and brought the laundry down to the basement. She didn't tell us to do anything. After the first week, Sister and I were used to being with her. One day she was making the Parents' bed when I walked in the room and sat on the floor.

"Where do you live?" I asked. She jumped a little and turned to me, grabbing at her chest.

"Baby, you scared me... Where am I from? Trinidad. And here I live in the Southeast," she said, picking up the dirty sheets and heading towards the closed door, "Gentlemen open the door for ladies. Could you get the door for me, Baby?"

I ran over and opened it, trailing behind her to the basement. She put the sheets in the washing machine, flipped the switch to on, then glanced around the room, picked up the bottle of detergent and shook it. Empty. She started sucking her teeth.

"What's that you're doing?" I said.

"What's what, Baby?"

"That noise you're making with your mouth?"

"It's something us tropical people do when we are mad," she said and then I tried to suck my teeth too.

"I'm hungry," I said.

"Baby, you need to learn the polite way to ask for things. Like 'May I please have something to eat?' and when someone does something for you, you need to say 'Thank you'. And if I say 'Thank you' you need to say 'You're welcome'. When you treat people with respect, you get respect back." She led me upstairs and made me a peanut butter and jelly sandwich, cut down the middle, with a glass of orange juice on the side.

"Thank you," I said.

"You're welcome."

I sat at the counter top that ran along the wall. The wall was covered with ugly prints of faded nautical themed clip art. Bubbles had formed from years of humid summers. Sunlight cascaded through the branches of the neighbor's trees and our small window which formed a patch work of shadows along the floor and sink. Patsy peeled me an orange. I slipped the triangles in my mouth while Patsy ate the peel.

"Why you eating that?" I said.

"There are more vitamins in the peel," Patsy said with a grin.

I walked into the living room. Sister sat on the floor. She handed me a pair of dull, child safe plastic scissors and asked me to cut off her hair.

"It's too long. I want it to be like yours," she said. Sister had a collection of dolls forced on her by our parents. She had never seemed interested in them until she cut off all their hair.

"You do it." I dropped the scissors. It looked more like work than fun.

"I can't see in the back." She picked up the scissors and placed them in my hand, then turned away from me. I wondered what it would have been like to be a barber. Snipping at the hair, it fell onto my feet. I kicked it off, then cut until no more large clusters were left. Then, I had a funny feeling like maybe I shouldn't be doing this so I stopped.

Her hair was uneven and dramatically shorter than mine.

Then Patsy looked in the room.

"Oh boy, what have you done!" she said, sucking through her teeth. Sister looked at herself in the mirror.

"Thanks Brother." She couldn't see the patch in the back that reached down to her scalp.

Mother's car pulled up front. Patsy had been sitting in the living room with us, but she looked outside every time she heard a car. By the time the car door shut, Patsy was already out front. Sister and I watched from the window. Patsy was saying something and pointed back at the house then at her own head. Mother tilted her head and glanced at us looking at her. They both came in and walked into the room where we were.

"What a beautiful haircut you have," said Mother and smiled, but that night she shaved off the rest, making it even, except the part in the back.

Father got home late and started fighting with Mother again. Sister and I were already in our beds.

"All you have to do is come home and spend some time with me," I heard Mother say. Every fight started out in a whisper, but over hours would grow into an all-consuming yelling match. Hateful words tumbled up the stairs, down the hall, and finally found their way underneath my door, passing through the pillow pressed against my head. I could only hear the bass notes, but they still kept me from sleep.

I tried drifting off, but woke to the noise of their bedroom door closing. The fighting had stopped. The house was quiet and lonely. The floors creaked and I was scared. I stopped asking my parents if I could sleep on their floor weeks ago when the fighting first started. I stepped softly, hoping not to alert the monsters, axe murderers, and Republicans that lurked downstairs when everyone was asleep. I tapped on Sister's open door.

"Brother, what do you want?" She sounded tired and annoyed.

"Can I sleep on your floor?"

"Sleep on your own floor."

"Please."

"Fine. Just be quiet." She sounded older than she was, like a grumpy old man.

The floor was hard on my belly. Wrapping myself like a burrito in my comforter provided some cushioning. If axe-wielding Republicans burst into her room, I would save her. I didn't care what happened to me. I didn't want to be left as the only one alive. I didn't want to watch the rest of my family die, even though I didn't really know what it meant to die. I thought that when you died it was like being sent to your room for a time out, but when the time was done you could come back out. Death wasn't real.

Maybe the fighting was making me nervous. Mother and Father weren't playful any more. They spent most of their time brooding in different corners of the house. Our family was changing and I didn't like change. It made me feel bad and I wanted to protect Sister.

I fell asleep, waking with morning's first light. Climbing into my own bed, I hoped Sister would forget I slept in her room. She might complain but she still looked out for me. Later, when they discovered I was dyslexic, she would be the first to stick up for me. Even when we fought, we still loved each other. When our parents fought it didn't seem like they loved each other. They didn't say they were sorry when it was over and they didn't forget why they were mad.

That fall, at elementary school, the first grade classes were divided into breaks for snacks and naps. I watched the other kids as they did their schoolwork, then looked down at my own. I didn't understand what to do; I never did. It seemed so easy for them, just like how it was easy for Sister. This is not fair, I thought. Why can't I do this? Was there something I missed that could help me?

"Just match the words with the pictures," said the teacher, noticing I hadn't done anything. "When you're finished, you can go out and play," she said with a smile, and walked off to check on other students. The image on the page was simple black line art. I looked hard at the paper; if I could, I would have set it ablaze. What was the right answer? I knew the image was a dog – it looked like a dog I had seen. But the letters arranged to mean dog meant nothing to me. I tapped my pencil, closed my eyes and cleared my mind. Letters floated in a jumble like a tangled fishing net and I couldn't untangle it. I could hear foot steps as kids quietly exited the room. I pulled a D from the tangle, but then I heard muffled laughter carried in from the playground. I opened my eyes and noticed I was alone. The rest of the class had moved outside and I could hear them playing. The teacher gazed at me curiously. I just wanted to play.

"Do your best," she said. Time was running out. I thought, if she just wants me to connect the image to a word I could do that. I methodically connected any picture with a word and ran out the door. The system worked and the next day I was one of the first to make it outside to play. I was back in control; the other kids were the slow ones. How come they didn't do the same thing? It was so easy, I was smarter than everyone, and the anxiety was held at bay. In the second week, my teacher stood beside me as I waited for Mother to pick me up.

"Did I do something wrong?"

"No dear, I just need to talk with your mother," she said. "Everything is fine."

There was a light rain and it felt nice on my face. Just beyond the school, the sounds of rush hour traffic whooshed down Wisconsin Avenue. I wanted to be in that traffic heading home. Mother turned the corner and pulled up in front of us.

"I have some concerns about your son," the teacher said, using that serious voice that I had learned to watch out for. "I think he may have a learning disability. I just read an article about it so I'm no expert, but you should consider getting your son tested." The teacher didn't realize it but she had just set the course of my life and everything good or bad would stem from an article she happened to read.

The Great Liberal Experiment

EMBRACE
 "Building"
  I can't get what I want
  I'm a failure
  Nothing I do ever seems to work out

And so started the Great Liberal Experiment. Soon after my parents took me to New York City for a weekend of tests to find out what was happening in my brain. By the second day, I wanted to go home. It felt like punishment. Maybe it was because I cheated and didn't do the work the way they wanted. I sat in a small chair as a man in a white lab coat flipped through cards with simple words. The room was white, with a long mirror that faced me. Overhead were fluorescent lights. One of the bulbs flickered, and the floor was an institutional gray carpet that was threadbare in spots from being vacuumed too many times. The man sitting across from me glanced up from the cards he held and waited for me to continue. I looked at the cards. They were white and slightly stained at the edges. The text was black, basic, and bold. Words as simple as CAT, BAT, and SAT. Trying to read for any extended time drained my strength. My eyes blurred and burned. The muscles in my fingers and shoulders tightened.

"Keep going. You're doing fine. Say the words as I flip the cards," he said and I did my best to stumble along. I sounded out what I could: Cha, Stra, Grrr.

When he was done, he left the room and I was alone. The room was cold. The bare skin on my shin brushed against the stainless steel leg of the chair and it stung lightly. *Why are they doing this to me? This isn't fair. I want to go home. Where is Sister? How come she isn't being tested? Why can't she be the stupid one?* A new man came in carrying a box of blocks with numbers on them and a few other odd contraptions. But I was busy watching his ears. They were large and wiggled as he talked. I wanted to touch them and even reached for one, but he took my hand and put it on a peg. I was supposed to move it around a board. It was supposed to help my hand-eye coordination, in relation to the way I scanned text across a page.

"We are going to test your motor skills," said the man but I didn't know what he meant. On the last day of tests, Father took me to F.A.O. Schwarz and let me pick out some toys. New York was crowded, dirty, and the people were strange. *I will never live here. This place smells like pee.* I just wanted to go home. My anxiety was like a thick rope around my midsection and, the more I struggled against it, the tighter it would become.

"I'm sorry I didn't do good at school," I said to Father. We were walking down 42nd Street back to our hotel. The pedestrians who had walked past us looked mean. No one made eye contact. It was like I was invisible. A dirty man sat cross-legged in the middle of the sidewalk. He held up a sign written in thick black marker on cardboard. His writing was shaky which didn't help my inability to understand the words. But from the look on his face and the way he held his open palm out, I could tell he wanted money from Father. Father wouldn't see him unless he was Nixon.

"Don't be sorry," he said. "You didn't do anything wrong. We just want to make sure you have the best possible chance in life. You are different, that's all."

"I want to be normal. I don't want to be different." Tears were welling up in the corners of my eyes but, since I hadn't cried all day, I didn't want to start now so I took in a long breath through my nose and settled down.

"Both your mother and myself have had learning problems. You just inherited it from both sides."

"So it's your fault."

He laughed. "I guess so."

Back in D.C., I had to keep doing the exercises with the peg and half wheel. They gave me a new diet to propel my jumbled thinking into order. They played with the lighting to see if it had any effect, but it just made things darker. The researchers, doctors and assistants looked official in their lab coats, but I was suspicious of them. How could they know what it was like to be me and, if they didn't, they couldn't fix it.

Sister was jealous of the attention I was getting. But she would have gotten over it quickly if our parents handed her the half wheel and made her move pegs around it for half an hour. I told her I didn't want to be different but she just said, "Why do you get gifts and get to go to New York?"

Patsy drove me in her muscle car. It was dark green with an FM radio. She liked to listen to the top 40 stations. A Diana Ross song was playing; the lyrics spoke of her love spinning around. It was disco, and I hummed the tune even though I didn't know the words.

"I don't want to go. Can't I stay in the car with you?"

"Baby, can't you see your parents are trying to help? Make sure you can do the things you want to do in your life. You're special."

"I just want to be normal."

"That's all your parents want too. This is going to help your hand-eye coordination."

"What is that?"

"Something about seeing something and doing it."

I held my hand in front of my face and wiggled the fingers to see if there was a problem. They seemed to work fine. *Stupid doctors.*

She walked me into the building with an indoor pool and brought me to the college student who was more concerned with the girl he was talking with than me standing there with Patsy. The college student was thin with bad posture. He looked like a green bean wearing shorts. The hall smelled of chlorine. The floors were tiled. I was already in my swim shorts. Patsy took my shoes off and pulled my shirt over my head.

"He's signed up for the swim class," said Patsy to the instructor. The college kid led me away. I watched Patsy walk out the door. Her jeans were very tight and I wondered if she was comfortable walking in them.

"I'll be back in an hour, Baby," she said and was gone.

"Well, everyone has a natural ability to swim, so we throw the kids in and they start swimming on their own," said the instructor to the girl.

"Then what do they need you for?"

"I'm here if they don't swim."

I was feeling bad about his plan. I didn't swim when I was at the beach. I didn't think I would do any better at the pool. There were other kids my age doggie paddling in the shallow end of the pool.

The college kid picked me up under my arms, holding me over the deep end. I looked down at the clear water. My feet dangled, wanting ground to touch. The sounds of other kids and the water splashing bounced and echoed off the tiled walls and mixed into odd sounds.

"You ready?" he said in my ear, but before I could say "No," he threw me into the middle of the deep end. My arms and legs grabbed at nothingness. Crashing the surface and being submerged in the lukewarm water, I opened my eyes and wiggled my arms in a circle as I sank to the bottom. I heard a second splash and felt arms wrapping around me, lifting me to the surface and handing me to the college girl.

I started to cry with snot bubbles and deep burst of breathing in between sobs.

"Why didn't you swim?" he asked.

"I don't know how." For the next hour I sat off to the side watching the other kids swim.

When Patsy picked me up, I was still sobbing.

"They tried to kill me."

"Who? The other kids?"

"No, the teacher."

I told Mother what had happened, and she went to the school the next day. I waited at the entrance as she walked over to the college boy. Calmly but sternly, she spoke to him.

"If I wanted to drown my son, I could do it in the bath tub. You should start at the shallow end and let them put their faces in the water so they get used to the feel of the water." I didn't go back to the swimming class.

I didn't like being thrown in the water, and drowning wasn't much fun either.

A few days later, I crawled into the back seat of Patsy's car as we headed downtown.

"You didn't like the swimming, Baby?"

"No."

"Well, everybody got to be swimming some day so you best learn when you can." She stopped the car in front of a small building with a dance school on the second floor.

"Does your car have a name?" I asked.

"Yes. Bubba," she said and led me into the building. The room had wood floors and a wall of mirrors with a stretching bar. The rest of the class were girls and right away I wanted to leave, but Patsy was gone. I didn't know what ballet was or why I had to have on a leotard. The girls bunched together in the corner and giggled at me. The instructor showed me the first position, plié, and a few other moves I wish I could forget.

"He's so cute with long blond hair," said one of the older girls. It was humiliating, but I did what I was told and kept quiet. It was in my second week that the school burned to the ground and I stopped going.

"I would suspect my son as the arsonist if it wasn't electrical," said Mother over the phone to my grandfather. She turned to me to see what my reaction was but since I didn't know what an arsonist was I had none. "...He needs to work on his motor skills... Well, it's affected by his dyslexia... No, he won't become a homosexual if he learns to dance," she went on.

I walked into the other room. I didn't want to be dyslexic.

"Come over here, Baby," said Patsy. I laid my head down on her lap and she ran her fingers through my hair, twirling and untwirling as she watched "Good Times". I fell asleep.

"Where are we going today?" I asked Patsy.

"Baby, you're going to a new school, special for you." Her car was almost an army green so I pretended it was a fast moving tank and nothing could penetrate its armor. We could roll over the cars in front of us or blast through walls to cut corners. Then I imagined both sides of Connecticut Avenue were lined with soldiers saluting us. But the closer we got to downtown, they slowly changed from soldiers to ballerinas. A special school for me, didn't sound normal. My stomach started tensing up and my palms began to sweat. The ballerinas faded into pedestrians on their way to work.

"I like my old school." I didn't want to go to a new school. I just wanted things to stay the same.

We drove to Dupont Circle. I felt far from home. I looked out of the car at the school as Patsy went around and opened my door. It was an old three story Victorian with details on the front made of concrete. A few older students lingered on the front stoop. One had sneakers with Velcro instead of laces. Another kid's head was oddly shaped like a twisted peanut.

"Will you stay with me?" I asked.

"I can't, Baby," she said and took me by the hand. "I'm too old to be going to your school, but I'll be right here when you get out." I watched her as she walked back to the car and drove off. I could feel the pressure building in my chest. What were they going to do with me? I wondered if there would be more tests like in New York. I wanted to be home.

In the lobby was a box with a pair of tennis shoes sticking out.

"What's that?" I pointed at the shoes and they moved around. They were still on someone's feet.

"Oh that's the Time-Out Box," said the teacher who then took me to a room. "Paul has a knack for getting in trouble." The teacher stopped in front of one of the kids, maybe 13 years-old, who was out front smoking. He had on a red and white striped rugby shirt with blue jeans and wore a pair of Chuck Taylors. His hair was coarse and black, with a crew cut. He was barrel-chested. His brow furrowed as his gaze landed on me.

"This is Sermon," she said. "He's going to show you around the school." He smiled until the teacher left the room.

"Okay, shit bag, follow me," he said, then slapped me on the top of my head when I didn't move fast enough. Right away I was scared of him, and I started feeling dizzy. We walked up the three flights, peeking into classes. The building was old and wasn't built to be a school. It looked like a rich family had lived there once. An older kid with white spiky hair, a beaten t-shirt and jack boots walked past us, unaware of our presence. A kid wearing a maroon Washington Redskins t-shirt stood outside the door. Sermon stopped before him and held out his open palm. The kid reluctantly dug in his pocket retrieving a crumpled dollar bill and handed it over to Sermon, who then smiled and poked the kid in the stomach with his index finger making the kid fold in half. Sermon left me in a class with kids around my age.

"See ya later, shit bag," he said and was gone.

"He's a dick," said the kid sitting next to me. He was a black kid with short cropped hair and the collar stood up on his Izod shirt. His eyebrows were thick and bushy.

"Pierre, do you need a time out?" said the teacher.

"No," said Pierre, and then he smiled at me.

My new friend, I thought.

It was The Lab School of Washington D.C., whose name in itself implied an establishment for the abnormal. It was a school for dyslexics. There were no grades. The classes were divided into groups. It was a tactic they used so that, when we tried to compare ourselves with other schools, we couldn't tell how far behind we were.

The student body at the Lab School was a cross-section of the city itself. Rich or poor, it didn't matter. If you couldn't make the grade within the standard school system, you were dumped at the Lab School. My classmates commonly lied to other kids about where they spent their days, naming any school but their own. The shame of being dyslexic was felt in and out of school. Pierre switched school names depending on who he was talking to.

When I got home, all I wanted to do was forget about school but the first thing Patsy said was:

"You should do your homework and exercises."

"I need to take the dog for a walk first."

Our dog Pepper was a mute with hair colored like salt and pepper. He was abnormal like me and I had never seen another dog like him. Pepper gave me an odd look when I held the leash in front of him, since I had never walked him before. We just let him go in the back yard. We went out front to play when some of my neighborhood friends came over.

"I heard you're going to a school for retards," one kid who lived up the block said. He was a rotund white kid with bad acne who always smelled of onions. His father was a senator.

"What do you mean?"

"You go to the Lab School right?" said another-- gangly tall kid with bright red hair that always dangled in his face. His father was some kind of judge.

"Yeah."

"What's the matter with you?" said a girl, whose father was a surgeon. I had a crush on her. She had a cherub face framed by straight black hair with bangs. She smelled of baby powder.

"I don't know. They said I'm learning disabled."

"Hi, I'm LLLLLLL...DDDDD....," said the kid from up the block as he contorted his arm slowly, swinging it back and forth for effect.

"I have to go," I said, pulling Pepper by the leash, and went back inside. Why did that stupid teacher have to say anything to Mother, I thought. Now everyone thinks I'm stupid. I started to tear up. Why can't my parents just leave me alone?

Patsy was vacuuming the living room when she saw me walk in.

"What's the matter, Baby? Why aren't you playing with your friends?"

"I just don't feel like it." I went up to my room.

"You need to be doing your exercises," she yelled after me. I picked up the half circle and placed it on the bridge of my nose, then moved the pegs around for close to a half hour. Sister walked by my room, looking in.

"No one's watching," she said. "Just say you did it."

I threw it in my closet. I never picked it up again.

It was two days later that I was sitting in a small white room in a building owned by the District of Columbia's public school system in Northeast. It was 8 am.

"As your school is paid for by city funding, you have to be tested every three years," said an older black man. His skin looked scaly. "The test lasts two days and is broken into segments: verbal, math, comprehension, and visual." I looked around the room for an exit in case I felt like running, but there was only a window that had a wire gate over it. I imagined what it would feel like if I tried to pry it open with my fingers.

"Okay. I want you to look at this picture. Then with these blocks, I want you to reassemble these blocks to match the picture," he said.

It was easy and I finished fast.

"Okay. I'm going to say some numbers in random order. I want you to repeat them back to me as you hear them."

At first I had it down, but the man kept adding digits, and I lost track at five. The tests frustrated me and even though having them meant getting out of school early, I would have rather gone to class.

When the second day was over, Mother was waiting for me when the man led me out.

"I have to go over the test, but from the information I have so far he exceeds the average college student's comprehension and understanding of complex theories," he told her. I knew that college was school for older kids. If I was doing better than them, it was a good thing. 'Comprehension' I didn't know, so I discarded it. Often, when I heard words I didn't understand, I would do my best to gather meaning from the words I did know and bridge the gap. There was a compliment in there and I felt a little bump of pride.

"But he is far below the norm when it comes to reading, writing, and math. He has difficulties with codes and symbols and their relationships between representation and meaning. Symbols with arbitrary meanings make no sense to him. Without a story, history or theory, his brain doesn't latch onto the abstract." *It's just random.* Then, I started thinking. *So someone made up what everything means and because I can't relate to it now I'm the strange one. If I was born before reading and math was invented, no one would have known.*

On the way home, Mother said to me, "You're a genius trapped by the arbitrary meaning of symbols in relation to language." She seemed proud of me. Maybe she needed to hear I wasn't retarded. I would have traded being a genius for reading normally.

I laid down in the back seat. My head hurt and I needed to close my eyes. They were sore from trying to read all day.

Father pulled out the knob, turning on the Sony color television. The TV flickered and made a popping sound; it came to life mid-sentence. The newscaster spoke of war. Vietnam was wrapping up and Cambodia was the newest hot spot. Images of fire, smoke, explosives, angry men and dead bodies splashed onto the screen. Father sat on the beat-up, second-hand couch he'd bought the week before from the Salvation Army. Holding his plate in his lap, he began cutting his steak into small cubes. After lancing each piece with his fork, he drowned it in an extra-large side of mustard. Like one of those cranes at a construction site, he proceeded to eat like a machine.

"The guerillas have strongholds in the northern province," the TV narrated.

"Why are the gorillas fighting?" I asked Father. A war between man and monkey. Well, why not? I'd seen Sigmund the Sea Monster; he lived in a cave and was on TV too.

"They're fighting over Communism. We want their people to have the right to choose their leaders." Mustard was dripping from the corner of his mouth. He ate too fast.

Walter Cronkite read off the day's numbers of those K.I.A., wounded, and missing.

"What's K.I.A.?" I was pointing at the TV.

"Killed in Action." His mouth was full.

A day later, at school, one of the teachers brought over a kid.

"This is Dash. He's new. I want you to show him around the school." She walked away and I just stared at Dash. He was chubby with blond curly hair and thick black-rimmed glasses.

"Hi," he said.

"Hi," I said.

I stared at him some more. He looked sad and scared. I felt the same way when I first got there.

"You want to make paper guns?" I said.

"Okay." I took plain white paper and rolled it into tight solid tubes, then cut and reassembled them with tape. Dash watched then copied what I had just done, but the roll was too thick.

"No, like this," I said and rolled him a tube. It was tight and hard. Dash took a piece of tape and wrapped it around the middle so it wouldn't unwind. The gun had a handle barrel and trigger with a rubber band on one end so it could shoot paper clips. When we had finished, Dash admired what he had just made. It was clear this was his first paper gun.

After school the next day, Dash and I were playing guerrilla war at my house. Dash didn't mind playing the Viet Cong. We tossed sharpened throwing stars at trees. If one bounced and either of us caught it, that person would get another chance to throw. We didn't wear protective gear, eyewear or gloves. We didn't think about getting hurt. Death didn't mean anything; it wasn't real.

It was fall, and Mother and Father headed home driving through Rock Creek Park, which runs the length of the city and deep into Maryland. Turning on its winding roads, the parents felt as if they were in a deep forest. They felt like they did before having two kids and full-time careers. Sister and I were at home with Patsy and there was nothing to worry about. Mother looked over at Father. He was mumbling quietly to himself, going over an argument on Nixon's behalf. But instead of bringing it up, she let him have this moment. Why bother she thought, he'll never change. He couldn't, even if he wanted too. She went back to watching the scenery go by. An occasional house peeked through the trees. It was quiet, with a warm breeze passing through the crack of Mother's open window.

The sedan coming from the opposite direction crossed over the double line and veered towards my parents' yellow Ford Pinto. Father was driving and turned the car off the road so that his side took the impact. Rigid metal folded like paper wadded up under the weight of a fist. Mother's window exploded when it embraced the stone wall. Two cars in motion came to an abrupt stop; the side of the Pinto was crushed. If Father had not veered, Mother would have been dead. She crawled out the front window and suffered just cuts, scrapes, and a few bruises. She scrambled to the other side calling out Father's name. The door of the Pinto had forced Father halfway into the car. The driver's side and the passenger seat had become one. Standing on the road facing on-coming traffic, Mother waved down the first approaching car. The driver stopped and told her he was going to get help and sped off. Mother ran back to Father and shouted through the smashed windshield.

"Can you hear me?"

Father slumped over the twisted steering wheel, blood trickling down his side. He tried to move, but was trapped.

"I'm okay."

"You're not okay. You have a car folded around you."

"I'll be okay."

"You better be."

The park police showed up a moment later and then an ambulance followed. Father spent the next few days in the hospital, and for the next year he would have to sleep on a board to heal his back. The driver of the sedan was a 17-year-old kid, who already had several DUI convictions.

Death was something I couldn't perceive. It wasn't even an abstract idea presented on the nightly news or in the movies I watched. I needed elaboration, so I brought the idea to Mother – the all seeing, all knowing mother.

"What happens when you die? What happens to those army men who die on the news?" I asked her, my big blue eyes peering out from my blond locks. She rubbed her arms, still bruised from the accident.

"Well," she said, "Some people believe when you die you go to heaven. Others believe you are reincarnated. You could come back as a cat or a cricket."

"What do you believe?" My mind was wide open. Each word and thought was etched into the tender recesses of my pre-pubescent brain.

"I think when you die, it's the end. Everything just goes black," she said very matter-of-factly.

"And then what?" This was her chance to discount her last statement or perhaps soften it, dilute it with other opinions.

"Nothing. There's nothing else. It's just over, like at the end of a movie or when you walk out of a room and turn the lights out."

I tried to imagine what it was like to be dead. I closed my eyes and sat quietly. After that, I didn't go out. I was afraid of getting a cut or breaking a bone. An infection would be the end of me. Watching the news one night, a story was covered on how a family had died when the coolant from their air conditioner leaked and infected their drinking water. I stopped drinking tap water and restricted myself to drinking orange juice from frozen concentrate. It wasn't until I made the discovery that Mother prepared it with tap water that I switched to canned Coca Cola. At night I lay in bed, eyes open, staring at the ceiling, afraid that if I went to sleep I might never wake up. Mother and Father fought downstairs in lowered voices. It had been a few months since the drunk driver had hit them. The fighting had stopped for a while, but since they both felt better, the war began again. I cupped my hands over my ears, wanting to drown them out. I rolled over onto my stomach and tried to push everything out of my mind by thinking of other things.

"Here you go," said Father as he walked in the house carrying two black mixed-breed puppies. Our first dog, Pepper, had died the year before. The puppies yelped at each other and then looked at me and Sister. It was Spring. The trees were already a vibrant green. We were outside in the large back yard. From the porch, I could see the hole in the ground where Dash and I had dug a fort. Father didn't notice. His face was awash with joy as the two puppies licked his bearded cheeks.

"Something is going to happen," said Sister flatly. She never showed emotion. She was seven, and I was eight.

"What do you mean?" I said.

"Whenever they get us dogs, it means they are planning something." She was always suspicious of the Parents like they were the enemy. In some ways I agreed. They were the ones in control of everything we did and their choices always seemed unfair or without reason.

When it was time for bed, Father made sure we were under the covers. He left my door open since he knew if he closed it, I would just open it again. He went in his room. A few minutes later their door opened and Father shuffled out, carrying his pillow.

"Well it was your great idea to buy the dogs!" barked Mother as Father went downstairs to sleep on the couch.

At school, I sat at my desk fighting off sleep. I couldn't keep my eyes open. I was like a zombie because my parents argued and screamed at each other all night every night. Why couldn't they just get along? Why did they even have us or get married? I blamed myself. Just by being born, Sister and I were driving them apart, or really we were the only reason they had stayed together so long. Or was it that my dyslexia added too much pressure to the already fragile relationship?

What they really wanted was to work all the time, to never come home, and concentrate on their careers.

"You act like Nixon is more important than my job," said Mother downstairs. It was Monday night. I could hear the dogs crying in the kitchen.

"That's not true, but I'm in the middle of the case. You, of all people should understand."

"I understand that you are never here and it's like I'm the only parent. Do you know what that's like? Can you understand what you are doing to me and the kids?"

"You work too!"

"I went to law school just like you! I have dreams just like you! What happened to you're becoming a law professor?"

"It doesn't pay as well and I'm lucky to have this job."

"You can have any job you want. You chose this one."

Then, I heard Sister voice at the top of the stairs just outside my room.

"Be quiet! You are keeping me up again. I have school!" She was almost screaming. The parents fell silent. Sister's foot steps slapped the floor on the way back to her room. Her door closed hard. The arguing downstairs turned back to a low muffle. A little while later, I fell asleep.

"We need to tell you something," said Mother. Her arms were crossed, and when she realized it, she unfolded her arms and let them hang loose at her sides. It was the morning. Her long blond hair framed her face. Her position was steadfast.

"Your mother and I are getting a divorce," said Father. His beard looked unmanaged and his hair was disheveled. His eyes were puffy, red with black circles.

"What's that?" I said.

"We will live in separate houses," said Mother.

"Good," said Sister. She seemed unaffected.

"I don't understand," I said and started to cry.

After they told us they were getting divorced, Sister and I were brought to see a child psychiatrist. The result would determine who would go with which parent, or if we should stay together with one home as the primary residence. I was sick of all the testing for my dyslexia, but at my parents urging I went in to see the psychiatrist anyway. Sister went in first, then me. He brought out dolls, had us draw, and asked many stupid questions.

"Do you like school?" He asked then scratched his nose. It was a giant lumpy nose and I wondered if he could smell more than me. "What is your favorite thing to do after school?" Talking to him was like talking to a friend's mother--boring and uncomfortable.

After the test, my parents had been brought into the room and went over the results.

"I asked your son if he was stuck on an island with wild and dangerous animals, who he would want to protect him. What do you think he said?"

Both parents answered the same, "Me." "Your son said Muhammad Ali. When I had your daughter draw a picture of her family, it was of her and her brother, neither of you were in it. I recommend that you keep them together and send him to a therapist. He seems to be taking it harder than her."

In the car on the way home, Sister mentioned her drawing. "I wasn't finished and didn't have time to do Mother and Father." The instructions were to draw the family so she would have done just that. I had taken enough tests to know they always underestimated the mind of a child. If they asked her to draw, in order, the family members she most loved, it would have been me, Father, then Mother. Sometimes I thought Sister hated Mother just because they were alike.

It was the end of summer. I went into the back yard and the dogs were gone. I ran inside to tell Patsy that they had been stolen.

"No, Baby," she said. "Your parents took them back to the pound."

I waited until Father came home. He walked in the door carrying his leather case filled with the same papers and yellow legal pads that he took with him every day.

"Where are the dogs?" I stomped my foot. My fists were balled up at my sides. *He had no right to take our dogs. You can't give something and then take it back.* It's not fair. I was sick of them just doing whatever they wanted.

"Son, they were very sick with heartworms and there was nothing they could do."

"Where are they?" My voice was breaking.

"I took them back to the pound."

"You can't do that! They are ours, not yours!"

"They were suffering," he said, almost pleading.

"Go get them. Right now!"

"I can't. They were put to sleep."

"Go wake them up and bring them back!"

"They can't be woken up. The Vet gave them a shot so they would stay asleep."

The big black void was chasing me again.

"You took our dogs and killed them!"

"It was the humane thing to do," said Father but I was already going upstairs to tell Sister what they had done.

A week went by with Sister and me mad at the parents. We had always been a team when we needed to be.

Father drove us to a pet store in Wheaton, Maryland.

"Are you sure these dogs are okay?" said Father to the clerk. "I heard that dogs in pet stores are crazy from having people looking at them from behind the glass." Sister and I looked at the round, stumbling puppies.

"That one," I said, pointing at what looked like a cotton ball. Sister found an ugly gray kitten. It looked flea bitten and its hair was out of place. When she heard that no one wanted it and the pet store would put it to sleep, she refused to leave until Father bought it too. We forgot about the old dogs. We forgot to be mad. When it came to pets, we were only loyal to the newest one. The Parents didn't become attached to the pets. Mother was a farm girl so she had pets by the dozens. Father had a parakeet when he was a kid. He tied a bunch of strings in the cage so the bird had something to land on, but in the morning he found the bird hung itself instead. For the Parents, we were the pets now.

Things were better after they divorced. Less fighting, more sleep, a new neighborhood for Mother that wasn't like Chevy Chase, D.C. At night, I lay in bed and the house was silent and a bit lonely. Now our world was split in two. Father stayed in Chevy Chase and Mother in Glover Park. I couldn't just ask them something, I had to call one. I had no reason to talk to them on the phone before and now half the week it was the only way to reach one. And when you are with one parent, you wonder if the other one is sad and lonely.

Our parents agreed to stay within the District until we left for college. They would share custody. Sister and I, and her cat and my dog were shuttled by our surrogate mother Patsy between the two homes on a weekly basis.

Dropping our things off at Mother's house, Patsy took us back in the car. It was still Fall and the sky took on a permanent cover of grey clouds. I had turned nine in August but didn't feel any older since I was still told where to go and what to do.

"Where are we going now?" I asked puzzled.

"New lesson," said Patsy. I looked over to Sister. She had been added to the Great Liberal Experiment and I liked the company. We pulled up to the skating rink.

"I don't want to skate," said Sister. I didn't either, but I kept quiet. My skates were tight and I wasn't used to the feeling of the shoe. Stepping on the ice, faltering, sliding forward, I leaned back to stop myself and my feet shot out from under me. I hovered, then fell with force on the back of my head. It bounced off the ice and I was knocked out. The great void had found me, and for a moment I thought I was dead. I wasn't scared; in fact, I embraced the darkness. It was quiet, calm, and I felt at peace. I came to in the back of the car. Patsy had driven me to Father's house. An ambulance met us there and I was hurried off to Children's Hospital.

"It's better to have the ambulance bring you in, otherwise you sit in the waiting room all night," said Mother as I looked at the paramedic flashing the light in my eyes and asking me to follow it. At the hospital, they put me in a wheelchair. My head hurt badly, but the other kids looked a lot worse than me. I was put in a room with a black kid from Northeast. He might have been sixteen. His hair was dyed a bright red. In the corner, he had a leather jacket with white lettering painted across the back.

"What does your jacket say?" I asked.

He scratched a scar along the side of his head. "It's a punk band from New York called The Ramones."

The Ramones sounded like a family name and I pictured the Brady Bunch but in black leather jackets.

"What's punk?"

"It's a scene."

"What's a scene?"

"It's like a bunch of guys who hang out and listen to music and go see bands. You're too young to understand. It's cool man."

I studied his appearance. In his ears I could see holes where rings might have been. On his wrist was a studded band of pyramid spikes.

He knew of a band from New York and painted it on his jacket. He didn't seem sick. I asked him why he was in the hospital.

"I have brain cancer," he said.

"I fell on the ice."

"Hey man, you want to trade?" He was pointing to his head and snickering.

I was trembling.

"You scared, huh?"

I nodded. I hadn't been away from home much unless I went to Dash's house.

"You'll be fine. I'll keep an eye on you." He winked at me and I felt better. "Here; listen to this." He hit play on a tape deck recorder that was laying next to him. The recorder was the kind I had seen at school. We used them to listen to books on tape. The music built up and then a voice squeaked out on the one tiny speaker. I lay there and closed my eyes as the music washed over me. It was a strange sensation. The sounds moved through the air with force and the reverberation stirred up new emotions of fury. It was like a drug. "*Hey, Oh,*" sang the voice. The kid stood up on his bed and began to hop up and down, singing along. I started to laugh and sat up.

"Come on, man. Your head don't hurt that much," he said. I stood on the bed too and bounced. "Look at that, you're doing the pogo!"

Suddenly a nurse popped her head in the door way.

"Settle down now!"

We both dropped back into bed and were quiet until she left the room, then burst into laughter.

By morning, the hospital was calling Mother asking her to pick me up. I was running around the hall with the other kid from my room, driving the nurses nuts. Just before I left, the kid from the hospital said to me, "I know I'm going to die soon. The doctors told me so, so I don't have time to worry about what is going to happen. It will happen no matter what I do, right?" He was right. I could live in a bubble and die just the same. I couldn't predict how it would happen and it was a waste of time trying to stop it. Instead of going out in a slow burn, it might be better to burst into flames and make a big show of it. On my way home, I thought about this kid. Why was he so cool? He wasn't afraid to die. And he was into punk rock. There was a kid at my school who was also into punk rock and he seemed not to care either. If I couldn't be normal, then I shouldn't care about anything. But secretly, I always would. You could never just completely stop caring; the best you could do was to put up a front.

Patsy was waiting for me when I got out of school.

"Baby, I won't be driving you every day to school. Your mother is making plans so that some of the kids who go to your school can take you."

"I like you driving me. Can't you keep driving me?"

"I can't Baby, but you'll be fine."

It was 8 am on the next day and the knocking at the door had been going on for a few minutes. It was Monday. It was the first day back to school after the winter break.

"Why don't you answer the door?" called Father, addressing me from the dining room. Since Mother had left, the dining room table had grown high with stacks of Nixon papers. It looked like a city of high rises. I just stood there looking out the window of the living room at Michael. He was an older kid from the neighborhood who went to the Lab School. He was tall with bony shoulders, and curly dark hair that needed to be cut. He would take me to school. I gazed back at Father, who was looking for something. He was always looking for keys or his briefcase. Before heading out the door, I pointed under the table where both Father's keys and briefcase sat from the night before. Michael and I walked up the hill and waited at the bus stop. Ten minutes later, the Metro bus pulled up in front of us and we stepped on. A few stops later, we got off to transfer. Sermon was there waiting for us. I stiffened up. On Connecticut Avenue, we passed the embassies and when Michael saw the Sheraton Hotel, he pulled the red cord, "the stop bell," and we all got off. I walked fast, trying to increase the distance between Sermon and myself.

"Hey shit bag", he called after me. "Where are you going?"

I ran into the school, but that didn't help. Class hadn't started so we waited downstairs for the bell. Sermon made the corner. He looked serious, intent. I had nowhere to go.

"Shit bag, hand it over," said Sermon. I just looked at him. Sermon came over and pulled my backpack off my shoulder, shoved me to the floor, and laughed. I went out to the front of the school, standing in the arch, waiting for my bag.

"Hey shit bag!" yelled Sermon from the third floor. I knew what was coming. The first book hit the last step, then the rest of my things followed, raining pens, papers, a paper gun I made, and about a dollar fifty in change. The bell rang and I was picking up my things when Dash's mom dropped him off.

"You're lucky you're late," I said to him as he walked up and helped me pick up the last few things.

"It's not luck," he said as he pushed his oversized glasses back onto his face. "I'm late on purpose."

Our school was above Dupont Circle, just below Adam's Morgan. Some suits, bums, and ghetto kids were waiting at the bus stop after school as Michael, Sermon and I approached. I was afraid of the ghetto kids. Two of them, one slightly bigger than the other, stepped up to the group of us. Their clothes looked like they were hand-me-downs and had been thrown in the washer a million times. This had never happened before, so I wasn't sure what to do, yet I was confident that Michael would handle the situation.

"Give me your money," one of the black kids said rather flatly. He had a moon face and a nose that was wide and slightly turned up.

At once, Michael and Sermon ditched the scene and ran away to hide in a nearby record store. I didn't run. Not because I was brave, but because it was too late. It would be impossible to outrun the two.

"Give me your money or I'm gonna fuck you up, cracker." The smaller kid stepped closer and eyeballed me from head to toe.

"I don't have any money." I was lying.

I had no clue what a "cracker" was either.

The taller kid punched me in the face, which didn't hurt, but I was terrified and dug deep into my pocket with a trembling hand. I pulled out the fifty cents I'd planned to save for the gumball machine. That morning I had stolen fifty cents from Father's change jar so I could get a toy from the machine at the pharmacy next to the bus stop. My muggers snatched up the coins and left. A woman at the bus stop had watched the whole thing. I felt helpless and that sense of control being taken from me just left me with anger. *I wish I was big so I could beat them up. I would take all their money and make them cry and feel ashamed.*

"I thought they were your friends!" the lady watching me said, rushing over to my side.

"My friends don't punch me in the face," I cried, holding my nose.

"Do you need some money?"

"No, I didn't give them all my money." I had enough to get back. I took the bus home--alone, miserable, depressed and scared. *I was punched in the face, but did it really hurt me? No. I would be okay.* Now I knew what it was like to get mugged and what to look out for. It was information vital to survive in the city. It was a dormant part of my brain that now began to function. I couldn't rely on Michael to protect me. I had to rely on myself.

The following afternoon, the same two ghetto kids followed me onto the bus, but there were too many witnesses.

"You better have the money tomorrow," the smaller one threatened and they jumped off at the next stop. I could feel the panic build inside of me. That night at Mother's house I told her everything.

"Well, I'll make sure that Michael is there with you this time," she said.

"I'm not riding the metro bus. I don't care what you say. I'm not doing it."

The Parents could make me do a lot of things, but not if I felt unsafe. It wouldn't matter if they punished me. I would sit on the floor and would not be moved.

"Let me see if I can arrange something else," she said.

That was the last time I took the Metro bus to school, opting instead for a ride on the "Retard Bus," as my friends called it. But it was still better than taking the Metro, better than the ghetto kids stealing my pocket change.

The Retard Bus was shorter than a normal bus, but that's not what made it stand out. Because dyslexia was considered a handicap by the city, the students were bussed together with the physically handicapped. My daily trip to and from school meant climbing on the Retard Bus with kids who had cerebral palsy, Down's syndrome, and back or leg braces. There was one kid who wore a helmet and bashed his head up against the side of the bus. From outside the bus, it looked like they were shuttling a ward of handicapped kids off to another hospital. I liked to pretend it was full of wounded soldiers coming from the front lines and we had to avoid enemy fire. Half the bus were kids from the Lab School. I sat in the back as we picked up more of my classmates. After me was Charlie on Reservoir Road. He was eleven. Charlie's head was so big it looked like a misshapen balloon. He had a bowl cut and wore a long sleeved, white collared shirt. His breath stunk like he brushed his teeth with vomit. How could his parents miss that? I had mine telling me every night to brush my teeth. I pictured Charlie's parents smiling and missing half their teeth. They were from Lithuania so who knows what the customs were there.

On my first day on the Retard Bus, Charlie climbed on and sat behind me.

"You want to see something?" he said.

I had to move my head away from him, his breath was so bad. "Sure."

He handed me a gold bar. It was heavy and I flipped it over in my hand.

"Cool," I said still looking at it.

"You know gold only goes up in value. I'm getting as much as I can. Someday I'll be rich." He once told me that his family had been royalty in Lithuania and the Nazis had come along and taken everything from them that they weren't able to sneak out of the country. Many years later, his father would became the Ambassador to Argentina.

We turned down Wisconsin Avenue and made a left on P Street. Burt waddled out. When he stepped on the bus, his weight made the bus lean to the side. His house was in Georgetown, close to the school, so the ride wasn't long for him but long enough for the other kids from the Lab School to pick on him for his weight. After years of abuse from the other kids, Burt had developed a nasty attitude. Charlie learned not to say anything after Burt told him "Your head is so fucking big and your breath stinks, it must be full of shit. I think I'll call you shit head." Anytime Charlie was about to say something, Burt would quickly interrupt by saying "What shit head?"

The past twenty minutes I had been facing the back of the bus talking with Charlie and Burt. The road was bumpy from years of poorly filled pot holes. I didn't feel too good. The driver kept stepping on the gas, and then slamming on the brakes. I felt nauseous. I didn't want to hurl into my own lap, so I threw open the window, leaned my head out and let loose a steady stream of vomit. It passed the window directly behind me and was sucked into the third one, where it came to rest on Charlie, spraying his face, jacket, and lap. The bus pulled in front of the school. I stepped off, perfectly clean and vomit free, as Charlie emerged covered in the little bits of my last meal. From the looks of it, I had eaten many yellow and red things. Sermon stood on the steps waiting. Sermon gave Charlie the once over, then bunched his face up in disgust. Charlie didn't say a word and marched up the steps. Sermon backed off of him, giving him the room he needed, then closed the gap, blocking my entrance. I handed my backpack to Sermon and he ran up the stairs. I sat on the steps and waited for my things to come back to me.

> *MINOR THREAT*
> "*Screaming at a Wall*"
> *It's like screaming at a wall.*
> *Someday it's gonna fall.*
> *You built that wall up around you.*
> *And now you can't see out. And you*
> *can't hear my words. No matter how loud I shout.*

Dash and I hacked our way through the dense brush of Rock Creek Park, both of us dressed in combat boots and camouflage. A jogger ran past on the trail, glancing over as I chopped at a small tree with a machete, my blond curly hair sticking out from under my army green cap. Dash wore his thick, black-rimmed glasses that he periodically kept in check by pressing between the lenses with his index finger. We were eleven years old. Earlier in the week, I was coming home from school when some kids in Father's neighborhood saw me getting off the Retard Bus. They made fun of me, saying the usual things: "Hey look, he must be retarded. He takes the short bus!" I imagined each kid's face on the edge of the tree trunk and slammed into it with the blade. I didn't talk with Dash about being picked on. He knew what it was like. I would never pick on someone for being different, I thought. *I'm not going to keep taking this shit. The next guy who says something to me I'll punch him in the face. Maybe I should carry this machete with me all the time. I'd bet they would think twice about saying something, but then I would feel bad. I have to learn not to feel bad after hurting someone and to not care what they think of me, or what my parents want of me.*

Turning onto Father's street, we ambled the three blocks back to the house and into the alley behind it. A couch had recently been thrown out

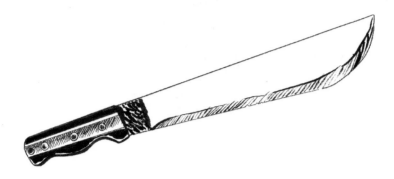

and we took turns attacking the furniture with our machete. I swung with the blade while Dash kicked and jumped onto the wooden frame that held its upholstery until it broke. We could do anything we wanted; no one was watching us. We weren't different, or retarded, just kids having a good time.

We walked in the backyard of Father's house, passing the hole we had dug as an underground fort, and went inside the house. Fluffball, my dog slept in the kitchen. Dash and I watched a movie on the Beta Max. There wasn't much else to do since I'd stopped playing with the other kids on the block.

Father's house was in Chevy Chase. The neighborhood was isolated. Rock Creek Park, the woods, the paths and its bordering houses provided little entertainment. A senator lived up the street, a district judge a few houses down, and Father, a lawyer for Nixon. They wanted their neighborhood kept quiet. I wanted to blow it up. The lives of the neighborhood kids were locked into a predictable future: politicians, doctors and businessmen-- all white-collar existences. If they were lucky, perhaps a cocaine addiction and rehab would follow, or infidelity and a divorce. I was told I was different, so I knew I wouldn't end up like them. At the time I began to question if I wanted to be like them. I had always assumed I wanted to be normal because it was denied. But the so-called normal kids were monsters. I didn't want to be like them. I wanted to be more like the punk kid I had met, but didn't know how to be. I remembered the feeling when he played the music. I forgot everything else. I wanted that feeling again. But I didn't know where to go and what to get.

Patsy drove me to school again because I told her how the other kids made fun of me.

"Thank you," I said after stepping out of the car.

"You're welcome." She nodded and smiled at my manners. My sneakers were too tight and everything was stretching on me; it was annoying to have to get new clothes every few months. I liked the camouflage shirt I had on, but knew it would be too small soon. At the end of summer, I would be thirteen.

I waited out in front of the school for the bell to ring so I could avoid Sermon. There was a group of kids standing out by the front steps. They weren't from our school. There was a girl with deep purple hair that covered her eyes, a boy with jack boots and a white t-shirt that he had written across with red spray paint: State of Alert. Another kid had a shaved head and a green bomber jacket. There were about seven of them. Simon, an older student with short spiky hair, handed out copies of 7" singles of his band, *State of Alert,* made on clear green vinyl. Later in the day, I listened as he handed one to our teacher and told her about his band. I wanted one of his green records but I was too shy to ask him.

"It's punk rock. I'm the drummer." I imagined I was the drummer playing a show in front of the kids who had been waiting for Simon. All my classmates were there too, so were Patsy and Sister. The spotlight was on me. My head was shaved and I had on a white T-shirt with S.O.A. spray painted in red across the front. My combat boots stepped on the bass pedal to the beat. Every time I hit the drums, the room shook and the crowd loved it; they loved me.

In May, near the end of that school year, one of the teachers had a barbecue and pool party out in Potomac, Maryland for all her students. I could smell fresh cut grass. The air was cold but my feet, submerged under the water, were warm. My swimming trunks were too tight. I had outgrown them since last summer. I never really thought of Dash as fat, but as he drifted by me on an inflatable raft, I noticed he had lost a lot of weight. "Baby fat", Mother called it. But his skin was still pale blue and looked like a sausage. He looked naked without his thick black glasses.

"Me next!" said Pierre to Simon. Simon grabbed him under his arms and gave him the heave-ho towards the deep end. Pierre's skin was dark against the clear water and light blue tile of the walls.

"Me too!" I said and before I knew it I was flying, splashing, then sinking. I struggled for a moment and felt Simon's hand pull me up.

"Don't you know how to swim?" he asked.

"Yeah, I just forgot."

"How do you forget that?"

"I don't know. I forget a lot."

"You want me to throw you again?"

"Sure." And he did, but this time I remembered to swim. His hair was short and spiked; he never dipped his head below the water. Comfortable in his own skin, he was cool without trying. He liked being different. I wanted to be like him. I asked him what was a good punk band.

"Generation X. You would like them; everyone likes them," he said to me with a smirk. I had been petrified to ask, but forced myself to do it anyway. Once I did, it was like I had conquered a goal.

Summer break came and my birthday would be in late August. I wanted a record player, but didn't want to wait until then.

"But we have a record player in the living room," said Mother after I asked for an early gift.

"I want one in my room just for me." I didn't want her to hear the records I wanted to listen to. She might try and take them away. After I promised I would take out the trash every day without complaining she bought it for me. The first record I got was Generation X's "Valley of the Dolls". I loved it and played it over and over. It was the same feeling I had when I first listened to the Ramones' song. Sister sat on my floor and she liked it too, though she didn't show any emotion. I knew she liked it since she didn't leave the room as she did whenever she was bored. In Georgetown, I had found a record store called "Smash". When I opened the door, a bell rang. The cashier glanced up at me from a magazine that read *Flipside* across the front. I would later find out he was the owner of the store. He looked normal, but then again so did I and I wasn't normal.

"If you need anything, let me know," he said. My eyes swept over the room. The walls were covered with band posters and flyers for punk shows. Band shirts were folded into squares and lined a wall behind the register; combat boots sat on shelves in the back, and there were lots of records in bins in the center of the room.

"Do you have the State of Alert 7 on green vinyl?"

"That was a first pressing," said the owner. "We have been out of it for a month. I keep asking for more, but it won't be a green vinyl. But maybe you might like the X record?" He came out from behind the counter and found the album. The bell over the door rang again. In stepped two guys who were about seventeen. One had a shaved head and the other pitch black hair in a bowl cut. They both had on leather jackets with lots of buttons on their lapels. The one with a shaved head had on blue suede creeper shoes. The other guy had on white Doc Marten boots. I flipped through the bins of records. It reminded me of the cards I was shown when I was being tested. I didn't read the band names, just looked at the cover art, stopping if there was a photo of a pretty girl. I didn't feel like anyone would have cared about my reading, not here. I picked up an album that depicted Reagan as a devil--horns, tongue sticking out, and a swastika on his forehead. Then I flipped through another stack and on a cover was a cartoon of a fat man eating poor people. On his back it said C.I.A. in bold. I guessed there was a lot of politics in punk too. I found that kind of boring. I didn't want to hear about Nixon or any other politician.

"Don't get that!" said the guy with a shaved head to his friend who was holding up a record a few bins down from me. "They are Nazis." The cover of the 7" said *Screwdriver*.

If you listened to Screwdriver, you were a Nazi or, if you had red laces in your boots, you were a communist. There was a code in the imagery and music of punk. If I had the wrong stuff then I wouldn't be cool. I needed to know the code more than I needed to know how to read. I picked out another record and paid. It was "Stand and Deliver" by Adam Ant. I chose it because the cover art was cool. Under the glass of the counter, there were a variety of one-inch band buttons, stickers and patches. I wanted everything in the store, but I didn't know what any of it was or if I would like it. Hanging around the store, I watched the punks and took mental note of their clothes and attitudes. "Piss off," I heard one say. I repeated the phrase as I walked home, looking at my records. Patsy walked into my room with clean laundry, and noticed my new t-shirt, which said "We are the Meatmen and you suck!" I was jumping up and down yelling "Piss off!" as Adam Ant's record played very loudly. I didn't hear her walk in until the sounds of sucking teeth made her presence obvious.

"Sorry." I sat down and turned the music down.

"Oh boy, you're going to be trouble now," she said as she left the room.

The Trade Off and New Liabilities

DAG NASTY
 "Can I say"
  Can I say
  What can I say?
  Why should I try?
  I tried to love
  what knew I hated
  I took a lie
  And I made a truth
  I defended
  what I should have denied.

Mother's house was in Glover Park, just above Georgetown. Our new neighborhood was middle class. The streets were numbered and lettered with a generic sensibility.

The house itself was old. The floors creaked with every step. The foundation had never quite found its comfortable state and liked to shift its weight ever so slightly from time to time. The house had a front porch, a small rectangular backyard with a one-car garage and a tall fence to divide it from other properties. It was identical to every other house on the block. The houses were tightly packed together and, looking across the alley into back windows, I could always find someone awake.

My new friend, Ted, lived two houses away and went to Georgetown Day School, a prestigious private school three blocks from the Lab School's new location on Reservoir Road. If Ted saw me outside of our block, especially if he was with his classmates or near his school, he pretended not to know me. It was a trade off I could deal with, to have a friend on my block. Kids from G.D.S. were proud to say they were students there. Kids from his school taunted my classmates and me.

I was thirteen. Girls were becoming more interesting. It started with cartoons. Ted's father had a collection of old R. Crumb comics depicting girls with oversized breasts and butts. I couldn't get enough. I had looked through each one, even taking a few on private dates in Ted's basement bathroom after he had fallen asleep. It was like a revolution going on inside me. I was obsessed with girls. Girls on the street, at school, on television. I envisioned them naked and doing things to me I had seen in the R. Crumb comics, but to actually talk to a girl was terrifying. It brought back all the old doubts about being dyslexic. How could I carry on a conversation knowing what would happen if I was somehow put into a position where I had to read something. Reading in front of anyone I felt great humiliation. My face would flush and I would feel like vomiting. Reading out loud there was no hiding my problem.

It was November and a kid named Scott and his gang were playing in his front yard. Walking by, I noticed a girl. She was the only girl I had ever seen hanging out with them, so she stood out. Busty with shapely curves, large brown eyes and an upturned nose, she had a voice that was high-pitched and girly. She looked older than Scott and his gang. I later found out she was. Her eyes fell on me and examined me carefully. She was adorable and reminded me of the comics. When I stopped, Scott eyed me suspiciously. I made no threatening moves and kept my palms up and open. Internally, I was freaking out. *What should I say?* Looking at her, I searched for anything that might point me in the right direction. But there was nothing. No band names on anything--nothing that said she liked sports or films. *Why is it that talking is so important? But without talking, what could you do?* I knew I couldn't touch her, not yet. I really wanted to touch her. The image of her naked was floating in the back of my mind; it was distracting me from thinking of something cool to say so I did my best to keep the image at bay. But the image kept trying to leap frog to the front of my thoughts. *Please don't get a boner, not now. I promise I'll beat off at home if you just wait,* I thought. Focus. Then all the negative thoughts bubbled up. What if Scott calls me a retard? Then they would all laugh at me, but if I don't try to talk to her I'll be so pissed.

"Hi, I'm Fiona," said the girl. Her gaze was penetrating. I quickly averted my eyes. She was younger than me, but more developed than a lot of teenage girls. She was a beautiful freak of nature.

"You're from around here?" I wasn't ready to talk to a girl. I was planning on striking up a conversation with the guys first, then easing in with the girl. But they were going to make that hard.

"Hey, don't talk to her," said Scott with a scowl. "She's my girlfriend."

"No, I'm not!" said Fiona, loud enough that the entire block could hear. She was unable to hide her contempt.

"I've seen you around," she said to me with a smile. I felt warm. I was blushing, but I pretended it wasn't happening. I didn't want to blow it and the only way I knew how to act cool was by pretending I didn't care. If a plane in flames crashed behind me, I would have shrugged and said "Whatever man."

"But he's a fucking retard," said Scott pleading with her.

I could feel the blood drain from my face and struggled to maintain my composure. I was working on a come back when Fiona turned to Scott and slapped him hard across the face.

"Don't say that!" she said. "You still piss your bed!"

The other kids started pointing at Scott and laughing. He denied it, but it was obvious that it was true.

"Where do you live?" I asked her.

"On 41st Street."

I felt awkward and ran out of things to say, so I went home. You are a fucking retard, I thought. A hot girl was right there and you blew it. I didn't even say goodbye. *Idiot! She thinks you're a total loser.* At home, I looked at myself in the mirror. I didn't think I was bad looking, but then again I wasn't sure if girls thought I was good looking. I heard Sister once say that Dash was good looking, but what did she know? I had slight muscles under my t-shirt. I slowly turned my head. My skin was clear. Squinting, I tried to picture myself older. Then I wondered, *What if I looked more like Dash. Would Fiona like me more?*

I thought about Fiona the rest of the day, that night and the next morning before school. I was thinking of her on my way to the bathroom in between classes. It was like she was on a loop and I couldn't shake her.

Walking into the bathroom, I noticed an older kid pissing at the urinal writing something with a magic marker next to some graffiti that was already there. His collar stood up on his Lacoste baby blue shirt. His hair was combed back, brushed and feathered into some kind of 80's look. The wall read, "I love cock" and "I love cunt" next to each other. On his wrist was a pyramid-spiked wristband. It looked like the one I had before the school had told me I couldn't wear it anymore. He finished writing "Then why don't you both fuck off". The few things I read well were curse words. He zipped up his fly as I took my turn at the urinal. He was making me nervous standing behind me and I couldn't pee. He lit up a cigarette, then walked over to the window and blew out the smoke.

"I see you wear that same t-shirt all the time. *We are the Meatmen and You Suck*," he said, not looking at me. I had a few other shirts I picked up from Smash but I didn't tell him that. "You listen to them?"

"No," I said, zipping up and washing my hands even though I hadn't peed.

"You should. Come over after school and I'll play them for you."

His name was Tyler Richards, but everyone just called him T.R. He was new and I had noticed him the first day he showed up. When I first overheard T.R. talking with an older kid about punk rock, I knew I wanted to be friends with him. After school I went to his house and he pulled out a milk crate filled with records. His basement had lots of different crates filled with records. The walls were covered with band flyers, just like Smash. "I DJ at parties on the weekends," he said as a cigarette hung from his lip. He found the Meatmen record and put it on the turntable. "*One down, three to go,*" the sound was raw, angry and fast. It gave me a tingling feeling, filled with energy.

"Do you know what they're saying?" I asked.

"It's about the Beatles. You know like, John Lennon is dead, so now there are only three to go before they're all dead!" I laughed even though I liked the Beatles and was sad when Lennon died. It was comforting hanging out with T.R. Whenever I was with Ted, I felt on edge even though he knew I was dyslexic. Another dyslexic would never judge me and Ted always acted superior. T.R. pulled out a dozen other records of local bands: Minor Threat, Teen Idols, Beefeater, Madhouse, Lunch Meat, Faith, Void, Iron Cross, and one I recognized, S.O.A., on green vinyl. The next day I went back to his house with a blank tape and recorded all of his 7"s. Carefully, I copied the names of the bands and songs. I didn't read the words, but built them by carefully penning each letter. T.R. educated me on the details of punk, like how it started in New York, then spread to England, changed, and came back to America. He taught me the difference between pop punk, street punk, hardcore, and new wave. He let me borrow 7" records and tapes.

I wanted to read, but no matter how hard I tried and wished for it, nothing worked. Holding the liner notes, scanning the handwritten text scrawled across the glossy black background, I needed to know the meaning. How could I call myself a punk if I didn't know what the songs were about? Wouldn't that mean I was a poser? I could picture my friends and those who I respected in the scene laughing at me, just as my old friends had done when they had found out I was dyslexic. That couldn't happen. I had found solace in the punk scene and feared losing the litte status I now had. I looked to the record player, picked up the vinyl and placed it on the turn table. I lifted the arm and put it on the track leading to the first song. How could I figure out what they were saying in the songs? The scratchy voice belted out the lyrics. I looked at the words. Some I could make out, the others I could guess as I listened along. I picked up the needle and placed it back at the start of the song, playing it over and over, reading along each time. Slowly at first, things began to make sense. I had never tried reading something I cared about and for me that would make all the difference. I started writing the lyrics down in a notebook, copying them word for word. Sometimes when I was trying to sleep, I would recall a line or a chorus and it would loop until I drifted off to sleep.

I shut the door to my room and pulled one of T.R.'s records out of its sleeve. The Cramps, Psychedelic Jungle. I bounced the needle around until I found the track I had been looking for, "Green Door." I put the headphones on so only I could hear the music. It was a private space and no one had been allowed in. I laid down on the bed and closed my eyes. The melody meandered around before I become lost in thought. I wondered what Fiona was doing. Then I pictured her laying on her bed in white cotton underwear with her breasts heaving out of her tight tank top and her eyes looking right at me. I had seen her a few times on the block. When she asked me about the Bad Brains record I was carrying, I told her it was D.C. punk. She was into Madonna and new wave, but I could tell she wanted to get into punk too. She had recently started dressing like Madonna, in white lace with a large crucifix around her neck.

It was a Friday.

"You want to come over and listen?" I asked her.

"Sure."

I felt a new wave of fear as I led her home.

Patsy eyed us as we went up to my room.

Fiona sat on the floor in a pool of afternoon light and read the back of "I And I Survive / Destroy Babylon", a 12" by the Bad Brains. The bass notes made the window rattle. I thought she might catch me staring at her breasts through her lacy white top, so I glanced down at her hands. Hands were safe. Her dark eyeliner, the large cross hanging from her neck, her tight little skirt and top made her look slutty. I didn't mind. I had already picked up that Fiona liked being the center of attention and that's why she dressed the way she did.

"I like this," she said.

"I'll make you a tape if you want."

"Okay." She flipped through my records: The Sex Pistols, Generation X, Misfits, X, Iggy Pop, Minor Threat, The Ramones. I grabbed the last one.

"Do you want to hear something else?"

"Okay."

I picked "Rocket to Russia" by The Ramones. The vinyl slid into my hand. I held the record between my palms, making sure my fingers never touched the grooves. I scanned the surface to make sure it was free of dust, then carefully placed it on the turntable. Picking up the arm, I dropped the needle on *Rockaway Beach*, then sat quietly next to Fiona. I wanted to touch her, but was terrified she wouldn't like it. Patsy came into the room to pick up dirty laundry. Seeing nothing fishy, she left us alone.

"The Ramones were one of the first punk bands," I said.

Fiona gave me a look of respect and, for once, I didn't feel like a retard.

"You want to make out?" she asked.

I looked out my door. It was open, but if I closed it Patsy was going to know something was up. I turned down the music so I could hear her coming. Fiona sat up a bit so I could get in a better position. My heart thumped away and I could hear it in my ears; it almost drowned out the music. Fiona didn't move. She forced me to take the first steps. I pressed my lips against hers. They were full and soft. Her lip gloss made them oily. Inside, I was jumping for joy. *I did it. I kissed a girl. Fuck all those guys who call me retard. I'm kissing a girl.* We kept making out. She lay down. I didn't dare climb on top of her. I put my hand on her belly and she pushed it away so I knew that was as far as it would go. We kept making out until she had to go home. My lips were red, puffy and sore. I didn't care; I wanted to do it again. A day later, she came over and we did the same thing but she let me touch her boobs over her shirt. At seven, she had to call her mom and I listened.

"No mom, I said I'm at Stephanie's house. Why do I have to come home? God, you are always on me. Why can't I just stay out a little longer?" She was a liar, and I still found her attractive. We started dating. Most of the time we spent together, we listened to new records and did a lot of kissing. Over the next year, I would make many attempts at getting her out of her tight jeans and top. If I got her down to her underwear, it was after many promises not to go further. When I went further, she would get up, get dressed and be out the door in a huff. But the next day she would be back over to listen to a new record and the negotiations would start all over again.

It was late one night after Fiona went home and I met up with Ted. We walked his mutt in the alley behind our houses.

"What's wrong with you?" asked Ted. I was walking bow-legged.

"My balls hurt."

"She gave you blue balls," he smirked.

We turned the corner and Stephanie was there waiting for us. I met Stephanie through Fiona. Stephanie had grown up in West Virginia and moved to Glover Park when she was nine. Now she was eleven and lived four houses away from mine. She was an attractive Persian girl with curly locks of hair that fell to her shoulders. Her eyes were large and brown, but she had a hairy upper lip and I couldn't stop staring at the hair. A gymnast, she could bend and twist her body into a variety of poses that she felt the need to show off. Stephanie was always up for sneaking out.

Ted had no patience for her long, drawn out stories. I didn't mind them as long as she rubbed my back. On the back porch of her house, behind the insect screen, she rubbed my back until the sky turned light blue. I thought of sex. I thought of Fiona who was her best friend. I thought of Stephanie's slightly hairy lip and it stopped me from going too far.

In the alley behind my mother's house, I skated back and forth trying to do some tricks, but failed. My ghetto blaster with a tape deck sat on top of a trash can. I got stickers at Smash and covered all of the blank space on my blaster with bands that I had never listened to but whose artwork I liked. I had just bought a record by a band out of London that T.R. had played for me, The Clash. I copied it onto the tape, and now it was squeaking out of the box. *"White riot. I want a riot white riot."* I hummed the tune. Over the winter, not much had changed. Fiona still hadn't put out and Stephanie was always lurking in the background to spend time with me. I had kissed her once. It was another late night after she had rubbed my back until the sky outside turned light blue again. I rolled over to go home and she kissed me. I thought to myself, if I do anything Stephanie will tell everyone in the neighborhood and Fiona will find out. But at the same time, I wanted sex desperately. I stopped her and pulled myself away. I didn't say anything and went home again with blue balls. I didn't think it was a big deal but after that Stephanie kept staring at me. With so much idle time, I should've known she'd be trouble. She liked to gossip.

I was walking in the alley with Ted and his dog.
"Stephanie's a pain in the ass," I said.
"That's cuz she lllllloooooooooovvvvvvvveeeeeessssss you," Ted said and laughed.
"Fucking Jews! Get in the oven and burn!" It was Nazi Shawn. We had walked onto his side of the block without realizing it. Shawn was sixteen and we were almost fifteen, yet he hadn't reached our level of maturity. I was only half Jewish so I was only half offended. Ted was fuming, but then again he was a full Jew. In a way, it was nice being called something other than retard. It was as if I were being treated like any other kid.
At Ted's, we plotted our revenge. Working as a team was fun; it was like Nazi Shawn had attacked us as a group instead of just me. That night

and every night after, when we were sure Nazi Shawn was sleeping, Ted and I walked Ted's dog by Nazi Shawn's garage, where we each emptied our bladders into the crack of the door of his family car. They never closed the garage door, making the car an easy target. Whenever I pissed in the car, I thought about how Nazi Shawn had once cornered me in the arcade in Georgetown, saying "You're a retard and ain't going to do shit. You're going to be a lonely loser who has to beg for change or suck dick to get by. You can't read a lick! Better start sucking dick now." I hadn't said anything back, I just walked away. But pissing into the crack of his car door gave me back a little of my pride. My pride had been gone so long that even a taste made my head swirl. *Maybe I could be the avenging angel of all dyslexics, pissing in car doors when needed*, I thought while I let the last little drop run down the outside of the car.

Stephanie transferred from the public school to the Lab school. It was a surprise seeing her walk down the hall. I stopped her by the water fountain.

"What are you doing here?" I asked, annoyed.

"I'm dyslexic too." She smiled. Her eyes darted back and forth between mine. She was always looking for some sign from me. I never gave it.

"What do you mean?"

"I wasn't doing well in school. My mother heard about you and then had me tested."

I gave her a once over and she seemed content.

"Do you want to be here?"

"They picked on me at the other school," she said.

"And you think it will be better here?"

"Isn't it?"

"No."

Up the hall, Sermon was pushing a younger kid around. He had stopped bothering me after T.R. had told him I was cool. T.R. had a lot of friends outside of our school which made him cooler then the rest of us. Dash, Charlie, and the others weren't so lucky. Sermon still pushed them around and threw their bags out the window. He never bothered Pierre, maybe because he was black. Just then Sermon smacked Dash across the top of his head as he scooted past. I heard the girls whispering about Dash. Stephanie didn't even glance at him and, even though I pretended

I wasn't interested, I liked the fact that she only liked me. It made me feel special and I needed that. Fiona showed every boy attention and when I called her on it she said, "But I only fool around with you." That didn't make me feel better, but what choice did I have? Fiona was the best bet for having sex and Stephanie was too hairy. Everything was giving me an erection. I had wet dreams about every girl I had met, even the ones I thought were ugly. It was making me crazy; all I thought about was sex. All the effort I put into beating off didn't help; but just in case it might, I kept at it. I did it before school, after school, in the middle of the night, in the shower. It was a miracle that I was never caught. But even if Nixon sat on the edge of the bed watching me with his beady little eyes, I still would have done it.

I met T.R. on the corner and we waited for the bus. I hated buses but it was the only way to get to his house in Tenleytown. A few kids were walking by.

"Uhhhh Duuuuuhhhhhh. I'm fucking stupid and looooook I can't read," said one of them.

"Oh look, it's a couple of fags," said T.R.. "You guys going to go fuck each other? Which of you plays the man, since you both look like a couple of bitches? Ugly little dick bitches." T.R. puffed out his chest and stood up straight. He was bigger than any kid in their group and they didn't want to fight, so they moved on. T.R. turned back to me as if nothing had happened and went on talking about his new Depeche Mode record.

"I hate our school," I said.

"Why? Because of those pricks? Fuck them. They get picked on by kids who go to Saint Albans High School and those guys are picked on by Wilson High School. It doesn't matter where you go, you will still be picked on."

"Yeah, but it's so easy to pick on us, because it's true."

"You don't think those guys are retards? Not one of their teams has beaten another school. They lose at everything."

"How do you know?"

"My sister goes there and she says they're a bunch of shit heads. She doesn't even hang out with any of them." I thought of my own sister.

The bus came and we climbed on. At T.R.'s house, we listened to some punk, and then he played Depeche Mode. I didn't like Depeche Mode, but didn't say anything since T.R. seemed to be really into them.

"Check out this video. It has all these runaways in it. This woman made a film on punks and she used real kids who lived on the streets of California." I took his video home and watched it over and over. The story was about a group of outcast kids who formed a gang and lived together. They protected each other and were like a family. They would go to punk shows, dance, and get messed up on drugs. But if anyone tried to pick on them, they would fight back together. The soundtrack was amazing. I bought the record and played it over and over. With my eyes closed, I would lie on my floor, lace my fingers across my chest, and imagine myself living in their home. When Dash or Pierre came over, I made them watch it too. The blue flickering light lit up their profiles. I wanted to be in a punk gang. Maybe then no one would fuck with us? And even if they did, we wouldn't care, just like the kids in the movie.

"We should start a gang," I said to them. Dash shrugged. Pierre nodded. We had a gang. "Let's call it The Rat Pack—but not after Dean Martin and his friends—or 'TRP.'"

"What do we do?" asked Pierre.

"I don't know, hang out?"

At first I wrote TRP across my notebook for school, then Dash and the rest of them did the same. Pierre showed up with TRP in bold black letters on his backpack. All at once, we were tagging everything, from chalkboards to books. Then we started tagging outside of school in all our neighborhoods.

"I want to be in the gang," said Charlie. I looked at his large head and I wondered if his neck muscles were extra strong. He had a habit of talking too much. Most of us ignored him, since listening to him drained our energy.

"I don't know man," I said.

"You're the leader." He averted his eyes from mine. "You could let me in if you wanted."

"You would have to go through our ritual."

"I'll do it." His breath wafted towards me. I backed up a bit, hoping some fresh air might weaken it.

We didn't have a ritual so we decided to tie Charlie to a gravestone for a few hours. Afterwards, on the way back to Mother's, we cut through the alley and stopped at Nazi Shawn's garage.

"Hold on a second, I got to do something," I said to the rest of the gang. I peed into the crack of the door like I always did when I passed the garage. The guys looked at me oddly.

"The guy who owns this car is an asshole." But it didn't really matter what I said, they were all going to piss in it. We went back to Mother's house to drink cans of Coca Cola and watch *Suburbia* on my Beta Max, again.

"Well, is Charlie in the gang?" Dash asked later. Charlie looked up expectantly.

"No," Pierre replied.

A few weeks earlier, Pierre had caught Charlie beating off in his bathroom during a party for his sister. For weeks Pierre had been calling him "jerk-off." It had been getting to him and I knew it was the real reason he wanted to join our gang.

"I can do something else if you want," he murmured. His shoulders slumped and his giant head hung low.

"Nah, it's okay, you're in the gang." I didn't want to be responsible for his suicide. Besides, we were starting to act just like the bullies we wanted to defend ourselves from.

"They have like over 50 members," said Stephanie a week later. "They fight all the time. To become a member, you have to sleep in the graveyard." Stephanie was talking to a group of kids at the park when Cross overheard. Cross was a big, mean, black kid from Southeast who ran with two gangs from his neighborhood. He was nineteen years old and part of the drug trade. Then he moved up and across town to Glover Park in Northwest where he became our neighborhood dealer. For Glover Park, Cross was a big deal, but for the rest of the city, he was nothing. I was tagging the school's fire exit and not really listening to her. I should have told her to shut up, but I liked it when she made us bigger than we were.

According to Stephanie's description, The Rat Pack was taking over Cross's territory and possibly his drug trade, or at least that's the way he took it. It didn't help when he saw "TRP" scrawled boldly on walls, posts and anywhere else a permanent marker could reach. I'm sure he was thinking he needed to launch a pre-emptive strike.

The next day, Stephanie came up the street. She walked with a purpose and I knew she was coming to tell me something.

Stephanie turned the corner and came up my walk.

"Cross said he was going to kill you," she said. Suddenly that feeling of fear crept up my chest and I felt a little dizzy. I still didn't want to die and the words affected me. I could picture the big black void.

"Why would he want to kill me?" I looked at Stephanie.

"Maybe I said something I wasn't supposed to."

"I wish you would stop doing that."

Patsy parked in front of Mother's house and came up the walk. I hadn't seen her much since Sister and I had been getting older and had little need for a nanny. I trailed behind her from room to room. She picked up clothing, made beds and emptied the trash.

"Baby, can you pass me those pillows?" she said, and I did.

"There is a guy named Cross who wants to kill me."

"Why does he want to do that?"

"He thinks I'm in a gang."

She sucked her teeth at me and I looked at my shoes.

"Boy, I see all that T.R.P. nonsense you be writing on your school books. You don't need being no part of a gang."

"We're not a real gang. It's just Dash, Pierre and a few friends."

"Boy, what do you think a real gang is?" Her voice went up a decibel.

"I don't know."

We moved downstairs.

"They have gangs where I'm from. Them boys only want one thing, respect. They never got it so they take it." She was right. I was tired of being called retard and that made me want to fight but at the same time I didn't want to get hurt.

"What am I going to do?"

"Don't be messing with that gang business any more and stay away from that Cross boy. He'll forget it after some time."

The phone rang. It was Dash.

Dash wasn't worrying about Cross since he lived out on Macarthur Boulevard, and was about to go on vacation to Assateague Island in Maryland. Summer break had started the week before and I decided it was best to go with him. We camped among the wild ponies that ran free on the island. There was nothing to do--no TV, no video games, nothing. I wished I could read. I was afraid to get into deep conversations with kids who weren't dyslexic. What if they brought up things I should have known? I watched the waves crash on the beach. The smell of salt was mixed in the spray. Dash sat at the water's edge building a sand castle. His back was to me and it was already a bright red. I wondered what I would have been like if I had been normal. I imagined myself standing in front of a crowed auditorium reading perfectly and everyone paying close attention to each word. After my speech I could carry on conversations on any number of subjects and remember the right names and dates of things. Everyone was impressed. Then I looked down at my bare foot under the sand. I stood up, brushed the sand from my hands and joined Dash at the water's edge. The island was isolated. In many ways that's how I felt all the time, cut off from who I should have been.

At the end of the week we drove back home. Dash's parents dropped me off at Mother's. The house looked the same, so did the street. I don't know why I thought it might be different. The whole way back I wanted to know if everything was okay with Cross. I dropped my bag off in my room and didn't bother to unpack. I went over to Stephanie's to get the most up-to-date information on my standing with Cross.

"Nothing," she said. "I haven't heard anything and haven't seen him around in a while. I think he has forgotten you." Then I had a thought, what if Cross hadn't said anything in the first place? What if Stephanie was just mad at me about something and was using Cross to scare me? Could it have been because she liked me and I was dating someone else? Maybe I should ask her. But if I ask her, she might do something really stupid like say something to Cross so that it becomes a real problem.

Then she said, "Fiona was hanging out with Pierre."

"What do you mean?" All my attention switched to Fiona.

"I don't know, he's been around whenever she is around." What the fuck, why is he trying to fuck my girlfriend?

"Did you see anything else?" I wished I hadn't gone out of town.

"No."

"Were they holding hands or kissing?"

"No."

"Well, then what did you see?"

"Nothing, forget it." But I couldn't forget it. It's all I thought about. So I went home and called Pierre and asked him to come over. Then I called Fiona, but of course she denied everything.

"Nothing happened," said Pierre. "I was bored, so I came over here."

"You better not be lying to me," I said back. "I won't be mad, but if she is cheating on me you should tell me."

"I would. Nothing happened."

"That's what she says, but I don't believe her."

Pierre smiled. It brought me no comfort.

"Thanks, brother," said Pierre after I threw him a can of coke. It was a Thursday night. Everyone else in the house was asleep. I liked it that way; it was like I owned the place. He popped the top and the spray hit him under his nose. The look on his face transported me back in time to when we were nine years old. He was making the same face when we watched a Ku Klux Klan march in downtown D.C. on the news.

"Why do they wear white?" I asked puzzled. They looked like they were playing ghosts. But the pointy hats made them also look like dunces who should sit in the corner of a classroom.

"It's their costume, like when you dress up at Halloween," said Mother. "They are afraid people will recognize them."

"Why don't they want to be recognized?" asked Pierre.

"They're ashamed of what they're doing."

"Then why are they marching?" I wanted to know.

"Well, they hate Pierre because he's black and they hate you because you're half Jewish," said Mother.

"But I never met them," was all I could say.

The march turned from an organized gathering into a bloody riot when a crowd of counter protesters began throwing bricks from the tops of surrounding buildings. White sheets turned red, soaked with blood. Pierre grinned.

Pierre lived in a row house in Northeast, behind the National Zoo. He had been adopted by his mother, a former Gray Panther. Pierre's house was run down and in a low-income neighborhood that was mostly black. Pierre's adoptive mother truly loved him and Pierre loved her back. Even if he stayed at my house most of the week, she always knew where we were and what we were up to, with the exception of our bad behavior. She didn't know about our gang.

Later that summer, Pierre and I were walking the alleys in Pierre's part of the city. We saw a buzz of activity in front of a row house. There were lots of cops in black and blue windbreakers with the letters "ATF" and "DEA" stenciled on the back of their jackets. The cops had about ten kids on the ground in front of them. Pierre recognized some of the kids from the basketball court who were about our age, 13 to 15. The house was being used to run guns, semi and fully automatic assault rifles and hand guns. Cops were walking out with arms full of weapons. It wasn't like the movies I'd watched at Father's house. Police weren't the heroes. They gloated over the boys lying prostrate in a horizontal line on the sidewalk, hands bound behind their backs by plastic cuffs that were more like garbage bag ties. It was different where Pierre lived.

A few days later, outside Mother's house, I was walking at two in the morning. I stopped by Nazi Shawn's car to take a piss, then went back to the street. Just then four cop cars pulled in front of a house on W Street. The cops drew their guns and rushed to the door; cops were in front and in back, at the side of the door and beneath windowsills. The biggest cop ran forward, gripping a metal ram by its handlebar, and bashed the door, while a few officers gathered behind him.

"Police! We have a warrant!" they screamed, darting inside.

Minutes later, the cops emerged, calmly and quietly, without their man. They propped up the door, sectioned off the area with police tape, and left a note tacked to the front door. I laughed and went back home. Maybe Pierre's neighborhood wasn't so different from mine. The drugs and violence that once covered only a few blocks were seeping into the rest of the city.

Kicked in the Face

THE DEAD BOYS
  "Sonic Reducer"
    I don't need anyone
    Don't need no mom and dad
    Don't need no pretty face
    Don't need no human race
    I got news for you for you
    Don't need you too

Mother's Mercury Zephyr came screeching to a stop and the dust trailing the car drifted forward.

"Get in!"

"We just got here!" I said.

"Get in the fucking car right now!" I had never heard her use the F word and I thought I was in trouble for something I didn't remember.

"Get in the back with your sister."

Pierre took the passenger seat and I opened the back door. Sister was lying down, face-up, blood coming from her mouth. I sat next to her. Her eyes were shut but she was awake. The car was moving fast. Pierre looked over the front seat and didn't say anything.

"Keep your sister awake if she starts falling asleep," said Mother. "She could go into a coma."

I slid over, putting Sister's head in my lap. "Anastasia, stay awake."

She mumbled something at me. Her mouth was cut all the way through and I could see the inside. The gash was in a crescent shape and her teeth didn't look so good either.

"Please Anastasia, don't die. I need you around." I started to tear but didn't make a noise with Pierre in the front seat. Where was her moon? The one that orbited her head. I needed to see it, to know she was okay. I had always hated it since most times it mocked me, but now I would have done anything to have it back. When it came to the battles between parents and us, we had always been together. I would be lost without her.

Earlier that day Mother dropped Pierre and me off at the nature preserve while Sister went to her riding lesson. She had been taking them ever since the Great Experiment had begun for me. She took ballet and tap dancing, but her passion was riding. At the nature preserve, there was a room with a living beehive that was kept under thick glass. We watched the bees wiggle past each other, climb up the tube that led out the window and fly away. Getting bored, we moved outside to play in the playground. There wasn't anyone else there, so we didn't feel too old to swing or climb even though we were fifteen.

Later Mother told me that she dropped Sister off and was heading up Western Avenue to pick up some food. Sister was riding in circles around the ring when the horse bucked and she fell off. Landing hard in the dirt, she stood up and brushed off. The riding instructor yelled for her to grab the horse. Even though she knew you're not supposed to chase a horse after you have just fallen off, Sister thought she should do as the instructor said. The horse kicked and the hoof made contact with her mouth, lifting her off the ground and throwing her in the air more than ten feet. Sister was out for a few moments, then came to. At that moment Mother was pulling into the parking lot at McDonald's and knew something was wrong. Without calling the stable, she drove back fast, pulled up to the riding ring and jumped out of the car. "Where is Anastasia?"

"Bathroom," said one of the students and pointed. Mother put Sister in the back seat of the car, and picked up Pierre and me.

At Children's Hospital, Pierre and I waited while Sister and Mother were in the other room. Sister was x-rayed and her mouth was probed. The TV was playing an episode of "In Search Of," narrated by Leonard Nemoy from Star Trek. The show talked of the predictions of Nostradamus: how America and Russia were going to unite against a prince wearing a blue turban from the Middle East. This was going to be the third world war, and most of the population would die. Mother came out of the other room.

"Your sister's going to be fine, but we have to wait for a plastic surgeon. That will take some time. The last time I talked with your mother, she said something odd to me". Mother was looking at Pierre. "If something happens and you have to take my son to the hospital, make sure you get a plastic surgeon to do the stitching if the injury is to his face. It was good advice." She smiled at us and disappeared. We went home eight hours later.

"The nurse told me it was going to hurt when they gave me the shot of novocaine," said Sister. "She said it was okay to cry. When they gave me the shot, I started screaming. She told me, 'Don't yell! You're scaring all the other children on the floor.' She was angry. I told her, "Well then, you have to be more specific next time." Sister stopped talking since her mouth was giving her pain. Her moon was wobbly and slow, but it was back. I knew she was going to be fine and I was happy.

It was a few days later when I made a suggestion to Sister.

"You want to try something that might make your mouth feel better?" She had been cranky all night. Mother was still at work, as she was most days. Patsy had gone home. Pierre and Dash had come up with the idea.

"What?" Sister was poking the side of her lip, which was still puffy, and looked first to Pierre and Dash, then to me.

"Mom's liquor cabinet" I said. Dash and Pierre smiled. Sister tried to smile.

I was formally introduced to alcohol. Before that, we had been nothing more than casual acquaintances. When I was very young, I would watch the adults drink at parties, holding glasses of rust-colored liquid that rolled around from one side of the tumbler to the other as they knelt to pat my head.

"Can I have some?" I asked one of Mother's friends.

"Oh darling, you wouldn't like the taste," she replied, tucking my curls behind my ear.

We had two houses and two parents who liked to work. Even though I had many chances to experiment with drinking, I didn't until I was fifteen. With Dash and Pierre, I was looking for something new to do. We poured a little bit from each of Mother's bottles of alcohol, no more than an ounce, into a glass and mixed it together with orange juice. Our concoction tasted awful, nothing like soda or chocolate milk. "Brother, are we drunk yet?"

I said yes, but didn't really know. Adding more alcohol to the mix and drinking more, I started to feel strange. I understood why adults liked it so much.

"I don't see why you like that Fiona girl?" she said.

Dash was watching Sister. She ignored him.

"What do you mean? She's hot."

"No she's not."

"What do you know about girls being hot? You like boys."

"No I don't. I like girls."

"You don't know what you're talking about."

"Yes I do. I like girls."

Sister was fourteen and hadn't shown interest in anything male or female. "Have you kissed a girl?"

Her face bunched up like the thought was disgusting. "No!"

"Then I'm not going to worry about it."

Pierre was chuckling. I punched him in the arm and he stopped. Sister had another big gulp and then noticed Dash staring at her. She fixed on him until he averted his eyes.

Sister and I developed our talent for drinking too much, getting sick, acting stupid and doing the whole thing over again the next night. Mother's liquor cabinet was being raided often. The bottles became more water than booze since I always refilled them with the same amount we had taken. A few blocks away, there was a mini-mart run by a Chinese family. The drinking age in D.C. at that time was 18. Walking in one day, I tried buying some beer. Milwaukee's Best was all I could afford. "I'm picking this up for my mother" I told the clerk even though he didn't ask me. He bagged it up. Walking out the door, I was scared that someone would see I had beer in the bag. Pierre was at the corner with Sister and two of her friends. Freedom was an ugly girl who wore thick glasses and had an over-sized forehead. She was almost a girl version of Charlie without the bad breath. Nicole was a small, sickly black girl who periodically coughed.

"Brother, we can't go home since Mother of the womb will be back soon."

"Mother of the what?" asked Pierre.

Never mind," I said to Pierre, then turned to the rest of the group. "Let's go to the graveyard."

We walked down the street and made our way into the graveyard on a path that led through the brush. It was quiet. You could see the city moving around us, but the graveyard was a dead zone. We sat on the gravestones. I ran my hand along the top of the coarse rock, beaten by the years and weather. I handed a beer to Dash. Dash smelled faintly of weed. He was becoming more handsome by the day. His baby fat had slowly disappeared and he no longer wore the thick black glasses. He must have had on contact lenses. In the last month he had started wearing a Grateful Dead denim jacket.

"You know if you're going to become a hippie I have to start harassing you," I said.

"That's fine with me. I tried to like that punk rock stuff and it sucked," he said back.

Pierre was looking at Freedom and sitting close to her. Sister's scar was thin and barely noticeable. She looked over my shoulder at something and I turned to see what it was. Fiona and Stephanie were walking between the head stones.

"What are they doing here?" she said, annoyed.

"I told them we might be here."

Fiona sat next to me and kissed me on the mouth. We had made up earlier that day. She had stopped by Mother's house and told me I was being an asshole and that she hadn't fooled around with anyone. I didn't believe her, but I also didn't like being alone, so I decided to go along with her lie. I noticed everyone watching us and turned red. Sister shook her head and I didn't have to look to know her moon was there.

Madonna's "Like a Virgin" was on heavy rotation. Fiona sported the latest Madonna flair: black rubber bracelets, a dozen or so on each wrist, crucifixes, earrings and sometimes a rosary worn around her neck. Everything she wore was lace and she had on thick mascara. A poor man's Madonna, Fiona had huge breasts, a cute face, tight clothes, and a little girl's voice. She was fourteen, a year younger than me. She exuded sexuality, my first true girlfriend. Young and inexperienced, I chose not to notice Fiona's personality defect. She flirted with other boys. I heard the faintest of rumors that slowly grew to a roar: that she'd made out with

Pierre in the phone booth at Roy Rogers in Tenleytown, given Dash a blowjob on a camping trip, fucked a punk in the squat. She was supposedly the biggest slut I knew; yet I was still a virgin. She was my first love, but each rumor chipped away at that love until there was nothing left but a shell. After Fiona, it would be hard to trust anyone again, but I stayed with her even after I didn't love her. She was my best bet to get laid. All I could do was love to hate her.

Each weekend we began to run off to Georgetown to see the Rocky Horror Picture Show. The show started at midnight and I wouldn't get home till 2 am. The theater was only eight or nine blocks from Mother's house, and even though the screening was rowdy, it was supervised. The film was a cult classic in which the audience participated by dressing up, yelling out comments, kicking, dancing and throwing everything from toast to toilet paper at the screen. The audience was full of oddballs, freaks and misfits, and if you looked hard enough you might find a fake Madonna and her punk boyfriend. We threw rice at the screen during the wedding scene. The biggest thrill of the night was the walk home, but not because of Fiona. Taking the fast way home, we walked the trail from lower Glover to upper. The path was steep with pebbles underfoot and dark. If someone hid, we wouldn't see them. The woods flanked both sides of the trail, but after a few months, we hadn't been murdered. In D.C. the murder rate had gone through the roof so I was always a bit paranoid. We upped the ante to drinking in the graveyard at the top of Georgetown on Wisconsin Avenue. We made out between the gravestones and it was a constant effort to hump her. It was only a matter of time before she would toss me aside and run off, leaving me alone with an erection.

After a particularly bad fight with her mother, Fiona spent the night at Mother's house. She would have to sleep in the room off of mine.

"She's not sleeping in your room," said Mother. "There will be no hanky-panky going on."

Mother's row house had a two-story add-on. Sister and I shared the upstairs add-on that was just off our two bedrooms. My old bunk bed divided the space. Fiona put on some of my old boxer shorts and a t-shirt. Her breasts floated under the shirt and I guessed where her nipples might be. The lower bunk would be Fiona's assigned bed for the night.

Mother yawned, rolled her hands into fists and spent a moment trying to push the sleep from her eyes, but instead she just pushed it in deeper.

"I'm going to bed. Be good." She went into her room at the end of the hall and quietly pulled the door closed behind her. Mother's room was twenty feet away from mine. She was a light sleeper, and even my walking to the bathroom next to her room might wake her up. I would have to mask any noise by turning on the air-conditioner. My air-conditioner only fit into the window of my room that separated the original part of the house from the add-on. The windows on the add-on were vertical and didn't open all the way. The exhaust would blow hot humid air into the add-on, forcing Fiona into my room, which was cold. I sat in bed thinking of her in the room next door. *I should just go in there and get her. What if that's not the right thing to do? She's upset about the fight with her mother so maybe I should just leave her alone? But I'm not going to get another chance like this. Maybe tonight is the night I have sex?* I could hear the sound of the door slowly opening and the creaking of floor boards as Fiona carefully stepped over to my bed and slipped under the covers with me. My heart raced. We kissed and dry-humped for hours. I could taste cigarette mixed with cherry lip gloss. Her breath on my neck gave me a tingling sensation. Her full breasts pressed against my chest. The anger I harbored for her vanished. It would come back, but while she was in the room with me I couldn't remember it. I couldn't remember anything. Mother wasn't there, Sister wasn't next door, I wasn't dyslexic, or retarded. There was nothing but me and her. Fiona had nowhere to run. She gave me my first blowjob and I thought things couldn't get any better than that. At least I knew then how Dash had felt with her.

The blowjob kept me at bay. Why did I need to lose my virginity? With a blowjob, I didn't have to work and she wouldn't get pregnant. I only felt half guilty that I didn't return the favor. The guilt was related to the uneasy feeling right after I came. What are you supposed to do? Hold her? Talk? What should I say? "Thanks" just didn't seem right. My mind was blank, so I said nothing and fell asleep holding her.

But even the mighty power of the blowjob would fade and my lust for more would drive me to the next thing. Fiona was still holding out, at least with me.

The row house was packed with friends, some from school and some of the neighborhood boys who skated plywood ramps in the alley behind Mother's house. We were drunk on Milwaukee's Best. Mother worked late again and had no clue that her house had been turned into a bar for underage kids. It was a weekday so we knew Mother wouldn't be bothering us. I noticed Fiona in the doorway. She was dressed in white lace and looked good, just like a cheap Madonna. She came over to me and took me by the hand and I saw an odd smirk persist throughout the room, as if everyone knew what was about to happen. One flight down into the basement, there was a guest bed on the far side of the room. The walls were painted a sky blue and the cement floor was green. Fiona led me to the bed and undid my pants. She broke free from my kiss, her lips caterpillared up my neck, stopping at my ear, "You know you can do anything you want to me," she whispered.

"Really?" I asked. She smiled and pulled my pants down to my ankles.

Mother had given me my first condom. "I don't think you should be having sex, but if you do, use a condom," she had said. "I don't want to be a grandmother just yet and you don't want any sexually transmitted diseases."

I had been carrying that condom around since. Now it was finally going to be put to use. I pulled off its wrapper. It was in bad shape, but I didn't care. I put it on, then put it in. Standing off the edge of the bed with my clothes and shoes on, there was no romance. I slipped out. She helped me stick it back in. I really didn't know what I was doing. I thrust my hips but was out of sync with her. She gave me a penetrating look, and I knew for sure that she had done this before. I found the rhythm. She laid her head back down and closed her eyes. I must have been doing something right. It happened fast. I didn't want to come, but I couldn't stop it. The orgasm felt like what I thought heroin must feel like, but shorter. If I were going to become addicted to something, it would be the orgasm. I lost myself, forgetting everything, the world, and her. There was nothing but a good feeling rushing over me, pumping through my veins, pumping through her. I melted into her, into the mattress, through the cement floor, past the foundation, through the soil. Sex became my new obsession. A few moments passed and slowly everything came back into focus, my basement, Fiona under me. I could taste the sweat on her breast, and I felt alone. I was drunk and it was over in a flash.

"Thanks," I said and, as soon as I did, I wished I'd come up with something more profound.

"You're welcome." She was still under me. I felt like I was crushing her so I pulled out and stood up. I pulled my pants up, and waited for her to gather herself. As she pushed her breasts back into her bra, I realized I hadn't taken it all the way off. We climbed the stairs together.

When I walked into the room where my friends waited, I received applause from the party and was relieved it was over.

Now that I had had sex, I was experienced. I was a man. I felt superior to all the virgins I knew, and I understood why all the non-virgins acted so smug. Something else happened, too. I started to realize that Fiona wasn't the only girl in the world that would have sex with me, that in fact there were going to be plenty of girls and they didn't care if I was dyslexic. I was sure Fiona was having sex with other people. I could do better than her.

Boarding School

"You've outgrown the Lab School and you need to start thinking about your next step," said Mother. She was sitting in the living room when I was about to walk out the front door. The Lab School didn't go all the way through high school and Mother had been bringing up the subject for months. It was the last thing I wanted to talk about.

"Why can't I just go to a public school like Wilson?" I asked. It could be my chance at being normal. I could start over.

"Because of your dyslexia, they will put you in the special education class. I've set up a tour of the one they have at Wilson."

"Did you look to see if there were any other schools he could go to?" said Sister as she came down the stairs. Her moon was out, but it was directed at Mother. Sister was wearing one of my old band shirts, the Clash. She had started borrowing my records and we would have a fight at least once a week when I would have to go in her room to track one down.

"This is his only option," said Mother and then she left the room.

"You're being set up," said Sister as I walked out.

The following Monday, I visited the Special Ed class at Wilson. Stepping into the room, I could see it was full of physically challenged kids, kids in wheelchairs or kids with Down syndrome. One kid was sitting in the corner with his mouth open wide. His tongue looked fat and spit drooled onto his lap. There was nothing special about the room - chalkboard, fluorescent lights overhead, desks and chairs - it was purgatory. I will drop out before going here, I thought. If I was picked on now, it will be a thousand times worse here. Fuck this place. Immediately I felt bad because I was treating these kids just like how I was being treated. They probably wanted what I wanted, to be normal. Any one of them would have traded what I had for what they had. Maybe I was a brat, a spoiled little rich kid, who cries because he can't read like the rest of the rich kids. And they would be right, but I could only look out of my own two eyes and until that changed I could only feel my own pain.

"Oh, you're here to see the class, right?" said the teacher. She looked tired and disheveled. She probably didn't want to deal with me.

I nodded.

"Well, have a seat."

"I have to pee pee," said a girl with a swollen head. She reminded me of Charlie but her breath didn't stink or at least I couldn't smell it.

The teacher ignored her.

"What other classes do they take here?" I asked.

"Oh, this is it. The homeroom is the only one they have. They stay with me here all day, but we do have a variety of different activities like drawing and story time. We take breaks and naps too." She paused and then went on, "But I can tell, you shouldn't be here. This is for the kids who need special attention." She stood up and led the girl off to the bathroom.

That night my parents took me to dinner. I knew something was up when I heard they were both coming and Sister was staying at home. *If they try and make me go to that special ed class I'll drop out, no backing down this time. If they push me too far I'll run away.* Father and Mother sat across from me. Father was in a grey suit that looked a size too big. He had lost weight since Mother had moved out. His mustache was thick and needed a trim. He was probably thinking about Nixon and really didn't understand why one school was better for me than another. Mother just stared at me preparing her case. Since the divorce, I hadn't seen them together unless it was to pass off Sister and me. "What do you think of the special education class?" asked Mother. The waiter still hadn't taken our order.

"I'm not going to go there," I said. They moved to Plan B.

Plan B was Landmark, a boarding school in Beverly Farms, about 45 minutes outside of Boston. I hadn't even eaten any food and wasn't in the mindset to make major decisions. I said yes without seeing the school or knowing much about it.

Back at Mother's house, I told Sister what had happened.

"Well, at least I'm not going to be in the Special Ed class," I said.

"How can you leave me with them?" She didn't like to show emotion, but I could hear the choking in her voice.

"I don't want to go, but I can't go to the public school. I have no choice."

"You always have a choice. You could go to GDS. They could get you a tutor. I knew they were planning something and that's why they didn't take me to dinner. I ask too many questions. You were tricked."

"What do you mean?"

"They send you to see the worst place possible, and then force you to make a decision between that and the alternative they have picked out. You can never complain. You never had a choice."

"They must have a good reason they want me there."

"They are crazy, so who knows? All they do is work. Now they don't have to deal with you. What am I going to do?"

That summer I had bought my first leather jacket after working a few weeks at a movie theater by Mazza Gallery Mall. I painted a white skull on the back and put pyramid spikes on the lapel and cuffs. One-inch buttons of my favorite bands were grouped just left of my heart. A plaid shirt tightened around my waist and I wore plaid golfer pants. Sister bleached my hair. It was almost white, just like Billy Idol's. The sides were cut short with side burns and the front left long in a devil's lock. I thought I looked cool, like real punk rockers I had seen. If I had to go to a new school and start over, I would do it the way I wanted. This time everyone would know me as that cool punk kid.

My parents never complained about my new look. Dr. Spock's book advised against it. "It's just a rebellious phase. If you say something, it will take longer for it to pass," said Mother to Father over the phone.

"When the rebel yells, he cries More! More! More!" I sang to myself. I had just bought a Billy Idol record that had a photo of him printed right on the vinyl. Mother took me to get new clothes that were within the dress code of the boarding school - corduroy pants and blazer, buttoned down long-sleeved shirts and ties.

"What color shirts do you like?" she asked.

"I don't want any of these, so what does it matter?"

"You will be the one who has to wear it." She pulled a blue and white striped long sleeved shirt off the rack and held it up against my chest.

"Here you go. This looks nice," she said and I rolled my eyes. It all looked like shit to me.

She picked up the ugliest tie I had ever seen. It was grey and knit. Mother held it under my chin and I looked at the mirror. It was as though my tongue fell out through the bottom of my jaw.

"Can't I just get a clip on?"

"These look better," she said.

It was the first tie I ever had and Father had to show me how it worked. He stood behind me and tightened it around my neck, choking me. It summed up my boarding school fears.

At Mother's, I packed the trunk with punk rock tapes, clothes and toiletries. On the inside of the trunk's lid, I had put stickers of every punk band I knew. Sister was standing behind me.

"You know you don't have to go. It's not too late."

"What else can I do?"

"Look at other schools. I don't believe the only school you can go to is in Boston."

"It's too late. They already paid for everything."

"I can't believe you would leave me with them," she stormed out of the room and slammed the door. It had always been the two of us. If I could, I would have taken her with me. We could have both started over.

Sister stopped talking to me after the fight. Our dog sat at the top of the steps and I patted her on the head and then scratched her butt. She wiggled with delight. She couldn't see any more so I wasn't sure she even knew it was me. Mother had told me not to say goodbye to a dog when you leave.

"It makes them anxious. They have no concept of time, so if you say goodbye and walk out it's like torture for the dog. It makes them feel abandoned and they can't tell if it's for a minute or a month. So it's better to just walk out". Maybe that was best for Sister too? I walked out without saying anything to her.

Mother took me to the airport and she looked like she was going to cry. I felt like crying but we both held our tears.

"Remember, if you get homesick, it's just a two hour flight," she said. She stood there until I couldn't see her any more. I shuffled down the hall to the plane. Over the runway, a low shelf of clouds blocked the sun. I wondered if it would be a bumpy ride.

At the Boston airport, I was picked up by the school van. Driving up the coast, we passed small towns, then the road narrowed to two lanes. The homes were further apart. We were beyond the suburbs, in the country. Turning up a steep drive and past a rock wall, I saw the view of the main building open before us, a Victorian mansion. Students carried duffle bags or dragged trunks. The driver pointed me in the direction of the Dean of Students. Everything was new. Waiting in line I made my way to the front. The Dean of Students looked up from his papers at all of my plaidness. I was checked off his list, and then he squinted at me. I knew we were not going to get along. He looked like a flunky lawyer in his cheap suit. I already understood our roles, him - authority, me - the rebel who fought him. What an asshole, I thought. Doesn't he know everyone can tell what he's thinking? Or at least I can.

The rooms were small and basic. A dozen buildings were spread across the property, classrooms, gym, printing press, and dorms. The main building, an old mansion, housed the younger kids and on its first floor was our cafeteria. The seniors had their own house that was connected to the art class and school library. My dorm was for the new kids and the ages were mixed. The first day I noticed there were a few other punks and one skinhead. Talking with a few of them, I knew I wouldn't have a problem making friends. That was the funny thing about punk rock. You could drop a kid anywhere in the world, it didn't even matter if they didn't speak the same language. If they were both into punk rock, they got along.

My new roommate had The Smiths playing in the background. The first night the teacher who lived in the dorm came by our room, telling us it was lights out. He made his way down the hall, saying the same thing to each room. I tried to sleep that night, but everything was so new. It was hard to relax. Then I started thinking of Fiona. *How long would it be before she cheated on me?* The next morning, the same teacher woke us. He popped his head in and turned on the light with "Time to get up. Up and at 'em!"

"You better get up," said my roommate.

"I'm skipping breakfast." My stomach felt nervous. Food might make it worse.

"They don't let you skip breakfast. You don't have to eat, but they kick everyone out of the dorm and make them sit in the cafeteria."

"Are you fucking kidding me?"

"No man, you have to go up there and sit."

The shower was open; I put on my flip-flops and walked in. Led Zeppelin was playing from the other room. Looking in the mirror at my new school uniform, I tucked in the shirt and tried to fix my ugly knit tie, but gave up after re-tightening it a few times. I took it off and just tightened it in a regular knot. I knew at the end of the day, I would have to cut it off with scissors. The teacher came back and collected all the stragglers (like me) and led us up to the main building. They did a roll call and I heard an odd name, odd because I didn't expect to hear it that morning. When I looked around the room, I matched it with its owner. Stephanie had followed me to a second school.

"Holy shit!" The teacher taking roll stopped and stared at me.

"Sorry," I said and was quiet until he called my name. I hadn't hung out alone with Stephanie over the last year, ever since I had had sex with Fiona. After breakfast I ducked out. I could see Stephanie looking around for me. I didn't want to talk to her. In our last conversations she reminded me that Fiona was cheating on me and that I could do better. I didn't want to think about Fiona with someone else.

I went to my first class. The room was white like all the other class rooms I had ever been in, even the fluorescent lights above had that same institutional look. But outside the window, it was a new world. The trees were evergreens and reached high over the roof. The smell of ocean spray filtered through the building and there was no sound of traffic from the street. The English teacher was the same guy who lived in our dorm. He was passionate about his class and I knew it wasn't going to be that bad.

The student teacher ratio was the same as at the Lab School. Seven students to one teacher. The major difference between the two schools was the emphasis Landmark placed on routine, organization and presentation. It was a never-ending checklist. Even after the school day, you were on a schedule. Dinner was six-thirty to seven-thirty, then there was an hour break followed by two hours of homework. Even if you didn't have any homework to do, you sat at your desk while the resident teacher make the rounds and checked up on you. After homework, you had another hour of free time, then lights out, which meant you had to be in bed in your own room. Prison, that was my first impression. The Parents never mentioned any of this to me. I imagined Sister's moon and her telling me "I told you so." I said I was going to go and had already told everyone I was leaving. I could hear Father and Mother's voices, "Give it a chance. It will be good for you." But in the back of my mind I knew it was only a matter of time. At home I could stay up and out late, and on school nights they were never home so I could do anything I wanted. You couldn't give a kid freedom then expect to take it away.

"Hey man, I'm Mark," said a kid about my age. We were in the hallway of our dorm. He was skinny with a mouth full of braces that almost made me laugh since they were in opposition to his shaved head, twelve hole doc martins, and all around tough look he was attempting to cultivate. He was anything but tough, but then again neither was I. He held out his hand, I shook it.

"You like punk rock?" he asked. When he spoke his words were mangled by the metal and spit tangled in his mouth. I nodded. "Come upstairs. I have some records." His room looked like mine but on the other side and one flight up. Beyond the windows the sky was black. There were no lights from the campus. If I were going to run off that would be the side to do it from, I thought. Mark flipped through a crate of records, his fingers looked like they were dancing across the top edges as his eyes flicked back and forth reading albums.

"You shave your head every day?" I asked. I didn't really care, but I thought he might want to talk about it and the best way to make friends with someone was to get them talking about themselves.

"I'm a skinhead," he said looking at me like it was obvious. When I gave him a blank stare he asked, "Don't you go to shows?"

"No." What happens at shows? I was never asked to go. The truth was I was scared to go. What if I was rejected from the punk scene? Then the illusion of being accepted would be over.

"Well, if you went to the shows, you would see a lot of skinheads." He found a record and pulled it out of the stack, then carefully placed it on the turntable.

"You heard of Agnostic Front?" he asked.

I shook my head.

"How could you not listen to them?" The music came out of the speakers, but unlike the other punk I listened to, this was more of a street fight. The drums were sharp and hard, the vocals raspy and shouting. The bass and guitar were on the attack. I liked it.

"This is a skinhead band," he said. "Skinheads in most cities are divided between racists and non-racists with two distinctly separate histories." He sounded like he was reading a book report in front of the class. Later he would confess that he had written one for his English class. "There are the non-racist skinheads called Traditional, Unity or SHARP Skins (Skinheads Against Racial Prejudice) – all the same thing by different names. Some of these guys date back to the '60s when the working class English kids would go to Jamaican dance halls. The white kids copied the black kids; they shaved their heads or styled their hair into a crop. Dressed in suits, they listened to Soul, Reggae and early Ska- bands like Desmond Decker and the Aces. I have a tape of some of that stuff you can copy. The Nazi or White Power Skinheads showed up in the late '70s with punk rock. In England there was a high unemployment rate that turned into hatred for immigrants. They got blamed for taking all the jobs." But what he didn't explain and I later realized was that all skinheads try to recruit new skinheads from the punk scene. It was like a war between rival factions and each side wanted bigger numbers. That's why he asked me up to his room to listen to music. I wasn't interested in being a skinhead.

"So if you listen to punk and you're a skin that means you're a Nazi?" I asked.

"No! I listen to hardcore punk and I'm not a Nazi." I was still confused but dropped the subject.

"Hey, we should go to a show in Boston," said Mark.

I was a little apprehensive, but at the same time didn't want to say no.

"They would let us go?"

"Sure, you just have to get permission."

The next day I went to The Dean of Students. He made me sit outside his office and wait until my break was almost up. I don't think he was doing anything since I couldn't hear anything from the other side. When he did let me in he had me stand as if I wasn't welcome.

"What can I do for you?" He didn't even look up.

"I would like a pass to go to Boston for the day."

"What for?"

"To see a band."

"You have permission from all your teachers and parents?"

"Not yet, but I will."

"How old are you?"

"Sixteen."

"After I get all the permissions back, I'll determine whether you can go." He handed me a sheet of paper with lines for each class. Then he dismissed me by going back to his work and ignoring me. What an asshole, I thought as I walked out. Stephanie saw me and I ducked down a hall before she could catch up with me. How was I going to start over here if she anchored me to home? By the end of the day I had gotten signed permissions from more than half my teachers. That night I was back in Mark's room.

"What is the deal with this school?" I asked. "They are so uptight."

Mark took out a Business record and put it on the turntable before answering me. "Yeah, they're fucking Nazis. I want to blow this school up."

"And all the students seem so strange."

"This is the best school in the country for dyslexics so all of the rich people send their kids here. You know the guy who always has on white pants and shirt? You know that cokehead guy? His grandfather founded a major Hollywood movie studio . One kid's dad is a famous racecar driver, another's mom is a big movie star. It's the thrown away children of the rich, powerful and famous."

There was a pile of flyers on Mark's desk. I flipped through them.

"Those are shows I did in Connecticut. I'm a promoter. I did all age shows."

"Can I borrow some of these?" I asked.

"Yeah, but be careful with them."

The teacher popped his head in the room saying, "It's time for bed."

The next day, I woke before the teacher knocked on our door. Led Zeppelin was already playing in the next room and I knew the order of the songs. It was tape 2, side 1 of a 7-tape collection of everything the band had ever done. My roommate helped me put on another tie and I walked up to the cafeteria for roll call. Stephanie was watching me and when she saw that I saw her, she waved enthusiastically. Walking to class, she ran up behind me.

"What are you doing here?" I said, annoyed, before she had a chance to say anything else.

"My mother talked to your mother and thought it was a good idea and I wanted to come, so here I am". She had on shorts that were tight. Her stomach was flat, but so was her chest. But what Stephanie lacked in the front, she made up for it in the back. She had a perfect ass. As she stood in front of me, I noticed the boys behind her sneaking a peek.

"Does your mother ever do anything without first talking to my mother?"

She seemed confused by the question.

"Well, sure, all the time."

"Great, now leave me alone." I was mean to make a point; otherwise she would have kept following me. We were in a new place and I could have dated her, but I was thinking about meeting new girls. I had seen a few around campus. Besides, I had promised Fiona that I wouldn't hook up with Stephanie, even though I was sure she was hooking up with some other guys.

That night before dinner I called home. Sister answered. She was crying. She never showed emotion so it made me upset too.

"What's the matter?"

"The Parents killed your dog." She was upset because she knew I would be upset. That's how we worked. We worried about each other.

"What do you mean? They wouldn't put Fluffball to sleep without telling me."

"They said they didn't want to make you upset."

"Put Mother on the phone." I could hear her calling for Mother. I was using the phone in the main building and there was a kid waiting to use it next.

"Hello," said Mother. She braced herself.

"How could you do that!"

"The dog was very sick. She was old and blind and couldn't walk. It would have been cruel to keep her alive. She was suffering." It was the same line of thought Father had used. No wonder they had found each other.

"You send me away and kill my dog the second I'm gone? Why wouldn't you tell me first? It was my dog, not yours!" I hung up the phone and went back to my room. At dinner I saw Stephanie and told her about my dog.

"I'm sorry… there's something I wanted to tell you… but maybe I should do it another time?" Her adorable eyes darted back and forth again between mine.

"No, tell me now."

"Fiona wrote, telling me about the boys she hooks up with."

"She told me on the phone that she can't wait to see me and that she isn't hanging out with anyone."

"Well, she's lying to one of us."

"Why does everything have to happen at once?" Stephanie put her hand on mine and I felt strange but I didn't pull away.

"Okay people, quiet down!" said my history teacher. She was standing on one of the chairs at the front of the dining hall. "Tonight there will be restricted access for the campus. A hurricane is coming up the East Coast and should be here in the next few hours. So we will be hunkered down here in the main building. Stay away from the windows…"

Later that night, the payphones were busy. It took nearly an hour before it was my turn and with a kid from my floor waiting behind me I dialed and turned as far away from him as I could, cupping my hand over the receiver. The wind outside picked up and I could hear it blowing against the walls, trees and everything else. The edge of the shelf on which the phone rested had the wood finish picked off by nervous fingernails and revealed the plywood underneath. I was now picking where the last kid had left off. The phone picked up on the other side.

"Hello" said Fiona. Her voice sounded cheerful, as if she were expecting someone else to be calling.

"You're a whore and I know it!"

"What are you talking about?" She sounded like a valley girl, even though she had never been outside of the D.C. area.

"I always heard you were sleeping around. Now I know for sure." I still didn't know it for sure, but I didn't want to see the letter. I wanted Fiona to trick me into being happy, even if that made me hate her more.

"I'm not sleeping with anyone. Who's telling you that?"

"Don't worry about that."

"How am I supposed to defend myself if I don't know who's saying bad things about me?" I could hear in her voice that she was searching for the name she already knew. Stephanie. "I think I know."

"I was so good to you and you shit on me. Why tell me you love me, and then go sleep with my friends?"

"I do love you, and I didn't sleep with anyone. I haven't done anything."

"I don't want to see you anymore. Don't call me!" I slammed the phone down, and felt a bit better. Or maybe I was redeeming my pride. I didn't make eye contact with the kid waiting for the phone and walked out of the room. I should have dumped her long ago, I thought. But then I started wondering if I should have put up with it, so I had access to sex. *Shit.* I had an urge to call her back and make up.

The lobby was packed with kids sitting in groups or by themselves. I made my way over to Mark and a few of the punk kids. Stephanie was sitting on the outside of the circle. Something crashed against the front door and everyone looked towards the sound. Thunder was breaking and the lights flickered out, with the emergency lights coming on in the doorways of each room. I wanted to be home. I missed my family and friends. Everything was happening at home and I was missing it.

"What did she say?" asked Stephanie.

"She denied everything." I sat down and Stephanie put her head in my lap like my dog used to.

"You know this place is haunted?" said Mark.

Wind slipped under the front door and whistled like a pipe organ carrying a long note. Then everything fell silent as if God had dropped a giant glass over the school. My ears popped.

The Rat

SLAPSHOT
"Back On the Map"
I'm going to get it back
Get back what we had
We're going to fight to make it right

The next day, the sky was clear. The grounds were littered with broken branches and garbage. The school staff was at work picking it all up when the van pulled in front. Mark, Stephanie and I hopped in and were dropped off at the T that took us to Boston. It felt good to be back in a city and see people just walking and doing their thing. The city reminded me of Georgetown. It was just as old, maybe older, made of red bricks and a few cobbled roads. Turning the corner, I saw a line waiting to get into the small club.

"It's the Ratskeller but everyone just calls it the Rat," said Mark. We waited in line, paid our money and got stamped on the back of our hands. As we walked down the stairs, all daylight vanished. The room was dark and packed with kids. The air was thick with moisture and the faint smell of teenage sweat. A small stage was at one end, bathrooms to one side and merchandise for the bands on the other side. I bought a Slap Shot shirt before even hearing the band. Fanzines, stickers and 7" records were spread out on the table. I flipped through the 7"s but didn't see the S.O.A. on green vinyl. Kids grouped together, some with mohawks, others with shaved heads, girls and boys with crazy colored hair. It was a room full of people that were all into what I was into. Sister would have enjoyed this, I thought. I walked over to Mark and Stephanie.

Stephanie's gaze had followed me around the room, but she always did that so I pretended I didn't notice.

A girl I had never seen before walked up to Mark and said hi. Mark turned to me and said, "This is Sally." Before she shook my hand, she handed me a fifth of vodka. She was a brunette with hazel eyes and big breasts. When she spoke, her voice was raspy and I was in love. I took a large gulp of vodka. It was warm and I tried not to notice the awful taste. I choked on the last bit and handed it back, wiping the corner of my mouth with the sleeve of my leather jacket. The first band went on. The music surged through me; the bass was so loud that it resonated in my chest and the back of my throat. The guitar sliced the air and the vocals made me wish it was me up on that stage with the mic in hand. I drank more of Sally's vodka and started feeling pretty drunk. The next band came on. More kids gathered by the stage and the circle of spinning bodies grew. Some kids ran onto the stage and dove onto the heads of the audience. They were picked up by the crowd, carried for a moment, then dropped when they reached a gap between people. Some kids just hopped up and down as though their legs were pogo sticks. From that point on I knew I was going to be at as many shows as I could.

I sat next to Sally. I put my head in her lap without asking and she began to play with my hair like Patsy used to. Sally was attractive, more so because she was new. None of the girls on campus paid me any attention except for Stephanie and here Sally was, staring at nothing else but me. Warmth bubbled up inside of me. I glanced over at Stephanie who was standing with Mark but glaring at me. I looked up at Sally.

"You want to make out?" I said. I knew this would make Stephanie upset, but if I made out with Stephanie, it could complicate things if I got back together with Fiona. I would be trapped.

"Sure." She pressed her thin lips against mine. I could taste the cheap vodka. I didn't mind.

The headlining band went on and I missed it. We kissed and rubbed on each other on the way back to the train, until Mark started to whine.

"Come on man, we're going to miss the last train back. You can see her next weekend" and he pulled me away from her. On the ride back, Stephanie wouldn't speak to me. She kept her head turned away from me, looking out the window. I think she might have been crying, so I left her alone.

I called Sally that night and she seemed surprised. We talked for the better part of an hour and I only got off the phone to let the next kid use it. On my door, there was a note that Fiona had called. I didn't call her back. And that felt good. I had choices. I knew I could have sex with someone else, and that Fiona had lost most of her power over me.

Sally and I talked everyday. The first things she told me were about being adopted and resenting her new parents, in part because they were Jewish and she was convinced that she was as pure as snow.

"An Aryan baby stolen by the dirty Jews," she said to me. But then again, she knew my last name was Jewish. "They're not my parents," she would hiss when I suggested that they could still love her.

A week passed, and I did everything I was told to do so I could get the thumbs up from all the teachers. My parents weren't a problem. They knew I wasn't happy at the school. They would let me go to Boston as much as I liked, but the Dean of Students didn't like me. He started making comments like "I think you should spend more time on campus and make some friends here. You will never get over being homesick if you keep leaving." After my third weekend in Boston, he changed the rules so that students could only get off campus every other weekend.

"He's a total fucking dick," I told Sally as she dyed my hair blue black in the upstairs bathroom of her parents' house. I knew it was against school rules, but I didn't care. If they were going to change rules on me then I'll change some on them.

"Yeah he was a dick when I was there. That's why I left the school." After she washed my hair, we had sex for the first time. It wasn't a struggle with Sally. We started kissing, and then groping. I was surprised when she touched me back. Fiona never did stuff like that; she made me do all the work.

"Do you have a condom?" asked Sally. She was asking me for sex. I almost tripped on my way back to my pants that had ended up on the other side of the room where Sally had thrown them. I had two condoms just in case this happened. She took it from me and put it on. *Holy shit, she knows what she's doing. I made the right choice, going to the show, and asking her to kiss me.* The sex was great. I didn't feel rushed or that we had to be quiet because Mother or Sister might hear. Sally's parents never bothered us. I think they were scared of her.

An hour later Sally asked, "Do you want to do it again?" And I did. The next time I would bring more condoms.

On Sunday, I walked into the dorm, already feeling tense about the week and weekend I had to be there.

"Oh shit man! You dyed your hair!" said my roommate when I walked into our room.

"Yeah, so what? You dye yours all the time."

"Yes, but its just highlights. Yours looks really unnatural. They are going to flip out."

"So maybe they will kick me out?"

"No, they'll just never let you leave the campus again."

"What the fuck? I can't stay here."

"Here, put this bandana on your head. At least it will cover it up around the campus."

"Well, if I'm going to hide it, you might as well give me a mohawk."

My roommate shaved the sides of my head and then we stood it up for fun. I went up to Mark's room and opened the door. He laughed.

"They are going to kill you." I was getting praise for being rebellious, which just made me want to do more. It was like I had gained punk points and they respected me more because of it.

The next day I put on my tie, slicked down my hair and covered it with the bandana and walked past the Dean of Students. He gave me a funny look but said nothing. I almost wished he had said something. I wanted to scream at someone, to tell them to go to hell, and fuck off. My first class was with the teacher from the dorm. The assignment was to bring in song lyrics and read them in class. He didn't say anything when I stood up and had on the bandana.

"I'm guilty of a racist crime that happened ninety-nine years before my time," I read the lyric sheet from a Minor Threat song. I noticed my reading was a little better. I hated Landmark but I was learning. I would never have admitted it at the time, thinking it would have just kept me there longer, but it was true. It was the routine, the very thing I hated most. They forced me to sit at my desk and muscle through the work. Even if my eyes burned I sat there until the time was up, trying to read. With no distractions I started coming around. It was slow, and almost unperceivable. I also noticed it was harder when I didn't care about the subject. If I was going to practice reading, it had to be something I was interested in.

I picked the Minor Threat song because I liked the meaning behind it. In Washington sometimes you got crap just for being white. Like I was personally responsible for slavery even though my family immigrated to this country sometime after. I then read over all of the lyrics on every record I had. My reading started with the lyric sheets. Songs are short, and I finished before my eyes began to burn. The lyrics revealed everything about the bands. Before I only liked the way the sounds made me feel, but now the lyrics told me a story, and the ones I liked most expressed my angst. It was like they were written just for me.

Winter break came and I went home. It was like work furlough from prison. The further away I got from the school, the better I felt. I smiled all the time and I must have looked like an idiot. But I did miss Sally. She would come down in a few days. I couldn't stop thinking of sex. I was an addict. If I moved back I would have to make her come see me every month, I thought. Though in reality that would only be a short-term answer and in the end we would have to break up. I didn't want to think about that, besides, I would see her here in D.C. in a few days.

It was common for Pierre to meet me at my house. Mother never turned on the porch light before leaving, so the front was often dark by the time I got home. She hid a key under the molding on the porch. Finding it meant searching in the dark, feeling around and crouching below the steps. Pierre knew where this extra key was hidden. He let himself in, had a bite to eat, watched TV and waited. Mother was at the airport picking me up and Sister hadn't made it back from her riding class.

Pierre had a habit of playing with toy guns. He bought a black plastic rifle, which was a convincing replica and had it with him as he let himself in. Our next door neighbors, who were new, didn't know Pierre. To them he was a young black man with a gun breaking into our home. They called the cops. Mother dropped me off at the house to go meet a friend. We had no idea the cops were on their way.

"What's Dash been up to?" I asked Pierre. Pierre was eyeing my new black mohawk. He didn't seem to approve. But they would all have to get used to the new me. I had changed, grown up and become a little more independent.

"He's been cutting down trees in the back of his house with a machete and smoking weed." Pierre was sitting on my bed, cocking the rifle and pulling the trigger over and over. "Paul shot him."

"What?" There was a knock at the front door. "You mean Paul from the Lab School who was always getting into trouble?"

"Yea, that Paul. He was playing around with a gun and shot Dash by accident or so that's what Paul says." The knocking from downstairs started again.

"Is he okay?"

"Yeah, it's not a big deal."

The knocking turned to pounding. I didn't move at first, thinking it was Fiona, but the knocking was too hard to be her and it didn't stop. As I made my way down the staircase, shouts came from the other side.

"Open up! It's the police!"

"I just got back! I haven't done anything yet!" was my automatic response. I hadn't known why I'd said that, but it had just flown out of my mouth.

As the door opened slowly, the barrel of a gun slipped through the crack. A middle-aged man with graying hair poked his head in, then seeing no threat, rushed in, followed by three more men. They scanned the living room, then spread themselves throughout the house. The gray-haired cop told us he was a detective from 2D (Second District). All the men were middle-aged. The gray-haired detective was obviously the boss.

"We got a call about a black man with a gun, breaking into this house," he said.

"That's Pierre," I said. "He's not a stranger. He comes and goes as he pleases. The gun's a toy."

Two more cops came in from outside.

"We're going to have to see the gun." The six cops ran upstairs with an enthusiasm rarely seen in middle-aged men. Pierre held the gun tightly and broke it in front of them as proof. As they left, the gray-haired man turned to Pierre.

"You're very lucky we didn't shoot you. You should know better than to play around with those things." I heard them outside, driving away. I walked into the room and sat next to Pierre and said, "If they'd shot you, Mother would've made it her life's work to ruin their lives and the neighbor who called them, and then she would have sued the city. You would have been rich if you'd lived."

"Yeah, but I would have been shot."

Sister walked in with a "Hi Brother" and vanished into her room with Nicole and Freedom. I walked in and sat on her bed next to Nicole.

"Where are you coming from?" I asked Sister, but I knew from the boots and pants that she had been at the stable.

"Riding."

"How can you ride again when a horse just about killed you?"

"I love them."

"I hate horses." I didn't tell her I hated them because one had tried to kill her.

"Why are there cop cars out front?"

"Ask Pierre."

Pierre came in the room.

"Where are you going to school?" Sister asked him.

"It's in Silver Spring," he said.

"How come you can't go there?" she asked me.

"I wasn't given the choice."

"You should ask Mother."

Looking around Sister's room, I noticed that she had painted it day-glo orange.

"Jesus Christ, this room makes me want to throw up."

"Well, then get out."

Pierre and I walked back into my room. Pierre was still looking at his broken gun.

Mouth Full of Metal

The next day Mother took me to an orthodontist. I got a mouth full of metal, just like Sister and Mark had. I had to put rubber bands on in the back to pull my teeth in the right direction. My teeth felt like they stuck out of my mouth and I had a hard time keeping my mouth closed. The metal scraped the inside of my mouth and my jaw hurt. The orthodontist gave me wax to cover the braces for what he called sports but I knew I would be using it for the punk shows, so that when I got hit in the face by some kid dancing, I wouldn't get cut.

"I didn't tell you that you were going to the orthodontist to keep you from worrying about it," said Mother on the way home.

"You kill my dog and when I come home you give me braces. Thanks Mother." She ignored my last comment. "Pierre and Dash go to school here. Why can't I?"

"Landmark is supposed to be the best school in the country for kids with learning disabilities."

"I hate it there."

"But you can go into the city anytime you want."

"That's not true. The Dean of Students hates me and keeps me on campus as much as he can."

"It just sounds like you miss your mother."

"I missed you and Father a long time before boarding school. You guys were never here, so what's the difference if I'm in Boston?"

"We are just trying to give you guys the best life possible."

"Come on, that's a cop out. You guys love your careers."

"Some day you'll understand."

"I doubt that."

"What time is your friend arriving?"
"Sally? 2:30. She's going to take a cab."

"You're different," said Sister when I ambled back into the house. Mother left to go wherever she had to go. She didn't tell me and I didn't ask.

"What do you mean?" I was looking out the window for Sally's cab. The sky was a sharp blue. Acorns lined the sidewalk. I was worried about my braces and kept running my finger over them.

"I don't know. But you're different."

She was right. I was different. Being away from home is something that most kids experience for the first time in college. I had learned to travel by myself, take care of myself and, most importantly, rely on myself. There was something else too, I thought. I had been going to the punk rock shows every weekend and was no longer frightened. I was becoming tough, or I was growing up. I guess maybe that was the same thing.

Sally's cab pulled up. I went out to meet her. Her clothes clung to her body revealing her curves. Other men could look and guess, but I knew.

"You have changed," she said.

I thrust out my chest with pride.

Sally hugged me, then her gaze fixated on my mouth. I tried to keep it closed. "You have braces."

I deflated.

She tilted her head and gave me a funny look. I couldn't help but smile. She examined the shiny metal and my awkward grin, then she seemed to accept it and led me into my own home. It was strange to have a part of my Boston life mixing with home. Each night she started out in the guest bedroom, off of mine, but by morning she was in my room.

By the end of the week I knew I would run into Fiona. I could feel her looming out there. Maybe it was like Mother's ability to know Sister was hurt, or maybe I just knew Fiona too well. Walking out my front door, I spotted Fiona coming up my steps. God, she still had a body like a short porn star, I thought to myself. But she's a fucking whore. Remember what she did to you? And anything she is about to say is a lie.

"Hi," she said. Her voice was buoyant.

"What are you doing here?" I could sense Sally in the house about to come out.

"I wanted to see you."

"Why? We're not dating anymore."

"I thought I could change your mind." Since I had been in boarding school she had grown up a little too. She no longer dressed like Madonna. Her hair was blond with dark roots. It was longer and pulled back. She had on a tight shirt and a little skirt. Her legs were in black fishnets, and she had on red creepers, with two inch heels.

Sally walked out the door behind me. My face flushed. I could feel it. Sally took a moment to realize who Fiona was.

"You're that bitch who cheated on him," said Sally.

"I didn't do anything, and who the hell are you?"

"I'm his new girlfriend!"

"I'm his girlfriend!" said Fiona.

"Wait a minute," I said but no one was listening to me. "You're not my girlfriend. We broke up months ago." They were trading insults.

"Fuck you, cunt!" said Sally and she moved towards Fiona. I grabbed her by the arm and Fiona made a retreat, yelling over her shoulder.

"He'll be with me when you're gone!"

The next day, I asked Sister where Mother was. Every morning I had gotten Sally to move into the other bed. But Mother was never there to see. The door to Mother's room was open all night. If she were here, it would have been closed. Now in the daytime I searched the house and only found Sister reading Mother's *New York Times*. She sat on a cheap white wicker chair that had a threadbare cushion as a seat. Our house was full of cheap furniture.

"Mother's been seeing someone," said Sister flatly.

"A new boyfriend?"

"This asshole."

"What's wrong with him?"

"He's fat, stupid and rude."

"Why is she with him?"

"She's lonely. She's never here anymore."

"She wasn't before."

"Yeah, but at least she slept here. You gotta come home. Where's your girlfriend?"

"Sally's sleeping in my room. That's why I wanted to know where Mother is."

"No, I meant Fiona."

"She's not my girlfriend anymore."

"Good, she's an idiot."

New Year's Eve came and went, it was now 1986. A few days before my break was over, Sally and I took the flight to Boston together and parted at the airport. The school van was white and could have been from an institution. Sitting in the back seat, I felt sick to my stomach and wanted to crawl out of one of its windows. The van passed the towns and went further from the city and drove me back to Landmark.

When the weekend came, I signed up for a day trip to Boston. As long as there were enough names on the clipboard, I didn't need to get permission from the teachers or parents. It was like a field trip. Mark came along. As we stepped out of the van, the driver warned us not to be later than 7:30 or the van would be gone. "Let's go to Newbury comics, then the record store in Harvard Square." I followed Mark. He looked at the records, then moved over to the tapes - The Ramones, New York Dolls and the Dictators. I searched for the S.O.A. on green vinyl. I doubted I would ever find it, but anytime I was in a record store I looked. Sometimes they put rare records up on the wall, but they never had the S.O.A. record. Mark picked up the Cure on cassette and stuck it down his pants, handing me one to do the same.

Patsy's words reverberated through my head when she once caught me trying to steal a candy bar. *"Baby, we don't steal because we don't have to. There is nothing more shameful than a man who steals when he already has what he needs."* My gaze pinned Mark to the spot. He was angular and bony.

"I don't steal and that band sucks," I said. "You should put the tape back." I threw the one he handed me back in the stack. "If you need to borrow money, you can." I thought of Pierre back home. He was broke but he didn't steal or at least not yet. I squinted, looking at Mark and reading the finer details of his character. He was going to grow up to be a sad little man. Maybe this was an attempt at recruiting me as a skinhead. And then I realized that Mark was an asshole. He was a rich kid who wanted to pretend he was poor. He would deny it but it was true and just because he was into punk didn't mean I had to be friends with him.

"You're so uptight. Relax, it's not a big deal."

I walked behind him as two large black guys grabbed him, then me. They brought us into a backroom and we sat up in chairs while the manager looked over at me.

"You can go. We have you guys on camera. We could hear you try to talk this one out of it."

"What are you going to do to him?" I asked. One of the big black guys folded his arms and gave me a threatening stare.

"We're going to call the cops and then your school."

"He'll be kicked out if you do that. I'm not leaving him here." *Maybe they would get me kicked out, too. That sounded good.* Then I pictured Father upset, crying in his hands and ashamed of his son. Mother would have shrugged it off saying, "Kids make mistakes sometimes and that's how they learn."

"Kid, this isn't your problem," said the manager.

"He's my friend and I'm not leaving him. If you call the cops, I'm going with him. Look, what if you call my mother, and his mother? I'm sure they will pay or whatever you want. If that doesn't work, you can call the cops and the school next."

Mark smiled and I realized I must have looked as stupid as him with my new braces. I didn't think I would ever smile again. The manager called Mother first, then Mark's parents. Our parents came up with an agreement and they let us go after taking a Polaroid of Mark's face for their wall of shoplifters. "Thanks man, you saved my ass, but if you want to get out of this school so bad why didn't you just let them call the cops?"

I didn't answer.

"We're late and we're going to miss the van," he said.

Turning the corner, I saw the end of the van pulling away. Picking up speed, I caught it at the first light. Mark was lagging behind but he didn't need to run anymore. He stopped, hunched over, trying to catch his breath.

The door to my room was open. Walking in, I could hear Led Zeppelin coming from the other room off of our bathroom.

"I'm going to break that tape," I said to my roommate.

"I don't think that would make things better. He would just bitch and buy another tape. Some other kid broke the old Led Zeppelin tapes."

"You mean he has been listening to the same band for more than a year?"

"As far as I know, it's the only tape he has ever owned."

"Fucking hell."

I looked around the room. We had covered the walls with flyers from every show I had gone to and a lot that I hadn't. I walked over and punched a hole in the wall right through a flyer of a show at the Lupos on December 5th; the headline act was Operation Ivy.

"Why did you do that?" asked my roommate.

"I thought it would make me feel better."

"Did it work?"

"A little."

"Do it again if you got to."

I punched a dozen more times. My knuckles were cut and bleeding. I sat on the floor and looked at what I had done. My roommate was already taking down the damaged flyers and putting up new ones to cover the holes.

The walls looked like Swiss cheese. Four of the ties that I had cut off my neck were pinned next to the door in a row like silhouettes of enemy planes shot down, painted on the nose of a fighter. The roommate of the kid from next door walked in and sat on the bed. "I need a moment away from the Led Zeppelin. What is all the banging about?"

My roommate pointed at me. "He's redecorating."

The next weekend came but the Dean of Students had stopped my attempts to escape to the city. Mark went without me and I stayed in bed until Sunday when he came back. Walking into the dorm, he avoided eye contact with me and walked upstairs. My roommate answered the public phone in the hallway and nodded to me. Sally's voice sounded funny, sad and tired.

"I have to tell you something and I don't want you to hang up on me. You always hang up when you get mad, so just let me finish before you cut me off."

"What? Say what you got to say." I was already getting mad.

"Last night I went to a party and Mark was there." I looked around the TV room to see if he had come back down. She went on, "We both got really drunk. Then Mark kissed me. I didn't kiss him back. He just pushed up on me and kissed me without any warning. I told him I'm dating you and he said it's okay, that you wouldn't mind, that we didn't have to tell you. I told him that I would tell you and he tried to kiss me again, so I punched him in the face and gave him a bloody lip. I fucking hate him... You still there... Hello?" Even if she was telling the truth I would still harbor aggression towards her. After Fiona I couldn't fully trust another girl.

"Okay. I got to go. I'll call you back."

"Wait a minute," she said, but I was already hanging up the phone.

What a dick, I thought. I sprinted one flight up to Mark's door.

Mark opened it, reading my face.

"Hey man, I'm sorry, nothing happened." Metal braces flashed as he spoke, and his lip was large, red and already cut from Sally. Mark's butt crashed to the floor. He grabbed his nose.

"All we did was kiss! Why did you do that?" he wailed. I felt good for a moment.

On the phone that evening, I told my parents that I wasn't coming back after that year.

"So you better start asking around or I'll just go to the Special Ed class at Wilson, I really don't care where I am as long as it's not here. Or maybe I'll just get a job." But I knew it wouldn't work. Mother had always said the more education you have, the further you can go in life, so there was no way she would let me get a job. Mark walked past me and I gave him the finger while I held the phone up to my ear. Mother was still speaking.

"They will hold you back a year."

"I don't care."

"It might mean you will be nineteen or twenty by the time you start college."

"I don't care."

"Maybe you're right. Your sister seems a bit lost without you here."

When the end of the year came, I wasn't ready. I could hear Led Zeppelin playing from the other room. Over the year, I heard those tapes every day.

"Fucking Led Zeppelin. If I go through the rest of my life never hearing that band again, it will be fine with me," said my roommate as he packed his things in a duffle bag. "You know we are going to get in trouble for these." He pointed at the holes I had punched in the drywall and I shrugged my shoulders.

"Just blame it all on me. Hey could you give me a hand with something?" I asked, pulling out a box of bright red hair dye.

He smiled.

While he was dying my hair, I looked at him in the mirror.

"Thanks for being my roommate." He nodded.

All over the campus kids were dragging trunks. Stephanie was sitting on hers. I took a seat next to her. She looked over at me with indifference and then to her fingers as if her nails held her interest. I knew she still liked me.

"What's the matter?" I asked her.

"Nothing."

I nudged her. "Come on."

"What do you care?"

"What did I do to you?" I had fucked another girl, again. First Fiona, then Sally. Who would be next? I grinned. What a bastard I was.

"You're not coming back next year."

"Yeah, so?"

"So, you could have told me," she said, annoyed.

"I didn't want to give you a head start. I'm sure you'll find me." I got up and walked away. I could feel her watching me.

I had to get a variety of checks from teachers and the last one directed me to the office of the Dean of Students. It was a dark, nasty, little room of leather and mahogany. The small, balding man was dwarfed, sitting behind his oversized desk. I could reach over the desk and palm his head, and wave him around the room like a rag doll. I started to raise my hand to bring thought to action, when he began to speak. "Take the bandana off."

I did as he said, and my ratty bright red mohawk fell in front of my eyes.

"What are your plans for the next year?" His tone revealed his deep dislike as he stared at my new hair color.

"I plan on *not* coming back here." I was smiling, since I was already enrolled at my new high school, close to Father's house.

"Good, because I don't want you here next year." He was speaking, but I was already walking out of the room without bothering to let him make his check on my list. I balled up the paper and threw it away.

Puke Boots

Dear Lover Boy,
    How's it going down there? I have been going to all of the Sunday shows. It's not the same without you guys from Landmark. I have been drunk since I got out of school and plan to stay that way as long as I can. How are the girls treating you? How's your love life? Getting any? Anyway I just wanted to send you a quick note.
    See ya.
    Sally.

"Why is she asking me about girls?" I said to Pierre and handed him the letter. We were sitting in the add-on room off of mine. It was just after twelve and the sky was a brilliant blue, the kind that hurt to look at until your eyes adjusted. Mother had put the letter outside my door before going out. I had only been home a few days. I immediately pictured Mark prowling around Sally and drunkenly making out with her. Anger bubbled up in me.

  "Maybe she is making fun of you?"
  "Like she knows I'm not getting any?"
  "Right."

I felt frustrated. I wanted to be home but I also wanted to be with Sally. Maybe she was already seeing someone else. Then I thought about what Fiona had done to me and realized I was putting myself in the same position again and knew I had to make a clean break.

"That pisses me off!" I didn't realize it at the time, but the overdose of teenage testosterone was affecting my judgment.

"Write something fucked up back."

"But I'm not seeing anyone right now." I wanted to call Fiona. I couldn't get the image of her out of my head. It started before I came home, first in a dream, then more and more when I was awake. Her large firm breasts bouncing in my bare hands. The smell of her skin and hair. My fingers tracing the line of her naked back. The crease of her ass. I knew it all too well. But so did someone else. *That stupid bitch! Fuck*, I had to stop thinking of her.

"She doesn't know that," said Pierre about the letter I was still holding.

I pulled the condom from my wallet, unwrapped it, spat inside and tied it off. I dropped it in an envelope with a simple note.

>Dear Sally My Sweet,
>Here is how my sex life is going.

I licked the edge and closed the envelope. Squeezing the envelope between my fingers, I wondered if it was the best plan to send it. Marching out the door, I took in the air of summer and looked down the block. Glover Park hadn't changed much. Ted walked by with his mangy mutt. Scott and his friends were at the end of the block and Stephanie was gone, still up at boarding school for the summer. I walked up to the corner and dropped the letter in the mailbox. Turning back towards my home, I saw Fiona and another girl standing in front of my place. Strong perfume wafted around Fiona. She had on a tight black mini-dress. Her breasts gave her buoyancy and seemed to float in front of me. I had an urge to touch them. I always had that urge. Lust and disgust washed over me.

"Hi Baby," she said. I furrowed my brow. *Baby* was a word Patsy used. It was reserved for her only.

"Fiona, what are you doing here?" I could feel my guard go up. I hadn't forgotten a thing. But at the same time I could also feel an erection building. I shifted positions not wanting to give anything away. I didn't have full control of my body yet and sometimes it did what it wanted to.

"I heard you were back and just wanted to say hi." She batted her press-on eyelashes at me. Her lips were glossed with strawberry. I briefly caught their scent. I hated her, but as much as I hated her I wanted to fuck her too. I thought about the letter I had just mailed. There would be no chance of hooking up with Sally again. I needed someone new.

There was another girl with Fiona whom I hadn't seen before. She had on a thick layer of white foundation. It made her look pale and sick. Her eyes were empty, devoid of sparkle, almost dead. A sardonic smirk rose to her lips. Her expression startled me, her profile like a laughing skull.

"Who's this?"

"Edgea. We've been hanging out since you've been gone," said Fiona with a touch of arrogance. "She's very punk rock."

"Hi. Nice to meet you." I shook Edgea's hand and she gave me a weak smile.

"You want to get something to drink and hang out?" said Fiona.

"I don't have any money." Mother was at her boyfriend's house and the thought of drinking sounded fun. Maybe I had more devious thoughts?

"I got money," said Edgea.

Pierre kept sneaking peeks at Edgea's round ass. It was nice but jerked to one side every time she took a step. I noticed Edgea limped oddly. There was something strange about one of her boots. One heel was larger than the other one. We walked over to the mini-mart and the guy behind the counter greeted me with a warm hello. He glanced at the two girls and their exaggerated make-up. *Prostitutes*, he must have been thinking. That would have made me the pimp. We bought what we needed. Pierre left. His mother needed help taking the dogs to the vet. I could tell he wanted to stay and drink with the girls. He wanted Edgea. Edgea was homely. Her eyes were dark and murky, her face looked like a skull, but she had some strange sexual appeal. Later, I would figure it out. She was easy.

Back at Mother's, I called Charlie.

"Yeah, I want to come over, but I have a friend from Argentina with me." I could imagine Charlie's stinking breath as he spoke. "His name is Juan."

"Sure, Juan. Bring him too."

Forty-five minutes later, I'd consumed a six-pack of Milwaukee's Best and a Fosters thirty-two ounce oil can. The girls dared me to drink a sixteen-ounce glass of straight vodka in one gulp. Edgea put down a dollar, betting that I couldn't do it. I let my arms dangle and shook out the tension in my shoulders. I was home and it finally sunk in that I didn't have a teacher looking after me and that I would never have to go back to Landmark. I was free. Fiona pulled an album from the stack. "Add it up" by the Violent Femmes came on and that song would play over and over in my head for the rest of the day. I picked up the tumbler. *It's clear. How can it be bad for me?* I peered into the depths of the glass and poured the vodka down my throat. For a few moments, it didn't do a damn thing, but then I started feeling a bit numb, euphoric, sociable and uninhibited. Fiona stumbled over to the turntable and started the song over. Maybe it was a hint.

> why can't I get just one kiss
> why can't I get just one kiss
> there may be something that I wouldn't miss
> but I look at your pants and I need a kiss

The vodka-beer mix was sitting at the bottom of my stomach, plotting to take over. Fiona was looking at her own reflection in the glass door of my stereo. Edgea was next to me. I reached out and touched the thick foundation on her cheek, then looked at the tip of my finger. It was white. She shoved me. I pushed her back. She fell off the couch.

"You think that's funny, buddy?" she said laughing. I got up and ran down the hall, then turned the corner into Sister's room. Sister was out. Edgea limped after me. I pulled a table over, blocking the entrance. She climbed over it, catching me and pushing me over Sister's desk, which I knocked over. I laughed and tried to pull myself up, grabbing a bookshelf, but it fell on me instead. The doorbell rang and I kicked open the bedroom door, which fell off the hinges.

"Shit!" The door was always coming off the hinges because in general I preferred to kick it open rather than use the doorknob. I propped it back up. The bell rang again.

"I'm coming. Hold your dicks, bitches!" Jumping more than walking down the steps, I reached for the door and opened it. Charlie looked in and Juan peered from behind him.

"Where are the girls?" said Juan.

"What? You're bringing me a horny Mexican?" I said.

"I'm from Argentina," he said with a slight accented twist on his words.

"I'm just fucking with you man." I swayed to the other side of the door catching myself in the frame. "Come on in."

I handed them blurry beers. There wasn't much left. I had drunk most of them. Fiona and Edgea sat on my bed giggling.

"Girls, these are my friends."

Juan's eyes flared open when he saw Fiona. He sat next to her with his beer in hand.

I walked into Sister's room. She had her collection of plastic horses lined up against one wall. I kicked over the first one and the rest fell like dominoes.

"That's not nice," said Edgea from the doorway. She leaned awkwardly since one of her heels was larger than the other.

"Aw, that's how a brother shows love for his sister." I waved my hand in the air like it was no big deal.

"You should show me some love." She took two large steps forward and stood nose to nose with me.

"Okay." I staggered forward, almost knocking her over, and kissed her. She pulled me onto Sister's bed and we made out.

> *grasp and reach for a leg of hope*
> *words to memorize, words hypnotize*
> *words make my mouth exercise*
> *words all failed the magic prize*
> *nothing I can say when I'm in your thighs*

"You're supposed to be making out with Fiona," said Edgea, breaking the seal of our lips.

"You want me to make out with her instead?"

"No. I'm just saying that was the plan."

"Yeah, I don't like that plan. This one seems better."

Rich Boy Cries for Momma

I was on top of her when I noticed Fiona standing in the doorway. Pure loathing washed over her.

"What the hell are you doing?" she howled. "Get off her!"

But Edgea and I kept making out.

"Edgea! Let's go! Get off my boyfriend!" Fiona demanded.

But we continued making out.

"I fucking hate you both! You fucking assholes!" Fiona stormed out of the room.

I could hear Charlie and Juan talking to her in the next room.

"Well, why don't *we* make out? It'll be your way to get even." Juan's proposal sounded simple.

> why can't I get just one screw
> why can't I get just one screw
> believe me I know what to do
> but something won't let me make love to you

"Fuck you, you dirty Mexican!" Fiona screamed and ran out of my house.

I turned back to Edgea.

"Let's have sex." Her skull face was blurry. It looked like a white blob.

"You're drunk."

"So are you."

"We'll have sex tomorrow when we're sober," Edgea said.

I kissed her some more, hoping it might change her mind.

Then from behind me I could hear Charlie.

"We're going back to my place."

"Okie dokie," I said and waved my arm over my back at them, but I kept making out with Edgea. Her boots were still on. I tried to pull off the one with the larger sole, but she stopped me.

> why can't I get just one fuck
> why can't I get just one fuck
> I guess it's got something to do with luck
> but I waited my whole life for just one

"Come on. Let's have sex."

"Not today. You're just drunk and I'm not sure you would want to have sex with me if you were sober." If I could have seen, I might have noticed the vulnerable look in her dark eyes.

"Sure I would. You're hot." I couldn't remember right then, but when I met her, I thought she was ugly.

"Not today. Get off me."

"Okay." I was drunk and horny but could still hear Mother's words, "If a girl says *no*, it's *no*."

"I'll see ya soon. I'm going to go find Fiona," Edgea said before hobbling out the door.

"Tell her I said hi." I suppressed a smile. Ever since I had found out that Fiona had cheated on me, I'd secretly wished there was some way to get even. I was blind drunk but clear on what I was doing. It felt good.

I staggered across town to Charlie's house. I spent a few hours hearing about his family's long history in Lithuania, how they were royalty and his grandfather had been the President or Prime Minister. *Blah, blah, blah.*

I suddenly felt strange. Hot flashes and a cold sweat washed over me. I knew the story was going to end with, "Now the Goddamn communists have our country. The bastards." Charlie always told it the same way. He was a capitalist and even when he was very young, he'd collected bars of gold. As Charlie talked about how rich his family should have been, I thought of all the gold he had upstairs in his room, locked away at the bottom of his closet. My dreams of gold were interrupted by the sweat that poured off my scalp. The hot flashes became overpowering. They were my body's warning signal to get home and quick, so I said farewell or maybe just walked out the door while he was still talking, I can't recall.

Stopping on the street, I glanced down at my boots and emitted a stream of vomit that completely covered them, the sidewalk, and the grass.

"Puke boots. Geez, that sucks," I said out loud, to no one in particular. I staggered onwards to a local Safeway supermarket on Macarthur Boulevard. Spotting a pay phone, I clumsily called Sister. I knew she would be home from riding lessons by now.

"Hey Anastasia, what's up?" I slurred.

"You knocked down my horses, you asshole. My room is a wreck, and what is this white powder all over my pillows?"

"Sorry." I tried to focus on something, but my eyes were going in their own direction. Everything kept drifting to the left. Above me I recognized a blurry rotating sign. It was red and white with a giant S.

"Brother! You wrecked the house."

"I'm at Safeway," I mumbled.

"Are you drunk?"

"I was. Now I don't feel too good."

"Where are you?"

"The Safeway"

"Which one?"

The phone went dead or I blacked out, but I could still hear shoppers walking to their cars.

"Mommy is that man dead?"

"No dear," said an older lady. "He doesn't have a home."

Time passed, then suddenly someone pulled at my jacket and made me sit up. My head fell back as far as it could go and my mouth opened.

"Christ, you smell like puke." It sounded like Dash. "Time to go, buddy."

Opening my eyes, I could see the world moving.

"Leave me alone you bastard," I said, tasting the vomit. I spat but it didn't go further than my jacket. "You are kidnapping me. Let me go! You fucking bitch."

"Fucking bitch, yes, I'm a fucking bitch," he said.

I opened one eye and saw it was a guy who looked like Dash, but older, more handsome, with tousled blond hair, his physique now rugged. I closed my eye, rolling my head the other way.

"Thank fucking god. I thought you were a rapist."

"Who said I'm not going to rape you," said Dash as he pulled me into the van.

We were moving. I was leaning against the door. I watched Dash driving. The setting sun washed everything in orange. He was rubbing his elbow in an odd way. When he saw me watching him he stopped and grinned.

Dash would later tell me that he had been at home when Sister called him since he was the closest one to Safeway.

Sister opened the van door and her moon was flying around her head and it said: "My brother's an idiot." Her arms were crossed but I was still too drunk to care. I reached for her imaginary moon. Dash pushed my arm down since it was crossing his face. I lay sprawled out on the seat.

"He's as white as a ghost. Maybe we should take him to the hospital!" Sister said.

I could feel Dash's finger running down the side of my face. He held the finger in front of Sister.

"What is that, clown make-up?"

"I think it was from a girl," he said.

"Was she a clown?" Sister's stare stabbed me.

I shrugged. I wasn't sure myself.

"Where did you find him?" Squinting, she looked like Mother.

"He was curled up next to a shopping cart holding onto it as if it were his baby."

Dash opened all the doors and the back of the Volkswagen van, trying to air out the smell of puke. They put me in Sister's room and when I opened my eyes, the day-glo orange paint made me feel like someone was screaming through my eyeballs. "Oh, God orange, who has an orange room?" I mumbled.

"Yes, I know you're sorry," Sister said, and then she put a cold, wet rag on my forehead.

Sister and Dash fixed the door I had kicked off the hinges, and picked up the shelves I'd knocked over, setting the house right and taking out the empty cans, dumping the bags in the neighbor's trash, all before Mother came home.

"Where is your Brother?" I could hear Mother's voice and buried my head under Sister's pillow.

"He has food poisoning". Mother came in and sat on the side of the bed. I pushed my face deep in the pillows to hide my breath. Years later, she would tell me she knew. Besides, I had punished myself. I was sick.

"How's the little soldier doing?" She placed her hand on the back of my neck.

"Not so good."

It took a few days before I felt completely normal. I was on my way out the door when someone knocked from the other side. Opening the door, I saw a girl with crazy spiked red hair and a face that looked more like a skull. One of her legs was longer than the other and her thick sole made up the difference.

"Yes?"

"It's Edgea!" Her name sounded familiar and then I remembered, Fiona's friend. Edgea didn't have on the thick white foundation. I could see the fine hairs she was trying to cover up. Or maybe she wanted me to see the real her.

"Oh yeah, I was just messing with you." I tried to act casual. "What's up?"

"Now we can have sex," she declared with a frightening smile that made her skull face look like a jack-o-lantern. I had seen her sober when we'd walked to the mini-mart to get the beer, but I'd forgotten. Seeing her made me think of how crappy I had felt just a few days before. I didn't find her the least bit attractive now. She was an oddity of pale skin, bad tattoos, mismatched colored hair and dark roots.

"Uh...I was drunk," I replied bluntly without smiling.

"Come on, fuck me," she demanded.

"I don't think so." I was taken aback.

"What, are you a pussy?"

"Just not interested."

"You seemed interested the other night."

"I was drunk and you had a part in that."

She limped over to me, clenching her fists at her side. Her smile was gone, replaced with a glare through angry, half-squinting eyes. I kept a watch on her fists. She had on cheap biker rings with an array of protruding spikes, making for great weapons. I saw a flash of cheap metal, and the blow bounced off my shoulder. I put my hands up in a defensive posture. Realizing I wasn't going to fight back, Edgea moved in for the attack, punching, slapping and scratching. She kicked me in the shin with her oversized shoe, a shoe that was meant to compensate for the lack of length in that leg. Its two-inch sole made it as much a weapon as a shoe. I wanted to hit her, but didn't think it was right to hit the handicapped.

A ring of spikes on her middle knuckle cut the back of my hand. Seeing this, she tried to hit me again with the ring. I palmed her oversized forehead and kept her at arm's length. I had seen this on the Little Rascals and was surprised when it really worked.

"You fucking asshole," she spat. "All you guys are the same. Let go, motherfucker!"

I started to laugh. This just made her angrier, but it was over. I had her by her head. Finally, she gave up and walked away, dragging her short leg with her. I had a new respect for that big orthopedic shoe and couldn't help but watch it as I rubbed my bruised and beaten shin. The scars on my hands where I'd blocked her blows remain a constant reminder to never drink vodka again. Even its smell makes me nauseous.

Walking in my room, I pulled the Stiff Little Fingers record from its sleeve and carefully placed it on the turntable. Picking up the arm, I blew on the needle to free it of lint. I had to get the Violent Femmes song out of my head. It had been dogging me since the day I'd gotten drunk. Bringing my face closer to the spinning vinyl, I could see the grooves racing past, like tiny, rolling waves of dark black. The phone rang and I dropped the needle on the record with a scratching noise. The song jumped to a start halfway in.

"Fucking hell." I picked up the phone.

"You asshole, motherfucking, cocksucking, shitbag, asswipe, degenerate fuck!" came out of the receiver.

"I guess you got my letter," I said, but Sally was still cursing me.

Chelsea

"Let's pick her car up and put it in a "no parking" spot," said Dash. He had on a denim jacket with a Grateful Dead logo painted on the back. He squatted, grabbing the car somewhere under the door with a cigarette still dangling from his mouth and biting down hard, while starting to move the small Japanese car. There were eight or nine boys lifting and slowly they inched the car over into the next space. Dash stood at the front tire, Charlie and his fat head were next to me, and Paul was on the opposite side of Dash. It was my first day at Chelsea and I knew most of the students there from the Lab School. Pierre was the only one missing from the old gang. He went to a different school.

"Good work, man," said Dash.

"Why did we just do that?" I asked.

"Because the girl who owns it is a bitch," said Paul.

Dash went inside to use the payphone to complain to the cops about the car. Half an hour later, a patrol car rolled up and started writing a ticket.

The school was in the center of Jessup Blair Park in Silver Spring, Maryland. The main building was colonial and rumored to have sheltered George Washington during the revolution or at least that's what the plaque on the wall by the smoking area said. There were a few prefabricated buildings on the lot that acted as classrooms.

I drove myself to school in Mother's old Mercury Zephyr. She gave me the car as a gift for getting my driver's license. The inside of the car was coated in graffiti and the outside had been silk-screened with the names of punk bands. My car was parked in the circle in front of the school, behind the car we had just moved. The car right behind mine was Paul's. It was a used, beaten-up old Toyota. Paul had cut off the roof with a blow torch. Old rain water lay on its floor, but since the floor was already rusting it wouldn't be long before it leaked out. I heard rumors that Paul played with shit to freak people out.

Sitting in class, I suddenly heard a voice come from outside.

"I didn't park there. Why are you giving me a ticket? This isn't fair." The girl was nondescript, boring, preppy.

"Hello!" The teacher snapped her fingers to get my focus back on the chalkboard. She went on with her lecture.

Paul had on new shoes and I wondered where he got the money, since I knew his family had none.

"Yo, snap!" he said, sounding like the black kids. He dressed like a GoGo, in Gucci glasses, Timberlands, baggy pants and a puffy North Face jacket. Paul's hair was faded into a flat top. It didn't look right at all. GoGo is a mix of Funk and Hip Hop with a largely black audience unique to Washington. Clubs such as the Black Hole or the Dome were infamous for their GoGo shows, and shootings happened on a regular basis there. Trouble Funk, EU, The Junk Yard Band and Rare Essence were some of the acts.

Paul looked at me from across the table and I smiled at him. My hair was now neon orange. He had his feet on the table and when the teacher walked passed, she knocked them out of the way to make room.

"So everyone is going to meet outside of the building and the van will take you over to the bowling alley," she said.

The first day they gave us the rundown on how things worked, then took us bowling. The school had a relaxed attitude and I already liked it more than the boarding school. Dash ducked into a back staircase in the alley and smoked some weed. He came walking out as if he were carrying a beach ball between his thighs, taking long awkward strides.

"Let's see this here," he said and picked up the ten-pound bowling ball with a thousand scuffs on its surface. He walked over to his lane and dropped the ball. It rolled to the gutter.

"Put on your bowling shoes, Dash," said the teacher, but he didn't move. It was obvious that he thought he was too good looking to have to adhere to the rule of the ugly. He had become cocky along the way.

Paul was in the lane next to mine. Paul was ugly. He had dark, sunken eyes, and an awkward build that made him seem unbalanced. He had on the bowling shoes. Running, he swung his ball down and threw it into my lane. The ball came crashing down bounced in and out of the gutter.

"Paul, we will send you home if you keep that up," said the teacher in the lane on the other side of Paul. But Paul was too ugly to care. He had learned a long time ago that when you are ugly it's easy for the world to ignore you, so to get attention he acted out. The teacher wandered down the lanes to bother Charlie. Paul handed something to Dash and Dash handed something back that looked like money tightly folded up. I suspected it was a drug transaction but wasn't going to ask.

"Fuck you."

"No. Fuck you!" Dash and Paul were yelling at each other, maybe about the size of the bag. Charlie came over to me, escaping the teacher's field of view. She was way down on the other side of the alley.

I turned to Charlie and asked, "What, they still don't get along?"

"Yeah, they hate each other ever since Paul shot him but it wasn't even that bad. He got like, two stitches."

"How did Dash get shot?"

"Paul and Dash were fooling around with a 22 rifle. Paul kept pointing it in Dash's direction and Dash kept pushing it away. It went off, shooting Dash through the fleshy part of his arm. In the hospital, he was questioned by the cops, but never told them Paul's name. Dash didn't want to have anything to do with him after that. But now Paul has cheap weed." Charlie smiled. "I don't like Paul either. Cheap weed. It's the only reason anyone hangs out with Paul."

The things that happened in normal society didn't apply here. Cops, shootings, drug deals under teachers' noses. The world of the dyslexics is a confusing place. I thought I had learned to navigate its waters, but apparently it held secrets I had yet to discover.

After school, I went to Dash's house.

"Hey, Ma," Dash said walking by a woman sitting in a recliner. She didn't move or make a sound, she just watched the TV. We went out to the back yard. A dilapidated wooden ramp took up most of the space. The grass around the edges had died. Earlier in the day there had been a few passing showers. The sky was grey and the ground still damp. A few leaves red and yellow dotted the landscape. A neighbor must have been cooking since the scent of pot-roast drifted in the air.

"I got a small scar right here," said Dash, pointing to where he got shot on his arm. Dash was sitting on one side of the ramp, smoking weed. "You want some?" He held the pipe out for me to grab.

"I don't smoke," I said. I really didn't do anything other than drink.

Dash took a drag, then got up and started rolling back and forth on the ramp.

"How come you didn't tell me?"

"I heard you were having a hard time, that your dog died."

"Who told you that?"

Dash didn't say anything; he didn't have to. Sister was the only one who knew what I was going through and also knew Dash.

His skateboard seemed glued to his feet as he made small hops. Slowly rolling higher on one side of the ramp, he would make it to the top, turn back and head in the opposite direction. He couldn't do tricks yet. I watched Dash come up the other side, try to kick his legs out and grab the edge of the ramp while still holding onto the skateboard. Coming down, he pulled the board under him but missed the landing. He fell hard. He cried out, grabbing his ankle. I leaped from my perch to help him.

"It's busted," I said.

The next day, Dash hopped along on his crutches, stopping in the center of the smoking area at school. His foot was in a cast. He lit a cigarette and smiled.

"What's up? I'm tripping." The sky was a brilliant blue and, as a back drop, it looked fake.

I hadn't done any drugs or even smoked a cigarette, but had seen Dash high so many times that I knew it put him in a fog.

"Why trip at school? That's no fun at all." I was looking at his eyes to see if anything looked different. Then I looked at all of him. I noticed his

Grateful Dead jacket was gone. It was replaced with a grey Eisenhower jacket with the name of a local gas station on the back. On the lapel he had one inch buttons of punk bands, the Misfits, Iron Cross, Generation X. I wondered if the change was meant to impress some girl. I was afraid to ask. Sister liked all those bands. Ever since I got drunk and passed out at the Safeway I had a feeling that something was up with Sister and him. But then again, Sister would have told me. The parents kept things from us, but Sister and I had a pact. We didn't lie to each other or keep secrets. If she was dating Dash and hadn't told me, I would be hurt. But worse than that, I would be alone.

"Sure it is," said Dash. "You want some?"

Dash held out a tiny piece of paper with the acid on it.

"No thanks." I said, then walked into school as the bell rang. In the hallway someone was calling after me.

"Hey freak boy, nice fucking hair! Nuclear Pukehead." He sounded white, but when I turned, I saw a big black kid built like a tank with arms as thick as his thighs.

"Who the fuck is that?" I asked Dash, who was hobbling in after me.

"Highwater? Forget him. He's a total pussy."

I tried to forget him but he still scared me. He was much larger than I was. I didn't want to deal with a new Sermon. I pictured my books landing on the front steps of the Lab School.

"We are going to try something different," said the teacher. He was young with glasses and wavy short brown hair. He had a friendly face. I was taller than him. "The students in this class have been picked based on their ability to comprehend theory. We will be studying an overview of the major philosophies, understanding where they started and how they apply to the real world." He drew on the chalkboard, dividing it and making a list - Machiavelli, Nietzsche, Darwin, Plato and others. On the top of the list he wrote "The Natural State of Man". The natural state of man, I thought. What would it be like if there weren't books or math? I would finally be normal.

I didn't smoke but liked to hang out with the smokers at school. Dash wandered off to smoke some weed. Paul was talking with his girlfriend when Charlie came up to me.

"You would think you would be cool since your dad's an ambassador," I said.

"Why is that? You think the ambassadors are the coolest guys?"

"Yeah, you're right."

Charlie had grown long bangs that he had a habit of brushing back so he could see. I wanted to hand him a breath mint and cut the bangs as he was talking to me.

"Jerk-off," I said, knowing he hated it.

"I wanted to know if it would be okay to be punk?" Charlie asked me earnestly.

The question had taken me off guard. Charlie had busted my balls for the punk rock thing and now he wanted to be one. I rolled back on my heels and realized it felt good to be asked. It meant that he respected my opinion, but it also meant I could give him a hard time.

"First of all, the idea of it is not to give a fuck what anyone thinks, so you should just do it. In fact, you would be twice the punk if you just did it. Go against authority and all that. It doesn't matter if you are dyslexic or top of your class. In punk rock, no one gives a shit how you do in school. All they care about is how cool you are," I answered, knowing he would do my bidding just like when he joined TRP. I held the key to his coolness.

"First you got to do something about your hair," I said.

"My hair?"

"Yeah, all the punks are defined by their hair. You have skinheads who have no hair, the mods who have bowl cuts, punk rockers who have colored and crazy hair, rockabillys who have pompadours, goths who have long jet black hair. What kind of hair do you want?"

He seemed to ponder the question. Maybe seeing himself in all variety of styles, then picking the one he thought suited him best.

"How do I bleach my hair?"

"Use Clorox bleach, wet your hair, and leave it in."

" What, like the stuff my mother uses in laundry?"

"Yes, that's it."

Highwater came out of the building and lit a cigarette, cupping it in his hand, then holding it like a proper lady might.

"What are you looking at faggot!" he said to me and I said nothing back. Paul stopped talking to his girlfriend and I could feel him watching us. Highwater stepped closer to me, looking me in the eye, and I looked away. His features gave over to disgust and then he burst out into raucous laughter. I was wrapped in a sense of desolation. I had a moment of joy and then he stole it from me. If I had had a gun I would have shot him on the spot. The bell rang and a teacher stepped outside, urging us to make it into class on time.

The following day at school, Charlie showed up wearing a black longshoreman's hat with its ends tightly rolled up all the way, the way punks wear them.

"Didn't it work?" I pointed to his covered head.

He pulled off the hat to reveal frizzy, yellow-orange hair. It was half afro and partially bare in patches where it simply couldn't stand the abuse and chose to split the scene entirely.

Dash hopped over on his crutches.

"Nice hair!" he said, then hopped on past.

"See. It's not so bad," I said and grinned.

"This is no good," he said, nearly inaudibly.

"Why don't you dye it black so at least it's all the same color?"

Highwater came over. "Hey guys, what's going on?" he said in the most friendly of tones.

"Not much," I said and felt like I was being set up for something. My guard went up. When it became apparent that I didn't want anything to do with him, he walked away.

"That was strange," I said.

Charlie nodded in agreement.

I looked over and saw Paul watching. Smoke swirled about him. The bell rang and I caught up with Paul.

"Yo, is Highwater still fucking with you?" he asked.

"No, why? Did you say something to him?"

"I told that bitch I was the only one in school who'd shot someone and he was going to be next if he kept fucking with you."

After school, Charlie called me.

"Okay, I dyed my hair blue black so it's all the same now, but it's all over my skin and around my hairline. It looks like one of those detachable Lego people wigs. How do I get rid of it?" he asked. "I keep washing it but nothing happens."

"Use Liquid Drano. It'll take it right off," was my advice. I hung up the phone. It was cold outside and starting to snow. On the record player was "Sonic Reducer" by the Dead Boys. I put Diggedy Doug in the ColecoVision and started playing the game. The joystick was awkward and it took a lot of effort to make my little man on the TV move where I wanted him to go. *Sonic Reducer I ain't no loser.* Blowing up the monsters and letting rocks drop on their heads was satisfying. The phone rang; I paused the game and picked up.

"And I'll be ten feet tall and you be nothing at all."

"What?" said Charlie.

"Nothing, just singing."

"My skin started to burn! It was smoking!"

"I didn't think you would really do that. It's an acid or something."

"It did work, though."

"Okay."

"Paul called and wants to hang out. Come over and let's do something."

"It's snowing." I wasn't sure I really wanted to hang out with Paul, but then again he helped me with the Highwater problem and I did owe him. I wasn't sure I wanted to hang out with Charlie, but then again it was nice having a protégé and, if I kept avoiding him, he would lose interest.

"So what? My head is burning. The snow will feel good."

"You washed it out, right?"

"Yeah I had to or I was going to die. I'm a moron."

"Don't feel too bad. I got a few girls to do the same thing. I'll be over in a few."

We met Paul and Dash and wandered through the surrounding neighborhood of Tenleytown. A fresh blanket of snow had settled. Earlier that day, Dash's cast was taken off and now he had a bounce in his step.

"Nice hair," said Dash, and Charlie pulled his cap down to cover it up completely.

"Thanks," said Charlie, and he gave me a dirty look.

"It's like we are on a mission, sneaking into some enemy base or something," I said looking down the deserted streets.

"Yo, like we're the last people alive on the planet," said Paul, and he pulled out a pair of nunchucks and held them in front of him.

"Yeah, and Charlie's got the disease and is dying," said Dash.

"Look at his hair. It's already falling out," I added.

"Yo, maybe we need to kill him so it doesn't spread," said Paul, and he started swinging the clubbed end of the nunchucks at Charlie.

"Hey man, those things really hurt," said Charlie.

Swinging around the pair of nunchucks and mimicking Bruce Lee, Paul threw them at Charlie's head. When Charlie ducked, they hit a house window. We all froze and looked at each other.

"RUN!" I yelled.

I could hear "All This and More" by the Dead Boys in my head. I had been listening to them all day. As we ran, it was as loud as it was when I put my head under the speaker. *"And would you feel right if I teach you tonight and put on the bite, all this and more little girl,"* I sang. Our furious sprinting stopped when we reached American University, a decent eight blocks away. Dash looked like he was about to pass out. He was hunched over, taking in air. He lit a cigarette without bothering to stand up straight. Walking through the campus, we stumbled across a party, a perfect place to hide. Without invitation; we walked in and started drinking beer.

The guy whose window we had broken and his neighbor had followed our fresh footprints in the snow. They led them to the party's entrance. Charlie overheard one of them ask a college student if a bunch of kids had just shown up. They scoured the crowd until they spotted Paul. I guess he didn't look like he belonged. None of us did. Singling him out, the men demanded, "Show us the bottom of your shoes!" They wanted to match them to the footprints in the snow.

"No," Paul huffed, puffing out his chest.

They repeated themselves and Paul declined a second time.

Stepping up in Paul's defense, I voiced, "Let me see the bottom of *your* shoes!"

I was answered with a sidekick in the face and I began bleeding profusely. My soft gums and tender lips pressed through the metal wire of my braces. I staggered outside, doing my best to hold my mouth together. Black belts? Ninjas? I didn't know, but as I watched from outside, I could see they knew how to kick the crap out of Paul. It was like a scene right out of a martial arts movie and Paul and I were the lackey henchmen who never get to win. Later, I would find out that they were students at Master Woo's Martial Arts School. It was the same one that Dash would eventually go to.

Walking back to my car in the snow, I dripped a trail of red dots. Paul limped behind me. Dash was still out of breath and trailed behind Paul, and last was Charlie.

"That was awesome," he said, and nobody bothered to tell him to shut up.

Break and Enter

GRAY MATTER
  "Burn No Bridges"
    I'm through with illusions just delusions for now
    I've took a step to the edge but
    I've been walking for miles
    It was a very temporary waste of time
    Is there really such a thing as a waste of time?

I didn't know how to pick a lock and couldn't bypass an alarm. But I didn't have to be a professional burglar to know how to get into a building. The trick to this was to be observant, because someone always left a door unlocked or a window open. The higher up on a building, the less likely that a window would be locked. This sometimes meant climbing up to a second or third floor. If a window or door wasn't left open, I could always come back the next day when the building was open and tape over the lock so it wouldn't catch.

I wasn't stealing. I didn't need anything. It was just something fun to do. Everything had become boring ever since the night we'd gotten beat up at American University. Not that I wanted to get beat up again, but I'd enjoyed the rush. High schools were now my prime target; large empty buildings with many small rooms to hide in, and most had no night security. I wanted to see if the schools looked different from ours, but they all looked nearly the same. I walked through the theater, gym and science labs. I was alone, surrounded by dark hallways. The risk of getting caught made me feel powerful, special and smart. But the thrill only lasted a moment. If I was lucky, I would be chased out by a janitor or one of the security guards. There was nothing better than almost getting caught and getting away with it. Most alarms emitted sirens that gave me plenty of warning to evacuate. If the alarm was tripped, I still had about five minutes before the cops were on the scene.

It was one of the smaller schools next to the National Cathedral. There was only one road leading up to the school and there were plenty of bushes to hide in. It was three weeks after I had been kicked in the face. The inside of my lip was still sore. Breathing in the cold air gave some relief. Earlier that day my braces had been taken off and now I was running my tongue over my teeth. They felt slick and clean. I had decided to call Pierre, since I missed hanging out with him and none of us had seen him in a long time. He showed up wearing a Fred Perry bumble-bee shirt with a British Army green parka and twelve hole Doc Marten ox-blood boots. His afro was gone and his hair was cropped short. He looked like a Mod, but when I asked him about it he said he'd started hanging out with some Rude Boys. Pierre was listening to Ska music and going to punk shows. I had sent him tapes of music when I was in Boston, but I didn't think he was listening to them. He never responded to the letters. Then again a lot of dyslexic kids don't like to leave any evidence of their learning disability, so it's hard to find anything they have written.

"I thought you said the whole punk thing was gay?" I said to him.

"Fiona was into it and so are a lot of other girls."

"So, you are just into the girls?" I was sure he had fooled around with Fiona. It was just one more thing that made me hate her.

"No. I'm into the music." I didn't believe him, but he did look cool. He had grown a lot over the past year. He was an inch or two taller than me. His build was lanky but muscular. He looked like he could take me in a fight.

Charlie walked up. Pierre and Charlie gave each other the once over, taking in each other's new personas. They nodded at one another. Then Dash ambled over.

"I thought he was a hippie?" said Pierre. We had all changed. I guess none of us liked our old selves.

I pulled the zipper on my black leather jacket all the way up, trying to cut off a sharp breeze. "He's still smoking lots of weed," I said in a low voice. "Dash, go look in the window and see if there is anyone in there, any lights on or windows open."

Dash walked out of the bushes with his hands in his pockets and calmly made it over to the front of the building. It was dark inside. He tried the doors but they were all locked.

"No sign of life," he said. Grabbing a metal pipe next to the wall, I pulled myself up to the second floor. A window was unlocked and I climbed in. I opened the front doors and Dash stepped carefully in, looking over his shoulder to see if anyone else might have followed us. We walked in with Charlie trailing. Charlie was wearing all black and still had on the knit shoreman's hat which covered the hair that hadn't fully recovered from the bleach and dye jobs. We toured the building, looking in rooms and trying doors that were locked.

I stopped in front of the trophy case, looking at photos of kids. I wondered what their normal lives were like. Charlie stepped into the girls' room. "I always wanted to be in here," he shouted through the door.

"Let's ditch Charlie," said Dash after a few minutes of waiting. I grabbed Pierre and we ran.

Charlie heard our feet slapping the floor.

"Come on guys, wait up for me!"

He stumbled after us with his pants at his ankles. It wasn't that we didn't like Charlie. He was like the little brother of our gang. He just never got it. He always tagged along and it was just fun giving him a hard time. If it hadn't been him, it might have been me. Just before leaving, I pulled the fire alarm and we sprinted across the soccer field. Charlie was lagging behind again, with toilet paper trailing from the back of his pants.

"Guys, wait up!"

"Shut up!" Pierre yelled back.

"Didn't you go to the Lab School?" called a kid standing next to Ted, my neighbor and sometimes friend. It was the next day and I was out on the porch getting the mail. Ted was walking out of his house with a few friends. The sky was a piercing blue. It was the kind of day that made you want to be outside even if it was cold.

"I used to."

"That's the retard school, right?" said a shorter boy.

"No. It's for dyslexics."

"I heard half the kids there have to wear helmets to keep them from bashing their heads against the wall," said the first kid, who had blond hair. No doubt both their parents had money and power. They had no clue what it was like to get beaten up or to break into a building. They didn't know anything other than what their parents wanted them to know.

"No. None of them have helmets." An image of me as a kid wearing a helmet flashed into my mind. "Ted, you going to hang out later?"

Ted gave a noncommittal shrug.

"You friends with that guy?" asked the blond.

"We're neighbors," said Ted.

I picked up the mail and went back inside.

Ted and I hadn't been hanging out much since I'd gotten back from boarding school. Later that night, Ted came over. Pierre played ColecoVision and didn't pay any attention to us.

"Are you embarrassed to be friends with me?" I asked him.

"No. That's not it at all." His guard went up.

"Then what was that all about?"

"My friends just don't understand."

"Don't understand what? They think I'm a fuck-up. They think I'm handicapped. They think they are better than me. Let me tell you something, they are assholes."

"You shouldn't care what they think."

"I don't."

"Then why are you giving me a hard time?"

"I care what you think."

"I don't think you're a retard. What are we going to do tonight?"

"Let's break into the Lab School," I said.

"Why?"

"You and your dumb ass friends think it's a school for freaks. I can show you it's not." Maybe I was still angry. "It's fun, and Pierre and I know the place."

"I don't know," he said. I handed him a beer.

After midnight we ventured over to the school. Leering in the darkness, we must have looked sinister. There was a window open on the second floor and I reached out over a ledge and pulled myself up. My feet dangled and I felt as if I was being held under the arms, above a swimming pool. It was a long drop to the ground and the landing was cement. My grip slipped and I imagined the fall. It gave me the adrenalin I needed to bounce into the room. I thought I heard something and froze. My ears perked up and I scanned the dark room. Nothing. I walked down the staircase and pushed open the emergency doors.

The classrooms were dead quiet, waiting for the students to bring them to life. I had spent so much time in those rooms and halls and wanted to find something that proved I had been there. A corner of a bookshelf was tagged "T.R.P." I pointed it out to Ted. He smiled but didn't care. Pierre pulled books from the shelf, flipping them open, then throwing them to the floor. I climbed onto a table, crossing to the other side, then jumping onto a desk that fell over with a crash.

"You see, Ted, there aren't any cages here, no rubber walls, nothing to shock bad kids. It's just a boring school with the same crap as yours."

Pierre stepped into the hall and ripped fire extinguishers from their perches and handed me one. I ran to one end of the hall and Pierre headed for the other end by the elevators. Dropping the extinguishers to hip level, we aimed our nozzles at each other. Pulling the pins, we squeezed the extinguishers' handles and a choking white cloud filled the room, killing visibility. I coughed, my tender pink lungs engulfed by the fine, white powder. Adrenaline mixed with the alcohol.

The school had a 100-gallon fish tank with $400 dollars worth of fish. Pierre dropped another fire extinguisher into the water, pulled the pin and squeezed the handle. The tank became an opaque white as the water swirled within the glass encasing, like snow in a snow globe. The noise of a door slamming came from downstairs.

"Let's go!" I shouted. We ran down the hall and hooked a right to a stairwell. I thought I heard the sound of footsteps, maybe the night watchman, but I wasn't going to look back. We burst out of the rear fire exit, and I jumped into my baby blue Zephyr. Pierre stood looking back at the school holding a fire extinguisher, as if ready to put out a fire.

On the third floor, I could see the beam of a flashlight, casting dramatic shadows on the walls. I was in the driver's seat throwing the car into drive. Ted and Pierre jumped in and slammed the doors. We left the scene fast.

"Let's go by Freedom's house," said Pierre. "It's only two blocks away."

"That ugly girl who hangs out with your sister?" asked Ted.

"Why do you want to go there?" I asked.

"I want to do something," said Pierre.

We slowly drove by. The lights were out and no one was on the street.

"Okay, now what?" I said. Looking in the rear view mirror, I could see Pierre rolling down his window and aiming the nozzle of his fire extinguisher. He sprayed her car. We drove to the end of the block, a dead-end, and we had to turn around. On our way back, he threw the extinguisher at her car. It hit the door and rolled into the middle of the street.

"Why did you do that?" I asked.

"Why not?" said Pierre. Why not? It was the answer to everything. Why break into a school? Why not? Why fool around with an ugly girl with a short leg and a big orthopedic shoe? Why not? Why steal a crappy tape in Boston? Why not? Why shoot Dash through the elbow? Why not?

"It's not the best way to get a girl to like you."

"I don't like her!" he lied.

"Okay man, whatever."

This was a mistake, since the fire extinguisher was embossed with a serial number that connected it back to the school. Freedom's parents called the cops. When Freedom learned where the extinguisher had come from, she told the cops that we were the only kids she knew who had gone there. I didn't feel bad about having sprayed her car or that she ratted us out to the cops. Pierre was the one who had had a problem with her. That was between the two of them.

Second District, or 2D, our neighborhood police station, was more like a small town Sheriff's Department. When I heard that the cops were looking for me and asking around at Mazza Gallery, I didn't know whether to laugh or be afraid. The lead detective was gung-ho, following all her leads, but hadn't come to my house to arrest me yet. I guess she didn't have anything solid. I was sure they were going to arrest me. I wanted to know if it was better to let them come and get me or to turn myself in.

Father sat in the living room behind a stack of Nixon papers. I had to peer over the stack of papers, so he could see me.

"Dad, if someone broke into a school and the cops were looking for him, would it be better for him to turn himself in or to wait until they came and got him?"

He glanced up from the legal pad and turned to me.

"What have you done?" He had a panicked look.

"Nothing, I'm just asking a hypothetical question."

"Are you in trouble? You must not lie to me."

"I didn't do anything."

"I'm an Officer of the Court and if you lie to me and it turns out you are in trouble with the law, it can get me in trouble. What have you done?" He started rubbing his hands together and pacing the room. "Really, you have to tell me." As I told him, it quickly developed into full-scale panic for my father.

"You've ruined your life. Now you'll have a police record. You'll never be able to become a senator or president!"

"I think the country would be in a lot of trouble if I were president."

When Mother found out, she shrugged it off and told me how she'd burnt down a forest by accident in her hometown of Scituate, and ended with, "Things happen." But Father insisted that I turn myself in.

I was pinned as the "ring leader" after Ted blamed me for coming up with the idea, which I had. Pierre wouldn't talk. Our parents worked out a deal with the prosecutor so no charges were officially brought against us. The total sum was $3,000 for the three of us. I had to pay $1,000 of the damages and the court ordered me to see a psychiatrist. I later found out that at the Lab School the students were advised by the principle to stay away from Pierre and me because we were "bad seeds."

A week after the judge made a decision, I called Pierre. He said, "My mom says I can't hang around with you or talk to you anymore. She says when we are together, we just get into trouble." Maybe it was true, but we also gave each other confidence. It took a lot of guts for us to do what we did.

"She doesn't have to know we are going to hang out. "

"If she finds out that I hung out with you, she will kick me out of the house, and you know she will do it. We will hang out someday, but it won't be for awhile, man." Ted said roughly the same thing when I talked to him. I had effectively ended two friendships in one night.

"Don't plan on having any fun this summer, my little friend," said Mother. "You've got yourself a job so you can pay off the legal bills and damages."

"Where?" I asked.

"At your father's law firm. You're going to be wearing your suit and helping out."

"Can't I do something else?" I hated Father's office. It reminded me of their divorce.

"Nope, its all been arranged. Besides, it would do you good to see your father more." No doubt she was thinking I needed more male supervision, but Father was really my mother figure.

"He doesn't give a shit about me. All he cares about is his reputation and Nixon."

She gave me a stern look. "That is simply not true. He gave up a lot for the both of you. He wanted to be a professor or a judge. Instead he works hard so you can have all the things you want. And if you're not ready to do the time, don't do the crime."

"I don't need anything and never asked him to work."

I still had a few months left of school and I was hoping they would drag out.

"What's up, gangster?" said Dash at school on Monday. The sky was gray and the clouds looked like a low ceiling.

"Very funny," I said.

"What were you thinking, trashing the place? I heard you ran into every room and sprayed extinguishers. You fucked up all their computers." He cupped a cigarette and pulled a few quick drags, then stamped his feet to shake off a little snow that had gathered from the night before.

"Well, I wasn't thinking. We got wasted. I heard when the kids showed up they started crying over the dead fish."

"Yeah, you're a fish killer now."

"But I like fish and didn't mean to kill any of them." I didn't mean for anything to happen. I just wanted to show Ted that it was a normal place and then something happened. I got carried away by the moment. I wasn't trying to destroy the place. I felt like calling up the principal and trying to explain, but knew I couldn't explain what it was like being me. I didn't even know.

Dash walked away to smoke some weed before class, yelling over his shoulder, "See you later, fish killer!" The bell rang and I went to class. There was a buzz about the campus of my new criminal image. The other students thought I was cooler, tougher, and street smart. I could see it in the way they looked at me.

My New Skinhead

STATE OF ALERT
  "Draw Blank"
    Always ask me how I feel
    You think the truth is part of the deal
    You'll never know
    I'll never show
    I'm not a book
    You can't read me

If you were going to do something strange like change your look, Friday was the best day to show it off. You would take a lot of crap on Friday but by Monday it would be old news. It was Friday. Dash looked stoned when he spoke. "Hey man, did you see Paul?" He put his hand out to lean on the side of the building but missed and almost fell over. Catching his balance, he stood up straight and looked around to see if anyone had noticed. I liked those moments because it made him seem more human and less like just a handsome mannequin. At home, gazing at my own reflection in the bathroom mirror, I noted how my features had slightly hardened. I looked more adult. I was okay looking. I knew that. I had girlfriends.

"No," I said back.

I could smell weed on his breath. "Dude you got to see him," said Dash with a sparkle in his eyes.

Paul came out from the building, pulling a cigarette from behind his ear. His head was shaved, and every hidden pimple was exposed.

"What the hell are you supposed to be?" I said.

The day before, Paul had been the Jewish kid who was into the GoGo scene and thought he was black. Maybe he felt left out, since the rest of us were into punk rock.

Paul tried to look dignified, puffing on a cigarette in the smokers' hangout by the back door of school. His head was clean-shaven, with the exception of an odd shaped patch of hair. His jeans were rolled up at the leg. He wore boots and wide suspenders (ones you might find a grandfather wearing) under an army green raincoat. Skinheads are supposed to be poor, yet they retain some fashion sense. Paul's own ensemble was a little off. Each article of clothing missed its mark and he knew it. All I could think of was his bar mitzvah and how he stumbled through the torah. What would his rabbi think? What would his poor Jewish mother think? I knew not all skinheads were Nazis, even though that's what the rest of the straight-laced normals thought.

"Yo man, can I ask you something?" said Paul as I craned my neck to see what was on the back of his head.

"Go ahead."

"Can you help me out? What do I got to do to be da skinhead?"

I was the House Expert on punk rock fashion. I looked over at Charlie. He was a mess. His hair was now dyed green. It was spiked out. It looked all wrong. Punk rock didn't fit Charlie, no matter what he put on. His head was just too large. I turned back to Paul and pictured him after his makeover. It was no better. Paul wanted to know not only how to dress, but how to act and to be introduced into the skin scene. I didn't know anybody in the scene. I hadn't gone to any shows since I'd gotten back. I guess I was afraid. But even if I had known someone, I knew better than to stick my neck out for him. His impulsive nature and sudden outbursts might gain him a few friends, but the vast majority of the scene would hate him.

He turned his head and I read "Erin," his girlfriend's name etched in his hair. I laughed a bit and stopped myself. Paul was a good guy at heart and I didn't want him to think I was making fun of him. He had been my friend for many years, and I knew that I could count on him in a fight, even if he'd lose. Besides, he helped me with Highwater.

"The first order of business...you've got to shave your girlfriend's name off the back of your head. You're not a billboard for love and I'm sure that your girlfriend won't mind if you lose her name in order to be fashionably correct. Get rid of the secondhand boots. You need black or oxblood 12-hole or higher Doc Martens, and what's with the poncho? It's not even raining. Go to the Army Surplus store in Georgetown and get a bomber jacket, not one of those leather ones, but a nice nylon black one. Make sure it's American made and not one of those cheap Indian ones. Get some thin suspenders and a Fred Perry or Ben Sherman shirt. You can find most of that stuff at SMASH next door to the Army Surplus store on M Street. What music are you into?"

He looked at me and I could tell that he was embarrassed to tell me. "Billy Idol?"

"Billy's fine. He used to be a punk when he was in Generation X. Now he's a sellout. When you're at SMASH, pick up the Oi Compilations 1 and 2. And stop all that Yo shit. You can't talk like that anymore," I continued counseling him. He only understood half of what I said, but still, he had a rough idea what I meant. "Oh, you need to get a lot of tattoos."

"Tattoos?" He said. "But I'm Jewish."

"Yeah I know, but all the skinheads have tattoos."

Hefty Lefty Tiny Righty

"Hey man, we used to ride the bus together, right?" The kid asking the question was obese. I pictured the Retard Bus, and grimaced with humiliation. His skin looked gray and unhealthy in the stark fluorescent light. I glanced down at his legs, thinking they must have been strong to hold up all that fat. I was standing in the 7" vinyl section looking through the old bin. It was Saturday and we were in Smash.

"Yeah, that's me." I clutched at the collar of my leather jacket, feeling to see if I had lost one of my band buttons. "Who are you?"

"It's Burt. We used to take the bus together to the Lab School."

He had transformed from an obese junior high student into an obese skinhead. He waddled like a penguin around the bin of records as I flipped through the S-R section of 7"s. Whenever I looked for a certain record I had to look through the entire collection since, if I tried alphabetically, I was sure to miss it.

"So I heard what you did," he said.

"Did to what?" I was looking for the S.O.A on green vinyl.

"Breaking into the Lab School and fucking the place up." His voice reverberated with phlegm. "The principal is a friend of my mother's. When she told my mom what happened. My mom said that if I saw you, I should stay away from you."

"Apparently a lot of mothers are saying that about me." I pulled the black army beret to the front so I would look tougher. I now had blue hair with black tips. The clerk put on "Surfer Rosa" by the Pixies and the song "Gigantic" came on.

"I think it's pretty cool," said Burt. "I hated that school. We should hang out."

I couldn't find the record so I gave up. I bought a GBH button and put it on the front of my beret. I walked with him up Wisconsin Avenue.

The incline was slowing him down. He was sweating even though it was cold out. I wondered if he was being nice to me just to try and recruit me as a skinhead. All the skinheads I had met were the same. They start with just wanting to be friends, then try and get you into their music. Then next thing you know they are saying things like, *you should be a skinhead*. As if you had passed some kind of test. But from the looks of most of the skinheads, I knew the bar was set low. Then before you know what happened, your head is shaved. I thought of Paul. I was helping him turn into a skinhead. *Maybe I should try turning him into a punk.*

"You used to be friends with that kid Pierre too, right?" said Burt.

"I'm still friends with him."

"I've seen him at the shows. He's getting into the skinhead scene pretty hard."

"No, I think you're thinking of someone else. Pierre's into the Ska thing."

"Man, don't you know that Ska is the gateway to being a skinhead? He was part of the Lab School thing, too, right?"

"Yeah, he was there."

"It's the same guy. I'm sure of it."

Walking by the Roy Rogers at Prospect Street, he led me in. Three of the tables were taken up by a motley crew of punks and skins. I wanted to walk out but it was too late. They saw me. I could tell these were the real guys who hung out. Not like me, who just listened to music in his room. They went to the shows; they hung out at Dupont Circle and were cool. They were boisterous. I hadn't been to any of the shows in D.C. I was working my way up to it. I wanted to know guys from the scene, but at the same time I was afraid I would be rejected. If I were rejected from the punk scene, what would I have left? The little respect I had accumulated would be washed away. There was also the threat that I could have my teeth kicked in, but I could live with that.

"Hey, this is my friend," said Burt gasping for air. "He broke into our old school and fucked it up."

I avoided the murderous stares and focused on the one kid who extended his hand for me to shake. He was a scruffy punk with a mohawk.

"I'm Lars. What's up, man?" he said, then smiled.

"Not much."

"Have a seat," said Burt. He waddled off to buy something to eat.

"We were called the Mirks," Lars was saying. I had shown up in the middle of his story. "Like mercenary." I thought of my old gang TRP. "All the Mirks had to have a mohawk hairdo. This is when I was in L.A. We all worked at an ice cream parlor where we sold two scoops and a dime bag of heroin on the side. If you pissed us off we gave you the "special" cookie which I jerked off on in the back of the store…"

Sitting in the back corner was the blackest man I'd ever seen. He was staring right at me. He was square-shouldered and menacing.

"What ya looking at, boy!" he said. Burt showed up carrying a tray filled with hamburgers.

"Hey, Tiny, he's okay," he said. "He's friends with that Pierre kid, too."

"I like Pierre," said Tiny. "All right, man. Just don't be eyeballing me, kid."

I looked to Lars. Lars was still smiling and looking at me.

"Tiny's alright when she's not on the rag." I gave a little fake laugh but was careful not to overdo it.

"So what'd you think of Tiny?" Burt asked outside. Testing the waters to see if I might want to join Tiny's gang.

"That guy's fucking scary," I answered.

"Tiny's a girl. Don't you know that?"

"No. You're fucking with me. That guy Lars said something about him being on the rag but he was just kidding around. Tiny's a dude."

"Her left boob hangs down lower than her right. That's where she got her name. Hefty lefty, tiny righty."

Burt talked as slow as he walked.

"She went to London to meet some skins she had been writing to for years. These guys were real bad asses, 'Made in England' tattoos across their foreheads. At the airport, when one of them noticed Tiny making a beeline towards them, he yelled, "Look at this fucking nigger. Piss off!" But she walked right up to them and introduced herself. It took them a few moments to realize that she was the one they'd been waiting for. Until her visit, they'd had no idea she was a woman, let alone black. They were Nazi skinheads, hooligans, and looked at her dumbfounded as she explained her pro-Nazi position to them. 'But, but, you're fucking black…' was all they could say."

"You mean she's a Nazi?"

"Yeah, but she only hates the Jews. She never wore Swastikas and she's never Zekhieled. Well okay, sometimes she Zekhiels."

"She looks like a gorilla."

"She initiates new members of her gang by making them have sex with her. It's her way of 'jumping' them in. Given the chance, I think they'd rather take a beating." I would never join her gang.

"Did Pierre have sex with her?"

"Not yet. But she has her eye on him."

Summer came and it was the end of my fun. I woke up at 7:30 in the morning and put on my shirt and tie from boarding school. I walked to the end of Georgetown and M Street to Father's office. I was the new file clerk, moving boxes filled with papers from storage to offices and other files back to storage. I worked with an old woman who spent the time prattling on about any subject that came to her. The air was dead, so were the fluorescent lights overhead. I felt they were sucking the life out of me.

"Your father is a wonderful man. He just walks the halls, mumbling, going over his lawsuits. When it's time for a conference, the secretaries track him down and lead him to the meeting." I knew the feeling. She went on as I tried to understand the letter and number system of the color tabs they used to organize the files. My mind wasn't connecting with the system and the dyslexia didn't help.

"Fucking Hell," I mumbled.

The old lady glanced up at me.

"I'm probably better at moving stuff than organizing," I said.

At lunch I ate with Father. He took me to his favorite restaurant on M Street. It was a family owned business as were many of the shops in Georgetown, before the large chains took over. In a weird way Father seemed happy to see me even though it was supposed to be punishment.

"How's Nixon?" I asked.

"I'm not allowed to talk about his case. Its confidential."

"You know sometimes you're no fun." As if he was ever fun.

"How's your mother?"

"She's fine." Father lived alone. I wasn't going to bring up Mother's boyfriend. "Why did you want to become a lawyer?"

"Well, Judaism is all about the laws of God. So it was an easy transition."

"But you're a terrible Jew. You don't do anything Jewish."

"This is true, but I'm a great lawyer."

I got to go home a few hours later. Walking up to Glover Park, I saw Lars panhandling from the tourists. A few passersby hurled insults at him.

"Help get a punk drunk," he said, holding his hand out at me.

"You're friends with Burt, right?"

"I wouldn't say that, but I know him." His eyes searched my face and then it came to him. "Oh yeah, I remember you. What's up with the tie and shirt?"

"Working for my father."

"That sucks."

"No kidding." I sat next to Lars and held my hand out as a family walked by and threw some change down on the sidewalk in front of us. Lars picked it up and dropped it in his cup. I noticed his bad tattoo as he reached out. It was a skull or a smiling face. I couldn't tell. Lars' mohawk didn't stay up even though he kept pulling at its tips.

"At his house, I once found a pair of Burt's shit-stained underwear, triple extra large, big enough to hold two whole watermelons. Burt's mom had to wipe his ass for him because he couldn't reach it himself. I took the poop-stained tighty-whities and threw them into a tree that stood in front of his house. They stayed there forever, an ass-wiped flag, until they dissolved. Everyone stays at his house but no one really likes him." Lars looked to me for confirmation. I didn't say anything. I wasn't going to bad mouth Burt even if that might have been an easy way to connect with Lars. The clinking of money in his hand averted his attention. A woman had dropped some change. Lars held up a quarter. "I got enough for a beer. You want to drink?"

"Sure," I said.

The next morning, I woke to the alarm buzzing. I grabbed the clock and pulled the cord out of the wall and threw it to the other side of the room. Wiping the sleep from my face, I felt sick, as I did every morning. My shirt was wrinkled and the tie was uneven. I didn't bother to fix it.

"Want something to eat?" said Mother and she looked like she was hurting, too. "No thanks." I slipped out the door and walked to work. I saw Lars coming up Prospect Street.

"What are you doing up so early?"

"I haven't gone to bed yet," he said.

"You going to the show tonight?" I asked. I was hoping he was going so I would know someone there.

"Yeah. It's Bad Brains. Hey did you know that Tiny got her ass kicked a few days ago by Rev?"

"But she's a girl."

"Are you fucking kidding me? She's no girl. Not anymore. She acts like a man so she can get treated like a man. Fuck that. If she hits me, I'm hitting back. Anyway, she has been laying low since Rev beat her ass. I bet she shows up tonight. She got to show she's still the toughest girl on the scene, you know. Top dog and all."

"Alright. Stop by later and you can get a ride to the show."

"Cool. I'll see you later."

A dull orange glow came from the entrance of the 9:30 club. I had slept too late and missed everything but the last few songs. Lars snuck us in by licking the back of some kids hand and rolling the stamp across the back of his hand, then mine. Inside, the last notes of "Re-Ignition" vibrated through the walls. The floor shuddered from the stomping feet. A kid fell in the pit, a few punks scrambled eagerly and helped him up before he was trampled. I had been terrified to go to the show. It didn't happen in Boston, maybe because Mark was always there babysitting me. The feeling started early in the day and grew, only to vanish sometime after I walked into the club. Whenever I had anxiety, it made me sleepy and that's why I had slept too long. I could feel the final hums of the bass falling onto my ears and hitting the back of my throat. After the show, the crowd spilled out onto the sidewalk and the street, reminding me of a glass of M&M's I once knocked over at my father's office. Lots of colors rolling out, spreading across the table's length in a terrible rush, then coming to a standstill. Those who had a niche or clique found their friends. Couples paired off. I stood with Lars. I had called Charlie and Paul before I had gone to sleep and I'd told them about the show. Now I scanned the crowd to see if they were there.

Tiny leaned against a parked car in front of the club. Two suburban punks who owned the car waited for their chance to get into it and leave.

"How long do you think she's going to sit there?" whispered the one with the bright blue hair. They were on the other side of me so I heard everything.

"I don't know and I'm not going to ask," said the other. "She can keep the car, for all I care."

Tiny's arms were tightly folded across her chest. She wore freshly shined black combat boots, eighteen holes laced up just below her knee, blue jeans with the pant legs rolled up so the entirety of the boots were seen, and a green bomber jacket. She had a head of tightly shaved hair. She pushed off the car and walked over to the club. She stood directly in front of the entrance. The crowd was forced to step around her carefully since most understood what would happen if they bumped into her. Flanked on either side by her new gang of skins, Tiny was prepared, perched in front of the entrance, ready for action and searching for victims. One of her gang was a good six inches taller than the rest, a white skin with no chin to speak of, whose neck flowed right into his head. Another was a chubby girl with a Chelsea haircut who was wearing a black bomber. She looked like a big nipple standing on two legs, puffing away on a cigarette, her mouth caving in around it. Off to the side was Paul, now a skinhead. Weeks before he had asked me how to dress like a skin and now he had on everything I'd told him to get. I hadn't seen it yet, but he had even gotten a portrait of the Fonze tattooed on one calf and the cover of the Kiss record *Rock and Roll Over* on the other. On his left bicep, it said D.C. Go-Go. None of which was very skinhead, but all of which were extremely Paul. I wondered how many drugs he had had to sell to get his new outfit. If I squinted, Paul looked like a real skinhead.

I carefully maneuvered around Tiny and tapped Paul on his shoulder.

"Yo man, what's up?" he said warmly.

"What are you doing standing with Tiny's crew?" I said in a low tone.

"I ran into them in Georgetown and they were cool."

"But Paul, you know she's a Nazi, right?"

"Yeah, but so what."

I whispered. "You're Jewish."

He shrugged. Maybe she didn't care. Tiny must have been desperate to let Paul in, or maybe she hadn't known he was Jewish. Tiny's eyes bulged.

She looked like a rabid dog about to bite. Tiny had to show that she still remained a threat or she'd have to leave the scene for good. Too many of her victims were waiting for the opportunity for revenge. More important, she wanted to retain the respect she had accumulated. I could understand that; sometimes it's the only thing you really own. I went back over to Lars.

"What are you going to do now?" he asked me.

"Nothing, why? What's up?" I said. I had on a new used leather jacket and was looking at myself in the reflection of a nearby parked car. The jacket was an old motorcycle cop's from somewhere in the Midwest. It was too big but it looked broken in. I had painted the edge of the lapel white and had already transferred my favorite one inch buttons. My other jacket looked too new. I hated it so I sold it to Charlie and he was wearing it now.

"I'm going home to listen to music, drink some beer, you know." He wanted a ride.

"Hey man, can I come?" said Charlie. Lars looked over at Charlie and took in the sight of his oversized head and sniffed the air. It was rank with Charlie's breath.

"Nah." Lars didn't know Charlie and it would have been rude to bring him along. Besides, Charlie would cramp my style. Later, when I felt comfortable with Lars, I would invite him. "I'll call you later in the week."

Charlie lit a cigarette and nodded at me. I walked off with Lars. The next day Charlie called me and told me what had happened next. He saw Paul and walked over to him. The tongues of Charlie's boots hung out, flopping around as he took long strides despite his short stature. Tiny noticed his leather jacket and decided she wanted it for her own, even though it wouldn't fit her.

Sometime before, at Mother's house, Charlie and I had listened to all of my records. Charlie had devoured each band the same way I had when I'd first heard them. I had worn my old black leather jacket, which I'd painted across the back with "The Misfits" in white and red lettering, and on the sleeve with the laughing skull logo and "Sham 69." Metal pyramid studs had lined the lapel. Charlie had loved that jacket. When I had decided to sell it, he'd taken it, paying fifty dollars more than I had. He was proudly wearing it that night outside the 9:30 Club.

"Hey kid, nice jacket," Tiny said.

"Thanks," Charlie answered, then brushed the hair out of his eyes, unaffected by her presence. He had no clue who she was. This was his first show.

"I like it. Why don't you give it to me?" Tiny phrased it as a request, but it was a demand, her eyes bigger than ever.

"No!" Charlie was taken aback by her bluntness. Suddenly, he was sucker-punched from behind by the No-Neck Skin. Charlie hunched over and threw his arms up over his head in an attempt to shield himself from the blows. He was encircled. Paul jumped in and pulled the No-Neck Skin off.

"What's your fucking problem, man," said No-Neck to Paul.

"That's my friend."

"So fucking what? Either you're in the gang or you're friends with him." He pointed at Charlie as Tiny booted him hard in the face over and over.

Paul tried to pull Tiny away, but then No-Neck hit him from behind and the gang jumped on him, too. Tiny was still booting Charlie in the face. Paul rolled in front of him and took the brunt of the attack. His extra thick skull protected them both. The two punks who were waiting to get in their car ran into the club to tell the bouncers.

In seconds, every bouncer working the place, eight in all, filed out onto the street. Seeing the crowd of spectators, they moved en masse. Tiny was kicking Paul in the back of his head. Paul resorted to curling into fetal position to wait it out. The first bouncer ran towards the fight, tackling Tiny and knocking her to the ground. The No-Neck Skin tried to run when he caught sight of Tiny being held by the bouncers. He didn't make it far. The smallest bouncer tripped him. He spilled across the sidewalk, slamming his head into the hubcap of a parked car. Nipple Skin and two others made their escape while Tiny and No-Neck were held for the cops.

"Paul wouldn't talk to the cops when I pressed charges against Tiny," said Charlie. He didn't sound that bad over the phone. I pictured myself looking up at Tiny as she kicked me in the face. I needed a crew. It was the same thing in high school. There was safety in numbers.

"I'm sorry Charlie," I said. "If I had known I would have brought you along. She really fucked you up?"

"Yeah, but I'm alive. Paul saved my life."

"Just when you think you know a guy, he goes and does a thing like that."

Charlie laughed on the other end. I felt bad for him and wondered if it was my fault. I was the one who made him go, got him into punk rock, and sold him the jacket. Then I left him because he had a giant head.

"When I walked home last night, I got knocked out by a muffler some redneck had tossed from his pick-up truck yelling, "Fuck you, punk."

"What, after you got jumped?"

"Yeah, last night! After I left 2D."

"Dude, maybe the punk thing isn't for you?"

"Man, that kind of stuff happens to me all the time. Fucking rednecks hate me because I'm a punk." But I realized it was because he had such a large head, which made for a great target.

Later Lars would tell me that when Tiny's court date arrived, she was sentenced to a year in jail for the assault.

Lars is Punk as Fuck

STATE OF ALERT
  "Girl Problems"
    You had better say the right thing
    She might think you're a fool
    You have gotta lie through your teeth
    To make her think you're cool

It was ten o'clock Friday night, and we were driving up Western Avenue at forty-five miles an hour in Edgea's car. Edgea hadn't said a word directly to me. Lars had called me up and said he and his friend would drop by and pick me up. When I opened her door, Edgea didn't even bother to look over at me. I got in and we drove without speaking. She looked the same, thick white makeup covering a skull face, that was lit from below by the green of the dashboard. Ugly, but at the same time, I bet she would fuck the hell out of you. The road was bumpy since the city didn't have the money to repave it. Lars leaned out the passenger window of Edgea's car. Two women were standing in the street's median, parallel to Mazza Gallery Mall. As his body wavered in the wind, Lars extended his arm, palm open, fingers spread wide. His speeding hand grew closer and closer to the attractive blond's bottom. A cracking sound was heard from outside the car. The woman jumped from her spot, rubbing her backside as we sped by. Lars slithered back into his seat, shaking the sting from his fingertips.

"Ow! I didn't think it would hurt! I sprained my wrist!" he yelped.

"I just realized who you look like," I said.

"Don't you fucking say it!" Lars raised a fist at me, and Edgea started laughing.

"Alfred E. Newman," she said and Lars socked me in the arm.

"Whatcha do that for?" I rubbed at the spot.

Lars provided a source of constant entertainment. He functioned as a spoon that mixed boredom and opportunities into trouble. Earlier when we picked him up, his cat was acting funny. When I'd asked him why the cat had been running in the same circle since we'd arrived he'd said, "I gave the cat acid." When I'd asked him why, he'd said, "Why not? I didn't want to trip by myself." Lars lacked concentration and had no work ethic, no drive. I wondered if Lars was dyslexic, too. His mother was a teacher but, if she didn't know about dyslexia, Lars also wouldn't know about it. Maybe it was too late for him, I thought. He was done with high school. Lars was short in stature, his body was peppered with prison-style tattoos. They were a faded light blue, child-like scribblings that he had given himself, using a single sewing needle. He wound a small piece of thread around its tip and dipped it into an inkwell, then repeatedly stabbed into the first four layers of skin, producing thick lines. He made up for his small size with the ruggedness of a man twice as large. He was short, but if he could get his mohawk to stand up, it boosted his height. As we drove up Western Avenue he told us about being a runaway living on the streets, dumpster-diving for thrown away pizza crusts. I asked him if he'd ever had a job. I wanted to know what kind of work I could do, since now I was comparing our lives. "Landscaping," he said. *No fucking way was I going to do that.*

Later that night, a pounding came from the other side of the door.

"Open up, you bastards! It's the police". Lars reached, stretching his body without losing his spot on the sofa, and rolled the lock over. The door burst open and there was Victor Da Skin, a thirty year-old white guy with a dirty bomber jacket, shaved head and potbelly.

"I scared the crap outta you," he said, and strutted in like he was king.

"You say that every time," said Lars.

Lars' apartment was a sanctuary for the outcasts of the scene. When Victor Da Skin stopped by, my mood sank. Lars had told me he was a Nazi. Victor had tried to recruit young skinheads to join his Neo-Nazi party. There was already Tiny and no need for another.

A majority of D.C.'s population is black. In the skinhead scene here, there were few true Aryans, which made it difficult for Victor to find recruits, and he was harassed at shows. Apparently Pierre prank-called Victor late in the night at his parents' house, where he lived. The late night calls and threats escalated until finally Victor cracked.

"Fuck you, man! If you think you're such a badass, come over here and do something about it!" he yelled into his phone, or at least that's the way I heard it.

Pierre and his crew, obliging Victor's request, paid him a visit. They kicked down his door and stomped Victor without mercy as he cried out for his parents' help. After Lars told me this story, I tried to call Pierre to confirm it. His mother said he wasn't staying with her anymore, but I wasn't sure if that was true. Pierre's mother had hated me since we had broken into the Lab School. I remembered how Pierre looked when we were kids watching the Ku Klux Klan march on downtown D.C. I wished he had been there when Victor showed up. I didn't mention I was friends with Pierre. I had nothing to say to Victor.

Victor mostly sat around attempting to be menacing, but I wasn't afraid. He looked anything but frightening with his bruised and beaten face. Besides, it was my friend who did it.

"Grab me a beer," Victor yelled at Lars, even though it was a small apartment and you could hear a whisper from its furthest corner.

"There ain't none left," Lars said with his head in the fridge.

"Then go get us a case," Victor demanded, even though he never had any money, or, if he did, wasn't sharing it with us.

I hadn't taken off my leather jacket yet, so I was ready to go out for more beers. Liquor stores in Maryland stay open later on Sundays than the stores in D.C. Victor, Lars and I went on a beer run. This symbiotic relationship grew out of Lars and Victor's ability to buy booze legally and my access to transportation and my parents' money. We were united in our search for cheap beer, though ultimately Victor would drink most of it.

When all the beer was gone, Lars broke into stories about his near-fatal stabbings. Both stabbings had happened while he was attempting to buy drugs, and he had six or seven scars around his kidneys and a slash starting at his shoulder and ending at his love handle on the opposite side. Lars had a habit of always turning his back on these knife-wielding maniacs.

"Every self-respecting junkie knows this is bad etiquette," he said. "Don't trust a junkie, but under no circumstances trust a junkie's dealer." Victor had been there for the big slash when Lars had come stumbling back to the truck. Blood had filled his boots, making sloshing sounds.

"You gotta drive." He'd stammered, groping his side. "That guy cut me pretty bad."

"But I don't know how to drive a stick!" whimpered Victor.

With no other option, he drove himself to the hospital.

As Lars spoke I could picture the scene: His already pale complexion was completely devoid of all color. Arriving at the emergency room, nurses slapped Lars onto a gurney. He tried to fight them off as they cut free his studded belt, leather pants and combat boots. He only relented after passing out due to blood loss or perhaps an inevitable drug crash.

"After they stitched me back together, I looked at myself in the mirror. I looked like Frankenstein." He sounded proud.

It was Thursday. I went home and changed out of my work clothes. I met Lars down on M Street and he led me to the spot where the punks and skins preferred to hang out. Georgetown is the oldest part of Washington, with roads laid in cobblestones and townhouses more than two hundred years old. It existed before the nation's capital moved from Philadelphia. At the base of Georgetown, below M Street, runs a canal that stretches far beyond the District's borders. Merchants had used the canal to transport goods into the heart of the city during a time when mule-drawn barges had made the journey from deep within Maryland. Now the canal had deteriorated into a manmade swamp, garbage lining its bottom and a stench of stagnant and rotting vegetation rising from its depths. Joggers and strollers leisurely bypassed the canal and only a few dared to venture there. Bums, junkies, punks and runaways had found it to be a sanctuary. From the street, the canal was hidden from view, making it a prime location for just about anything.

My eyes swept over the group.

"Rev hangs out here," said Lars. "If you're lucky you might see him today." As if Rev were some rare animal.

Lars pointed at some of the other punks hanging out. "That's Ronnie Motherfucking Collins." The finger moved over to a girl with jet black hair. "That's Safety Pin. And you know Victor Da Skin."

I nodded.

The sky was a blinding blue and the sun beat down with an oppressive heat.

"Nice shirt," said Lars.

I looked down at my "We're the Meatmen and You Suck" shirt. Spots of black had dripped around the collar. I had just dyed my hair blue-black. Father complained about it at work, but since I wasn't breaking any laws he had to deal with it. Lars handed me a beer. It felt like I was being handed a shield and we were about to walk into a battle.

"I thought Victor was scared of Rev?" I asked Lars in a low voice.

"Victor is desperate to prove himself. The scene is like meeting a woman with a short-term memory. Even though he's a joke, that could change. With Rev's respect, the rest of the scene will have no other choice but to accept Victor."

Victor finished off a can of beer, crushed it with his hands and kicked it into the canal, where it floated.

"D.C.'s such a drag. We should go to New York; that's where everything's happening."

"Why don't you go back to Maryland?" Lars said as he fingered a spot on his head that he'd missed shaving in order to keep his mohawk in form.

"Fuck you, asshole."

"Poser."

Blood stewed in their bodies. The only relief was from cheap beer. The hottest days made the beer taste great; it was the fuel of banter, political diatribes, passionate embraces of first time lovers, and the prelude to every fight. Lars, staring at the window of a restaurant that backed onto the canal, searched his reflection for imperfections in the height and straightness of his mohawk. He chugged down a full can of Pabst Blue Ribbon. He tossed the empty can into the water and it landed with a splash where it floated next to three other cans. The girl they called Safety Pin walked off to M Street, intent on panhandling change from tourists. The older black skinhead, Ronnie "Motherfucking" Collins, stole some sleep after having given it away the previous night to drinking and drugging. Shaded by the only tree that lined that part of the canal, nothing could wake him, not even Lars, who periodically was touching his nose or flicking his ear with a steady index finger.

Everyone lazed alongside the green water, where the details of a discarded tricycle could be made out from below the muddy depths. A shopping cart, a safety cone, who knew what else lay deposited beneath its sludge. A kid my age turned the corner on his bike, trailed by two older guys. He was shorter than me with a shaved head. He wasn't white and he wasn't black; he must have been a mix of both or middle eastern. He wore Adidas Samba classic indoor soccer shoes, and a black track suit with yellow stripes. I could hear his high pitched voice when he spoke. He didn't seem threatening.

Lars nudged me in the ribs, giving me the signal that this was Rev. This is who they are all afraid of?

"The other guy who squints a lot is Rev's best friend, Blitz," said Lars. "Watch out for him too."

Rev rested his ten-speed bike against the stone blocks and sat on the wooden deck of the restaurant with Blitz as they drank Busch, a slightly better beer.

Lars slapped Ronnie on the ear. Ronnie groaned.

"I'll fuck you up, motherfucker," and rolled over onto his side and continued sleeping. Lars walked over to where Victor was sitting. He wasn't guarding his beer and Lars leisurely picked it up and popped the top. Victor heard the snap and fizz of the fresh beer and turned to see if it was his.

"Give me back my fucking beer." Victor stood up, pushed out his chest and sucked in his beer belly.

Lars chugged, and then handed the empty can back to its owner.

"If you say you're a skinhead, then fight Lars," squeaked Rev. "He's a punk."

Knowing Lars would not be easy to beat, Victor politely declined.

"Well then, I'm gonna throw you into the canal," said Rev. He sounded somewhat like Mickey Mouse.

I envisioned the canal turning into the Roman Coliseum, Lars and Victor its gladiators and Rev its Caesar, with Blitz at his side. I wasn't worried about Lars. He seemed like he could take care of himself.

"Fight," Rev commanded. "You're no skinhead."

Victor began to hop around, holding his guard up, waiting for Lars to throw the first strike. Lars finally interrupted Victor's hesitation by throwing an opening punch that sent Victor reeling backwards. Blows were exchanged. The fight looked like two puppies playing and was anything but serious. Lars was moments from claiming victory when Rev, deciding he'd seen enough, tossed them both into the canal with two quick heaves. Lars stood waist-high in the water, and Victor floated for a moment with his hands flailing behind him. Their own beer cans bobbed around them.

"See! You're no skin," Rev affirmed as he walked away with a bow-legged strut, pushing his bike along with Blitz trailing behind. I wouldn't see Victor around much after that.

It was exciting. This is the scene and now I have my own story, I thought. I felt like I was part of it, even if I was just on the fringes. I wanted to call Dash up and tell him what had happened. He probably wouldn't care. Maybe I would tell Sister? She wouldn't care either. The one person I knew who would listen and care was Stephanie, but she was still at boarding school. Wait a minute, did I miss her? I wondered. But then I suppressed the thought. Victor was trying to climb out of the water now and it was funny watching him.

Lars' mohawk was slicked to the side of his head, washed free of its hairspray and the wood glue that had given it height. Sitting on the steps of the deck, Lars peeled the t-shirt from his back, exposing skin speckled with pink freckles and a few poorly executed homemade tattoos. He balled up his shirt, squeezing the water out, and tossed it onto the back of a chair to bake in the sun. Noticing Ronnie hadn't finished his beer, Lars pried it from his sleeping hand and drank down the last third. It must have been warm with Ronnie's backwash but Lars didn't care. Victor sulked and didn't say another word for the remainder of the day. That was fine with me. I was glad Rev hated him, too.

It was dusk. Lars walked up the street, still wet. Charlie was sitting at the intersection of M Street and Wisconsin Avenue, panhandling.

"Did you go swimming?" asked Charlie.

"Why is your head so fucking big?" said Lars and marched up the street.

I stopped in front of Charlie and asked why he was panhandling.

"It's what all the punks do. Why not?"

"Well I just saw some punks get thrown in the canal. You want me to throw you in there, too?"

"No thanks."

"You want to come get records with me?"
"Sure."
"Do you have enough money?"
He opened his wallet. It was full of cash. I shook my head.
"Did you hear what happened to Pierre?" asked Charlie.
"No. I tried calling his mother's place. She said he wasn't staying there anymore. It sounded like she'd kicked him out, but I could tell she was worried about him."
"He got arrested for beating up a bus driver. The guy is in a coma."
"Why?" My voice went up a decibel.
"I don't know why."
"Shit man, what the fuck?" We started walking to Smash. I told him the story of what he'd missed at the canal. On the way, we stopped in Burger King. We waited in line. When I got close to the cashier, I realized it was Tiny.
"Can I help you, sir?" she said. I wanted to tell her to stop eyeballing me or I was going to complain to the manager but that would just have given her a reason to kick my ass. She pretended not to recognize either of us and I was fine playing my role. It was sad in a way, seeing the mythical monster trapped behind the counter in a paper hat that looked a size too small, wearing an orange and tan uniform. She was reduced to being nothing more than one of society's lackeys. I ordered my burger and then Charlie stepped up to the counter. For a moment he said nothing, then he ordered his food and we met back at the table.
"There is justice in the world," said Charlie. I looked back at Tiny, who tried to look busy behind the counter, but there were no other customers.
"Why is she out?" I said.
"She was sentenced to a year; which means she would only have to serve a month or less, you know. It's like on the news. Some guy gets sentenced for a murder and then only serves six years."
"Oh… I almost feel bad for her."
"To hell with her."
 "You know, we are like a dyslexic mafia."
"How do you figure?" Charlie asked.
"Think about it. Paul saved your ass with Tiny. Pierre is most likely going to jail. You're into punk rock and now Dash is leaning that way. We

all went to the same schools and have known each other forever. We have a connection that outsiders just don't get. It's like a family or a mafia."

"But you and I are different, you know," he said.

"What do you mean?"

"I mean Pierre and Paul are poor. We have parents with money."

"What difference does that make?"

"All the difference. We are going to go to college. They will stay here."

"I don't know if I'm going to go to college," I said, truthfully.

"You don't know it yet, but you are going."

The Motherfucking Circle

SWIZ
"Won't Breathe for You"
When your teeth fall from your face
I'll be there to catch them
And with your smile in my fist
I'll do all your smiling

"Dupont is where all the punks hang out," said Lars. "You've never been there?"

"I know my old school was close to it, but I don't think I saw it. Where is it?" I said as he passed me his beer. It was just backwash so I didn't drink any. It was a muggy Monday after work. I found Lars panhandling on M Street again. It was too hot to wear the suit and I desperately wanted to go home and change. I also wanted to get home before Mother so I could go back out until late. She had been giving me a hard time about staying out all night when I had to work the next day. But I figured it was my summer break. It would be my birthday soon and then I would be back in school.

"It's downtown," said Lars. "Connecticut Avenue and Massachusetts run through it."

"What do you do there?"

"Hang out. Drink, fight, talk, whatever."

"Why there?"

"Why not?"

After I went home and changed, I pulled out of the driveway just as Mother pulled in. Lars and I drove down to the Circle and parked in a lot off of P Street. Walking by the businessmen heading home reminded me that I was straddling their world and the punk scene that summer.

"Fucking yuppie scum bags!" said Lars as he gave the finger to some guy who was looking at him funny. We crossed the street into the Circle, which had a fountain at its center. It was ringed by benches and, on the outside, cars that drove past. Bums, messengers and punks mixed in small groups to one side of the benches.

"Help get a punk drunk," Lars panhandled from the yuppies who walked past, and when he had enough money he bought a case of cheap beer. I noticed a girl stealing looks at me. She had brilliant blue hair, tomboy looks, a freckled face, a slight chest and a big can. She wasn't pretty but there was something sexy about her. Maybe I just needed sex. So anyone who would have me was sexy at that moment.

"This is Ronnie Motherfucking Collins," said Lars later that night. "He's like the Prince of Dupont Circle." I remembered him from the other day at the canal.

Ronnie held his hand out for me to shake. He was a light-skinned black with a short afro. Ronnie smiled and Lars went on with his introduction.

"All the women are in love with Ronnie and all the men wish they were more like him – except that no one wants his addictions."

"It's a pleasure, sir," I said and took Ronnie's hand and shook it.

He had become a legend to me. Lars had told me countless stories of his old friend. My favorite was how he had gotten his name.

Ronnie had just finished the last drops of a 40-ounce bottle of Old English Malt Liquor and was walking down M Street in Georgetown. His hair was cut short and he wore a plain white shirt, blue jeans and combat boots. He looked like he was ready for war. He passed a man in his 40s who was wearing a Dallas Cowboys baseball hat and T-shirt, which is something you just didn't do in the town of the Redskins. The man stared and shook his head in disapproval at Ronnie's appearance. Ronnie wasn't paying any attention to him. He just assumed the guy was cruising for young boys. But after a moment, he heard the man call out, "Nigger!" Ronnie stopped and slowly turned in the direction of the man, who was smiling.

"That's right. I'm talking to you," said the man. Maybe he was drunk.

Without warning, Ronnie punched the man in the nose. The man fell to the ground and a gun that was on the back of his belt dropped onto the sidewalk, just out of his reach. Seeing the gun, Ronnie became more furious and continued punching and kicking the guy on the ground.

"I'm a cop!" the guy screamed in between blows.

"I'm Ronnie Motherfucking Collins!" he shouted back, continuing to tear the undercover officer apart. It took four cops to pull Ronnie off. From then on, the scene deemed him "Ronnie Motherfucking Collins." He spent a few nights in jail, but in the end they let him go.

After introducing me to Ronnie, Lars walked off to get some beer.

Some of the low-lives and bums loitering around the fountain came over to me.

The biggest one said, "You got to be paying the white boy tax."

"What?" I said.

"You is a white boy, right?"

"Ah...yes."

"And you in the Circle, right?"

"Yeah."

"You need to be paying me some tax or I might have to fuck you up, son."

Ronnie stood up. "Leave him alone, Motherfucker!" he ordered. They left me alone. From that point on I considered him a friend. If there was trouble, he was by my side, no questions asked. I felt safe around him. I didn't have to prove myself to Ronnie. He just accepted me, whereas with most people in the scene I'd had to seek out their approval.

"Listen here, motherfucker," he'd say. To him everyone and everything was a "motherfucker" and you could almost have a normal conversation with him if you could blank out all the "motherfucking."

"Listen here, motherfucker," he leaned towards me, tilting his head in my direction, eyes wide open as if great knowledge were about to spill from his brain and slither into my ear.

"You got to think like the Criminal Minded if you want to survive the Circle. These motherfuckers don't play. Never look for a fight, but if you're gonna fight, motherfucker, win. If you have the slightest doubt, then you've already lost, motherfucker. When you're in the act of fighting some motherfucker, it's like you're gonna kill the motherfucker. Only stop when the motherfucker can no longer defend himself, motherfucker.

There is no honor in beating a motherfucker who can't fight back, motherfucker. Here's how you deal with the mother fucking cops:

Rule Number One: Never look guilty, motherfucker.

Rule Number Two: Never run, motherfucker. That's how they pick the motherfucker out of the crowd.

Rule Number Three: Change your motherfucking clothes 'cause they be looking for you, motherfucker.

Rule Number Four: Be motherfucking nice to the policemen. The motherfucking pigs deal with motherfuckers who have bad attitudes. Say 'Yes Sir, Mister Motherfucker Pig Man.'"

Ronnie's rules of the Criminal Minded were often violated by his followers. You were never to hit a woman, but Rev insisted, "She was acting like a man, so I treated her like one," after bricking Tiny. Punishment for breaking the rules worked on a sliding scale. The higher up you were in the scene's status, the more you could get away with, like when Blitz knocked out a girl for calling him 'the Geek'. Blitz the Geek was his nickname before he became Rev's sidekick and a terror in his own right. There weren't any complaints. Nothing was done about it and the overall response from the scene was, "Everyone knows he hates it when you call him the Geek."

Ronnie's afternoons were spent panhandling and in the evenings he drank, smoked rock, or shot up. It was two days after we were introduced when a young businessman cut through the Circle to save time on his way to Massachusetts Avenue.

"Excuse me, sir. Sir, could you help me out? Some motherfucker just stole my wallet. Could you help me out with a few motherfucking bucks? I need enough to take the motherfucking bus home. My motherfucking wife and baby are waiting for me. She must be worried about this motherfucker now." Ronnie held out his hand, spreading his fingers wide to make his hand look bigger and more desperate at the same time. The businessman pulled out his wallet and gave Ronnie a five dollar bill so he could end the one-sided conversation and be on his way.

Ronnie turned back to us with a large smile, holding the five dollars by its ends, high over his head.

"Looky here, motherfuckers! Let's get a case of motherfucking Milwaukee's Best." What he lacked in manners, he made up for in charm.

Even when he was playing the starving bum with his hand out for change, people liked him. Well, everyone liked him, except Mother.

A few days later, I was shaving Ronnie's head in my backyard and drinking the cheapest beer I could get. The curls of his hair fell to his shoulders, sticking to his shirt. I heard the hum of the garage door as it rolled open. Mother's red Le Baron convertible pulled in. I grabbed the beers, prying the one Ronnie was drinking from his hand, and hid them under the cover of the grill. A few moments later, Mother passed through the yard on her way to the house.

"Hey Mom, this is Ronnie." I left out the Motherfucking Collins part, thinking she wouldn't appreciate it.

"You are a very lovely woman, " he said casually, watching her with his hand frozen waiting for the beer to return to it. I was shocked he hadn't cursed.

Mother's face tightened and her eyebrows sloped into a "V" formation. She turned to me.

"Never bring him here again." With that, she went into the house.

A day later, Lars, Edgea, her friend Jenny and I, waited for Ronnie. He came stumbling into the Circle, escorting a beautiful girl on his arm. His head looked clean. I'd done a good job. Maybe I should be a barber, I thought.

"It's never the same one," said Edgea.

"But they are always hot," said Lars.

"He doesn't care about the girls. He uses them to get drugs from the dealers. He trades them," added Edgea.

But the drugs were rotting him from the inside. Unkempt, he would slowly lose his wit. Over the next year we would have to watch over him like a child. Ronnie contracted HIV from his heroin addiction because of dirty needles and bad blood. He would be my first friend to die from AIDS. But that would be later. For now he was still on top of his game.

Jenny drank a wine cooler. Lars and Ronnie returned from panhandling and didn't have enough to get beer. Lars pulled at the tips of his mohawk. Edgea limped behind Lars, dragging her orthopedic shoe along.

"Let's get out of here and go to Georgetown," I said, standing up and holding my leather jacket. It was just too hot to wear.

"I don't want to go yet," said Jenny.

"Come on, it's not cool here, and I don't want to leave you two with the bums."

There were new guys hanging out and I didn't trust them. Ronnie had already ripped one of them off for drugs twice and I overheard him threatening pay back. They called him Screwdriver Skip. I thought it was a stupid name, but he looked dangerous.

"We'll be fine," said Jenny.

"Yeah, we're fine," echoed Edgea.

I looked to Ronnie but he was passed out again.

"I don't know," I said, looking to Lars. "Maybe we should stay?" I had a bad feeling, but Lars knew the Circle better than me.

"Come on, they're fine," he replied. We left with the plan to meet later and go back to Jenny's place.

When we got there, she was drunk. When I asked her what had happened to Edgea, she didn't remember. It was the next day when Edgea called from a pay phone. She was at the squat downtown and asked me to pick her up. Lars came along for the ride.

She was waiting on the corner. Climbing in the back seat, she looked like she had been tossed inside a duffle bag and thrown down a flight of stairs.

"What happened to you?" asked Lars.

"We were hanging out with these bums, Screwdriver Skip and his friend Angel." As she spoke, her eyes avoided ours. "They seemed pretty cool. Skip told me to come with him to help carry the beer, so I did. Then when we walked past the parking lot he pulled me in and he had a screwdriver at my neck. He said he was going to kill me if I made any noise, so I didn't."

"And what happened?" I asked.

"He raped me." Her voice broke.

No one spoke for a few minutes and I drove.

"No one saw or tried to help?" I asked and I knew it was a stupid question. She didn't answer.

"Skip killed a guy with a screw driver and went to jail for six years," said Lars. "He's only been out for a few weeks."

We dropped Edgea at home. We asked her to go to the hospital but she refused, scared her father would find out.

"My father's an asshole and wouldn't understand," she said.

"Where are we going now?" said Lars. It was getting dark.

"I'm going to kill Skip." I was angry. Angry at Skip, at Jenny and mostly myself for letting them stay at the Circle when I knew it didn't feel right. It was dark when I parked. Stepping out of the car, I thought of what had happened there the night before. As we walked up the block, Lars pointed out Angel.

"Where is your friend Skip?" I said, holding my fist tight at my side. I wanted to hit him. "We need to talk to him."

"I ain't seen that brother all night, man." Angel looked nervous and walked off fast. We crossed over to the Circle and found Ronnie Motherfucking Collins. He was already high, but seemed to understand what we were saying. One of his rules had been violated and now someone had to pay.

"I'm going to beat that Motherfucker's ass," he said. "Come on Motherfuckers I got some friends who can fix this Motherfucker." Ronnie led me over to a group of black guys I had seen around. They were drug dealers, but Ronnie hadn't ripped them off yet.

"You know that motherfucker Screwdriver Skip?"

"Yeah man, he's a scum bag," said a guy with a giant Afro.

"That motherfucker raped a friend of mine."

"For real?" said a guy who wore sunglasses even though it was dark.

"Who that be?" said the Afro. He looked over at Lars and me, sizing us up.

"Little motherfucker with one short leg and crazy hair."

"Little shorty? Fuck that. If you find Skip, bring that bitch to us. We'll take care of him." While the guy with the afro ranted about what he was going to do to Skip, I noticed a group of skins walking along the outside of the Circle, then stopping at the light and waiting to cross.

The guy with the sunglasses tipped them down over his nose so he could better see the group of skins and then said;

"Yo man, it's those crackers. You better get Manny". The guy with the afro ran off and came back with three other guys. The light changed and the skins walked into the Circle. I saw Paul but didn't know any of the other guys. The skins recognized the black guys standing next to us and immediately started pulling out of the ground two by four stakes that were supporting young trees, holding up the stakes over their heads. The guy with the afro pulled a gun from the back of his pants and both groups started yelling at each other.

"You know those guys," the guy with the afro said to Ronnie after noticing Paul giving me a confused look.

"I've never seen these Motherfuckers before."

He held the pistol but he looked like he had never fired it and then said to me, "Your boys came down here the other night starting shit and tonight we're going to end it."

There was nowhere to run; the two groups moved toward each other. I was sure I was going to be shot. A screeching of tires came from outside the Circle, then the headlights bounced light across the path in front of me. The lights on top flashed red and blue. It was the cops. The guy with the gun pushed it into his afro where it was hidden from view. The officer looked over at him and assumed he was keeping his hands on his head as an act of submission. The skins dropped the two by fours. The cop rolled down his window and shouted.

"What's going on here?" Everyone was quiet.

"Nothing, officer," said the guy with the sunglasses. "Just talking with our friends."

"Well you better keep it that way or I'll be dragging you all in." The cop's window rolled up. He drove off slowly and parked outside the Circle, watching.

"Thank fucking god for the cops," I whispered to Lars. Then I looked at Paul. "What the hell is your problem? These are friends of mine," I said to him.

"I don't know you motherfucker, but you better come corrected around these parts or those motherfuckers be shooting your ass," said Ronnie to Paul.

"Paul, you are fucking something up that has nothing to do with you." I still wanted Skip. "You better fix this."

The two groups started talking.

"Now what?" asked Lars.

"I don't think Skip will show up after that," I said. "We should go to the canal just to make sure he isn't there." But he wasn't at the canal either. After that I had had enough for the night and went home.

I slept late, enjoying the fact that I didn't have to go to work until Mother woke me up with a phone call from Lars.

"You remember that guy Angel?" Lars asked.

"Yes."

"After Edgea got raped by Skip, Angel took her back to the squat and raped her again. Last night, when we went looking for Skip, Angel ran off and told him. They got caught breaking into someone's home. Skip got sent right back to Lorton and Angel will end up there, too. I guess they were trying to get money to split town."

"I don't know if I'm supposed to feel good about that or not," I said.

"Forget it. There is nothing else we can do." He hung up. What would I have done if I had caught Skip? I was so mad at the time I might have done something very stupid. In the end I would have gone to jail. My life would never have been the same.

Getting Drunk and Meeting Baxter

VOID
 "Who are you?"
  I walk up next to you everyday.
  You never hear anything I say
  I came to you with all my problems.
  You don't care you couldn't be bothered.
  So who are you why am I here.

I was at a party late on a Sunday night in September on Reservoir Road about a mile from Mother's house. It was too hot during the day and now it was too cold. Fuck I don't want to go back to school, I thought. Nothing good happened this summer. I'm so sick of the same people at these parties. My eyes swept over the room. I was out because I didn't want to feel like I missed out on something, but there wasn't anyone I wanted to talk to either. Then the door opened and the laughter of a girl came bouncing in as if to announce her entry. Her physique was slim, her black hair in a long braid, her voice buoyant. *I could be exceptional with her by my side.* I couldn't stop watching her and when she noticed, I turned bright red and looked at my shoes to make sure they were still on my feet. She casually looked away.

I imagined holding her hand, her long black hair brushing against my face, and looking into her blue eyes. Being so close to her, I would have to keep one eye closed so I didn't see a double image. Putting my hand on the curve of her hip, grabbing her around her small waist, pressing her breasts against my chest, taking in her scent, kissing her full lips and freckles, and feeling her tongue against mine. Then a boy I knew walked into the room. He nodded hello to me and did all the things I wanted to do to her. He was a skater who sometimes hung out at Dash's house. We never talked and I hadn't paid any attention to him until now. Then he sat down and she climbed on top of him, straddling him. Her back arched and her braid whipped around to her front.

Dash walked up to me with a joint in one hand and a can of beer in the other.

"Who's that?" I asked.

"I don't know," he said as his eyes swept over the two intertwined bodies. "She's got a boyfriend."

"No shit. She's so hot."

"You think so?" he said as he took a drag of the joint and then held it out for me to take. I didn't take it so he took another drag.

"Yeah, don't you?"

"She's not my type." *WHAT was his type?*

Charlie wandered into the room, his eyes darting wildly in search of a beer. He noticed us both watching the girl.

"Her name is Maggie."

"How do you know?"

"I just met her brother."

Balmy summer air blew through the house. I was drunk. I had driven over without any intention of drinking, but it was the last party of the summer. When Charlie suggested finding someone to drive my new car home for me, I figured why not? The Zephyr had died and my new white '87 Oldsmobile with its blue velvet interior was parked outside. As I walked by the front window, I made sure it was still there.

I had just turned eighteen. D.C. had had a drinking age of eighteen but had just changed it to twenty-one after a bunch of kids from Maryland had driven into the city to get drunk at the bars and then had killed themselves on the way home. If I had been born a few years earlier I would have been grandfathered in. I had a strict rule about not driving drunk.

Since my parents had almost been killed by a drunk behind the wheel, I wouldn't put myself in the same position.

I noticed a kid who lived close to my house. I had seen him in the neighborhood, walking down Wisconsin Avenue towards Georgetown and at Smash. He was a punk with white liberty spikes and he seemed sober. All the beer was gone and the girl whose house it was wanted us out.

I didn't trust my friends with my new car. When I drove Dash or Charlie's cars, I treated them like tanks, smashing into trashcans, cutting across curbs, leaving their cars dented and beaten. Their cars were shit. A hubcap flying off didn't matter. I had a new car now; well it was Mother's hand-me-down, but it was new to me. I didn't even trust my friends to change the tapes in the tape deck; I had to do it. So I stood up straight and rolled back on my heels to catch my balance as the buzz interfered with my coordination. I looked around the room and found the kid standing in the corner. He was pulling at the tip of one of his liberty spikes, a hairstyle of his own doing, then puffing at the cigarette held in the grips of his teeth. His face was long. He was tall and had gangly limbs. He would have to do. Charlie had already left so I didn't have to worry about getting him home. Dash lived right down the street and could walk.

"Hey man. You live in Georgetown, right?"

"Yeah," he said.

"Me too. What are you doing now?"

"I don't know, walking home, I guess?"

"You want to drive my car back to the neighborhood?"

"Sure. I'm Baxter." He held out his hand and we shook.

"You haven't been drinking, have you?"

"No way," he said.

In the car I asked where he went to school. He went to Georgetown Day School and even knew Ted.

"What do you think of Ted" I asked.

"Well, he's kind of a priss, if you know what I mean. Last year he got busted for breaking into the Lab School down the street from our school. He totally freaked out, like he had ruined his life. It was kinda sad, in fact. He had finally done something cool, something he hadn't been expected to do and then he'd freaked out about it. He's a pussy. You know, my school is filled with assholes that will be running this country someday. It was nice to think one person might have had a thought of his own."

"What do you think of the Lab School?"

"I don't think much about it. The kids who go there seem normal enough to me. The guys who go to my school pick on them because it's easy. It's embarrassing, really."

"I used to go there."

"I figured."

"Why, cause I act different?"

"No. You wouldn't have asked what I thought of the Lab School."

I nodded. This guy's alright, I thought. We could be good friends.

The ride home was fine. I hadn't noticed anything odd since I was still drunk, and we made it to Mother's house. The Oldsmobile glided into its parking spot. Baxter stepped out of my car.

"Thanks for driving. I'm too drunk and I owe you one," I said.

"No problem. I'm wasted but I drive better drunk," Baxter said, and then he turned to stumble in the direction of his home. "And I'll get my driver's license next month!" he shouted over his shoulder as he turned the corner.

The next day he came knocking at my door.

"You want to come with me to Smash to pick up some records?" he asked. He pulled the zipper of his tight black biker jacket up to his chin with a harsh yank.

"Sure." I grabbed my leather jacket even though it was still too hot to wear.

We walked into Georgetown under a rain-laced sky. Baxter took a long time, meticulously flipping through every record. I looked for the S.O.A. green vinyl, but of course it wasn't there.

"Come on, man, you're worse than a girl," I said, hoping it might move things along, but it didn't. I thought I was bad, but this guy took forever.

"You have to look through all of them sometimes. When these guys find something really great, they hide it in another section and come back for it later, like this. Here you go." Baxter pulled out a rare copy of an Addicts record. An hour later, he paid for the dozen records he'd picked out and we walked up to R Street, where he lived.

"Come on up. I'm the only one who uses the back steps." He showed me a side entrance that led to his backyard. We pushed past the hanging vines and the space opened up into a lawn with a pool and the back of a modern mansion, rectangular with plenty of glass so you could see into most of the rooms. He was the first person I knew who lived in a house so big. *Rich boy.*

Sitting in his TV room, we watched a video. I could hear the light footsteps of a girl coming down the hall. She was humming a tune. She appeared in the doorway. It was Maggie, the girl from the party, the girl making out with someone else. I sat up straight. Her eyes caught mine. She studied me a moment.

"This is Maggie," said Baxter.

I stood up to shake her hand. She smirked at the oddity of my formality. Maggie sat on the ottoman, with her back to me. Her midriff was showing. She leaned to one side, holding herself up with an arm, her hip slightly turned over. I began to feel queasy.

"Where do you go to school?" she asked.

"Chelsea."

"Where is that? I've never heard of it."

"It's in Silver Springs." That was the good thing about the new school – no one knew it was for learning disabilities.

"You're friends with Dash, right?" *Did she have a crush on Dash?*

"Yeah, why?"

"Nothing, my new boyfriend knows him."

"God, you're chatty today," said Baxter to Maggie.

"Don't be an asshole," she fired back.

Maggie was a few years younger than Baxter and me. She was beautiful and sweet. I was looking at her when I noticed Baxter watching me watching his sister and I looked back at the TV. Maggie left the room to make a phone call.

"I don't trust her new boyfriend," said Baxter.

"Did you give him a hard time?"

"No, I don't do that kind of thing."

The door bell rang and Baxter got up to get it. A moment later Maggie's boyfriend came into the TV room and sat across from me. I remembered the back of his head and how her fingers had run through his hair. I could hear Baxter making noise in the kitchen next door and Maggie was just out of ear shot talking on the phone in the hall.

"Hey, I know you," the skater kid said to me. He was puny, scruffy, and good looking.

"Yeah, and I know you, too. Before you get all chummy with me, let me say this. Maggie's your new girl? If you fuck with her or make her upset, I'm going to fuck you up," I said. *Why did I do that?* I meant to be nice and before I knew it I said the wrong thing. If I couldn't have her at least I could protect her. *Fuck it.*

"I won't."

"I am just saying, if you're going to do something like that, it's not cool with me and I'll take it personally."

"Okay, okay."

Maggie collected her boyfriend and Baxter walked in carrying a sandwich stacked high with meats, mustard, mayo and lettuce.

"Did you meet the new boyfriend?" he said just before taking a bite.

"No," I said.

Fuck School

SOUL SIDE
"Baby"
It's hard not to be depressed when you're sick and I'm sick of questions.

First day back at school hit me like a terrible hangover. I was now a junior. All the students seemed dazed by the same feeling. Dash skated back and forth in the driveway, high on something. I hadn't seen him much over the summer, so that was the one good thing about being back at school. Paul stood next to another one of his junked cars. The white doors didn't match the blue rusted out body. He had taken off the hood and I wondered if the car would run in the rain. Paul was trading drugs for cash and trying to look like he was doing anything other than that. When he was finished he spotted me watching him and pulled his shirt over his head, revealing a giant, fresh black and gray tattoo that stretched across his back. It was a zombie standing on top of a mound of skeletons. "Who did that?" I shouted over to him.

"Yo, some crazy Indian named Running Bear." I wanted a tattoo. What would I get? Maybe the name of a band? The Bad Brains, but what if the band did something stupid, like turned into some crappy rap act? Paul moved on to show some of the girls his new ink.

Charlie walked outside and rubbed his head, feeling the shortness of his new haircut, which was meant to make his head seem smaller, but had had the opposite effect. "I've already applied to two colleges," he said. "You can never be too early."

School? Why is he so obsessed with school? College wouldn't be easy. They expect you to read lots of books then write papers all the time. How could I get by?

Then, two small hands covered my eyes from behind. They were cold. The air around them was heavy with perfume. The scent was all too familiar.

"Guess who?" a prissy girl's voice said, tugging at some distant memory.

"I don't know? Daisy Duke?"

"No silly, it's me!" She brought her face around to my front. Fiona. I prepared myself for what was next. A smile quickly overtook her lips.

"How do I look now?" she asked.

"Good," I lied. Her once voluptuous breasts had begun to lose their shape. She had developed early and now I guessed she was going to start aging early. She had dark circles under her eyes, as if she had been up partying too late. Her clothes seemed tighter. She had to try harder to look alluring, where before it had been effortless. I imagined her flesh squishing through my fingers. She craned her neck to get a better look at me. I had grown since the last time she'd seen me, muscle tone enlarged my frame. We'd dated when I had been a boy and now I was midway to being a man. She gave me a look, like she had already conquered me, taking my virginity and a bit of soul along with it. I didn't bat an eye, even though I could feel my anger building.

"What the hell are you doing here?" I said, annoyed. I didn't want her to be part of my life again. She had hurt me and I didn't want her around to remind me.

"I go to school here now." Her lips glistened slightly. Her hair was a natural chestnut color. If I squinted, I could see that she still had a few years left as a sexual deity.

"But you're not even dyslexic."

"At my school, I was having a hard time so they gave me some crazy tests and they said I had Attention Deficit Disorder, and now I'm here."

"Great. I have to get to class." I walked into the building, then sat at a desk. Memories of sex with her crossed my mind. Don't do this, I thought. I couldn't help it. I would think of sex with her, and I knew at some point I would give in. Losing my virginity to her made it hard to forget. *Fuck her, why did she have to come here? Why can't she leave me alone?* For the rest of the day it was all I thought about.

After school, Dash came to my house and we picked up Sister. We went down to the Lincoln Memorial to sit on the steps and do homework outside. I looked up at Lincoln sitting in the chair and heard a tour guide say;

"Notice that one side of his posture is tense. With a hand clinched and foot drawn in, and the other side is relaxed. The artist wished to express the two Lincolns, the wartime president, and the peacemaker who attempted to heal the nation." The group moved on. The statue looked as if it were made of dried toothpaste. I walked over and touched the foot, stretching to reach it before the park police came over and asked me to unhand the president. Sister was watching me with her moon spinning around her head. I sat next to her and she helped me with my homework. Dash flipped through his books and threw them back into his backpack. I guess the good looking don't have to worry about being smart, I thought.

"You're done?" I said.

"Oh yeah, sure I'm done," said Dash and he lit a cigarette. The park ranger motioned for him to put it out. He did under the heel of his foot.

"Brother, I have to tell you something."

"What is it?" I was trying to read something and was about to ask her help.

"I might be getting into college early." Dash looked over at her.

"That's great," I said, but I wasn't really paying much attention.

"Won't you be upset?"

"I guess so. I won't know until it happens."

I read more as Sister asked Dash about the schools he wanted to go to. But Dash wasn't planning on going to school. He wanted to move to New York and become an actor. Or at least that's what he said that week.

The week before it had been a musician in LA, and last year it had been a Marine. He didn't know what he wanted to do. Neither did I.

"Are you going to the party this weekend?" Dash asked Sister, changing the subject.

"What party?" I wanted to know and wondered why he was bringing this up with her.

"Just someone I skate with."

"I'll go," I said.

"All right," said Dash. Sister said nothing as she went back to reading a textbook. I thought I saw her stealing a glance at Dash.

"Whart derar hell arrrarrrr Dars place eirs a freaking," I heard coming from the other room. It was Saturday.

Is someone beating a dog? I thought to myself.

Baxter and I had met Dash at the party. Dash was wandering the rooms in search of beer, vanishing around the corner. The guy who lived there had gotten an eviction notice, and the place was going to be demolished for new construction. The party included an odd assortment of people. Skins, punks, hippies, jocks and preppies were all mixing about the house. A kid kicked in the drywall, then smiled at me. I looked into the hall as a skinhead was bashing out the rungs of the banister leading to the upstairs. As the former renter stood and witnessed, the guests destroyed the house.

"Go ahead. I don't care. They're kicking me out anyway. To hell with them." Rev and Blitz watched ominously from a corner. Lars and Ronnie played the hand slapping game. Lars was winning. Ronnie wasn't looking so good. He was showing the first signs of HIV, though we didn't know it yet. As I passed some kid, I heard him talking.

"Yeah, he's a black skinhead named Pierre. Now he's in jail up at Lorton." It was old information. I thought I saw the back of Sermon, my old tormenter, walking out the front door. Paul high-fived me on his way down the hall. It was overwhelming. I looked at Dash, wondering why he'd invited Sister. He gave no sign.

"Where is Charlie?" I asked.

"He couldn't come out. He is writing an essay to get into some school."

Dash ambled off to talk with Paul; no doubt he wanted weed. Baxter handed me a beer. It was warm. I drank it anyway.

"Dang dwart dart dis neart beer"...."

"I heard it again," I said to Baxter, but he wasn't listening to me. He was watching a skinhead girl punch out a window. I walked into the kitchen and saw something digging in the refrigerator. It was foraging, hungry and desperate. I felt safer backing up a few feet. It sensed my presence and quickly stood up, towering over me and everything else in the room. It's gaze found me. I let out a loud gasp.

Twenty-five years old and still living at home, Ukala stood over six feet four inches in height and had straight black hair drenched in grease and styled in a Ramones long bob cut. His body was lanky, making his head seem stretched, and his face reminded me of a fun house mirror reflection or Silly Putty that had been pulled. His skin was gray and covered with festering pimples that oozed a yellow pus. His eyebrows drooped. The cuffs of his unwashed jeans were frayed from dragging on the ground. He was monstrous. He embodied what my dyslexia felt like on the inside, and I wanted to collect him as a new friend. Maybe hanging out with him would make me feel better about myself, I thought. I wanted to show him off to Baxter. I walked up to him and introduced myself. Then I picked up a brick that was used as a doorstop and threw it into the television. The renter darted into the room when he heard the noise.

"Hey, that was mine!" he yelled, and Ukala smiled. We could be friends.

The best shows with the worst bands were at Fort Reno. Free to everyone, the entertainment was funded by the city in an attempt to keep the youth busy, out of trouble and away from drugs and alcohol. But everyone drank and did their drugs in the parking lot of Wilson High School, directly across the street.

Fort Reno was originally a Civil War fort, one of many spread throughout the city. The fort itself sat back on the crest of a small hill, surrounded by a fence and signs that read "Government Property. Keep Out." Encompassed in green fields that you could run in barefoot, there was a small wooden stage only a few feet off the ground where the bands tinkered away. Our reason for going wasn't the music; it was a socializing event. We flirted with girls and looked for that night's party. The shows would end in a month. It was Tuesday after school. Baxter picked me up in his minivan and drove us over.

"Hair man, gravele mar monage fre ah beer dun," said Ukala, which meant, "Hey man, give me money for a beer run." It didn't matter if he was sober or drunk and I wasn't sure if he was retarded but he always spoke like that. It was his own language. I began to understand him. Maybe it was because of my dyslexia. Maybe it was because he spoke the way I read. He asked again. I knew if I gave Ukala the money, he would drink most of the beer, saying he had had to do all the legwork to get it.

"Piss off. I'm busy," I said, even though I had nothing to do.

As he spoke, I mentally translated his words. "Come on man, give me some money and drive me to the liquor store." Ukala didn't have a driver's license, and expected me to chauffeur him.

"Take the bus."

"Come on man." Now he was whining, and I wanted to punch him in the face when he acted like that. I wondered if his mumbling was an act. Why could he say some words fine, like beer and man, then sometimes sound like someone had knocked him in the mouth while he was juggling marbles with his tongue?

A kid standing behind us started laughing at something and Ukala turned to him.

"Whart dar hell errs yoll prebrm?" he said.

"What?" said the kid.

Ukala made a fist and punched the kid in the nose. The kid fell on his back and Ukala moved in to hit him again, but I jumped on him, climbing him like a tree and keeping my weight up by his shoulders. His knees buckled and he came crashing down next to the kid, with me sitting upright and comfortable on his chest.

"What, are you fucking nuts? He's half your size. If you want to fight someone so bad, there are plenty of other people who need it a lot more than some small kid," I said looking over at the other guy. "You okay?" I asked. He nodded, and Baxter helped him up. I got off of Ukala, who was having a hard time breathing with my weight on him.

Maggie's boyfriend walked up to me, already speaking. He had been watching us the entire time. I caught the last part, "Just so you know, we're not dating anymore."

"Dating who?" I said. But I already knew. I just wanted to make him say it.

"Maggie... Baxter's sister."

"Okay."

He walked on. I searched the crowd for her, but didn't see her.

I wondered if she was okay. Maybe I shouldn't have said anything.

Ukala went back to his original plan, asking kids to pitch in for beer. Baxter waited until Ukala was out of hearing range, then said;

"You do know that the kid Ukala hit is a student of Master Woo's?"

"What's that?" I asked.

"Master Woo is the Tae Kwon Do school Rev goes to. If you get in a fight with one of the students, even if you lose to them, Rev will find out. He'll kick Ukala's ass," said Baxter.

Unaware of this new threat, Ukala walked over to the parking lot.

"Are you going to tell him?" I asked Baxter.

"No, I'll wait until the right moment."

Charlie walked between the kids standing around Fort Reno, stopping when he saw someone he knew.

"There is a big party tonight," he said to us.

"I got school in the morning," I said.

"Well, the chick whose house it is is really hot."

"Who's that?" asked Baxter.

"It's Stephanie. You remember her from the Lab School. She went to some boarding school outside of Boston and just moved back."

Later that night, half of the scene was at Stephanie's new house in Alexandria, Virginia. I guess everyone wanted to see the new hot chick. I hadn't seen her since I'd left boarding school. I had thought about her many times, but I'd never contacted her. It would have been too weird, or maybe I'd been so used to her chasing me that I hadn't wanted to flip things around. Boisterous noise came from the house as I walked up the path, trailed by Baxter, Edgea, Lars, Dash, Charlie, Maggie, and Ukala. I was filled with anxiety. It was the same feeling I had before going to the shows. Baxter stuck out a bony finger and rang the bell. Some kid I didn't know swung open the door with an unfocused gaze on me and snorted. He turned around and disappeared into the crowd. Stephanie's face, the face I last remembered seeing at boarding school, floated up before me in my mind. I wondered if she had changed. Her house was packed. Did she know all these people? I spotted Paul's lumpy shaved head. It took a moment to squeeze past kids to get to him. I had already lost the group I'd come with.

"Check this out," he said, rolling up his sleeve. It was a portrait tattoo of Madonna from one of her record covers. It looked like she was coming up for air.

"Really, do you like Madonna that much?" I had to shout so he could hear me.

"She's fucking hot."

I shook my head. "Do you know the girl having the party?"

"Yeah, she's upstairs in her room."

I nodded and pushed my way up the stairs, stepping over kids who sat there and maneuvering around some girls as they came down. I pushed on down the hall, looking into rooms and searching the faces of kids I didn't recognize. Then I came to a closed door. I knocked. There was no answer so I turned the knob and went in. Stephanie was gazing in the mirror, brushing her hair. Long strands of dark wavy hair ran along each cheek. Her face was narrow and her features symmetrical: almond shaped eyes, long eyelashes, brown irises with green flakes, fine eyebrows hemming her eyes dramatically. Her skin was a dark olive. Her back and hips were slender. She had grown up and filled out nicely. The fuzz on her lip was gone; I didn't ask where to. Stephanie was beautiful now. I stared at her with blank amazement. It was the same feeling I'd had when I'd first seen Maggie. But Maggie was Baxter's sister, therefore off limits. My heart throbbed. Stephanie's eyes shifted over to me. She glanced at me warily. I didn't expect the chilly reception. My euphoria evaporated. I thought nothing had changed but then I remembered I had left her in Boston. My palms were clammy and I couldn't put my thoughts together.

The only thing I could say to her was, "You look really nice."

She gave me a suspicious look through the mirror.

"How's Sally doing?" she asked. I noted sarcasm in her tone. She stroked her hair. It went midway down her back.

"Oh, we broke up a long time ago." Gradually I could feel my courage returning.

She turned around to look at me directly.

"I hear Fiona is going to your school now." Had she been checking up on me? My confidence began to soar.

"Yeah, but I avoid her."

"You should avoid her," she said.

"What have you been up to?" I should have left the room and found the rest of my friends before I blew it.

"I'm going to go to school here this year."

She made me feel ugly, clumsy, stupid and insignificant. I began looking around the room and was happy to see one of Maggie's friends open the door and come in.

"Dash is in the next room with Maggie and the door is locked," she whispered, cupping her chubby little hand around her mouth.

Stephanie eyed me doubtfully, the corners of her mouth turning down in a smirk. It was clear I would have to work hard to get her approval again. Maggie's friend led me out of the room. I watched her giggle and excitedly clasp her hands in anticipation as we stood outside the locked door.

I knocked. There was no answer.

"Dash, open up!" No answer. I knocked harder.

Stephanie showed up and unlocked the door. "I don't want you knocking it down." She stepped back.

I rushed into the room. It was dark except for the light pouring in from the hall. I could hear heavy breathing, and when my eyes adjusted to the dark I could see Dash stroking her thigh. I found the light and flipped on the switch. They separated quickly, like roaches caught in the kitchen looking for an escape before being crushed. I grabbed Dash by his collar, pulled him away from Maggie and threw him into the hallway. Dash laughed and Maggie started to cry. Maybe I'd made a mistake, but I didn't care if Maggie hated me. I knew that if my sister was hooking up with my best friend behind my back, I would feel betrayed. But then again, Baxter and Dash weren't best friends. Maybe I was just jealous. My thoughts were a jumble. I wanted Stephanie. I wanted Maggie. But I also didn't want either of them. I should just go back to Fiona, I thought. She would fuck other guys. It would be easy.

It was late; the party was over. Stephanie's house was a mess, but she wouldn't get in trouble. Her mother was one of those liberal throwbacks from the sixties who believed in letting kids have independent spirits. She understood that her house would smell like spilt beer for the next month. We climbed into Baxter's minivan; Maggie sat in the last seat, drunk and upset with me. Dash and I sat in the middle and Ukala sat up front with Baxter. Edgea and Lars had left hours before.

"We are always safe in the minivan," said Baxter putting the van into gear.

It was the next morning and I was hung over. My eyes had dark circles. I felt poisoned like fine grains of sand were in my muscles and every time I moved it hurt.

I was starting to doze off when the teacher shook my arm.

"They need to see you in the main room."

"What did I do?"

"I don't think you're in trouble."

The main room was really the living room of the house our school was in. There were five other kids standing around with looks as confused as mine.

"It's the big round up before the slaughter," said Charlie.

Then a teacher came out, handing us certificates, and lined us up into two rows with me in the center. Dash took a photo with the school camera.

"What just happened?" I asked.

"Read your certificate, man," said the black girl next to me.

"Honor Roll" it read.

"Shit man, if I'm on the honor roll, this must be one fucked up school," said Charlie.

"How did I get honor roll?" I said, baffled.

"You do all your homework, right?" asked Charlie.

"Yeah."

"There are only sixty students here. Half of them don't do their homework. The other half do it but don't understand. We are the small group that does homework and gets it."

I felt like shit from drinking, but the honor wasn't lost on me. It felt great to be one of the smartest kids in school, even if it was a small school for dyslexics. I wanted to tell my parents.

When I pulled up to my house after school, Dash was already skateboarding out front, with Sister sitting on the steps watching his attempt to bunny hop his board over a stick in the street.

"What are you doing here?" I asked him.

"Nothing. Just waiting for you." His cigarette dangled from the corner of his mouth and I wanted to smack it free. I looked over at Sister and caught her looking at Dash. I walked inside and Dash stayed outside with her.

Later that night, Lars and I were hanging out in the parking lot next to D.C. Space. D.C. Space was a small club downtown where a lot of the punk bands played. You didn't have to go in since the stage was opposite a large window. You could watch the show from outside. Ukala had met us there. Lars was sitting on the back of my car, drinking a beer out of a paper bag.

"Ronnie Motherfucking Collins is in the hospital," said Lars. "He wants you to stop by and see him."

"Me?" I asked.

"Yeah, you."

"Why?"

"Why not? Ask him." Lars was trying to look over my shoulder. Two girls walked past us. "Hi ladies," he said.

"So you know Baxter has a pool," I said to Ukala. I was thinking of Maggie in a bikini. Then it switched to Stephanie. I bounced between the two girls. Then I put them in the pool together. Then they were kissing. I didn't want to think of either. I could feel Fiona lurking in the dark recesses of my mind.

"I don't swim," said Ukala.

"You don't have to swim. Just stand in the shallow end of the pool"

"Errr okay," he said.

Dash had said he'd meet us, but he never showed up. I wondered what he was up to.

After school the next day, I pulled up to Mother's house. I had forgotten about the plans we'd made the night before to go swimming. Lars and Ukala sat on the porch in their swimming trunks. Ukala's legs were lily white and sparsely covered with fine, sickly hairs. He tugged at the shorts that were already too high up and rested on his navel as if he were some degenerate senior citizen.

"Come on then," I said as I opened the passenger door for Lars.

"You don't need swim trunks?" asked Lars.

"Na, I'll wear these shorts. Just remind me to take out my wallet."

We had to pass through the neighbor's yard to get to Baxter's. His neighbor's house was another mansion, slightly larger and with a traditional architectural style that screamed money to anyone who saw it. The lady who lived there owned the Washington Post.

We stopped momentarily to sneak a look at her house. We didn't get out of the car, but simply parked. Her bodyguard stepped up to us, gripping his Uzi submachine gun.

"Can I help you?" he asked cautiously, peering into the car and noticing our bathing suits.

"We're here to see Mr. C's stepson," I declared.

"Go on through. His house is right next door," he motioned.

We drove through to Baxter's. Getting out of the car, we walked up to the house. Baxter's mom pointed to the backyard. We turned the corner of the house just as Baxter was unfurling an American flag. It rolled out of his hands smoothly from where he was standing on a second floor balcony off of his room. The end of the flag stretched out to its full length, a good twenty feet, and grazed the grass below. Mr. C, peeked up from his kneeling position on the lawn, where he had been trimming blades of grass with a pair of scissors, searching for perfection. He was slow and methodical. The snipping was Zen to Mr. C, something therapeutic. The flag rustled in the breeze and my attention focused back on that.

Up in his room, I asked where the flag was from. I listened for Maggie's footsteps down the hall, but since I hadn't seen her on the way up I gathered she was out of the house.

"At about three in the morning, I got dressed all in black," he said. "Black gloves, black combat boots and a black knit sailor's cap and drove out to Rockville Pike, past the beltway. You know, where the car dealerships are. I parked the minivan down the road and walked back to the dealership. Then I took a tire iron and a hacksaw, sawed through the line that held the flag and watched it drop. It was bigger than I'd thought it'd be. I mean, from the road you think, 'That's a big flag.' But when it's falling on top of you, you realize how big it is. Bigger than a parachute! So I scooped it up and ran back to the van, but I could barely see the road because the thing was so goddamn big!" Baxter beamed.

"Were you by yourself?" I asked.

"Yeah," he said excitedly, like he had single-handedly accomplished something of the utmost importance.

"You can't hang this on your wall," said Lars. "It's too big."

"I know." Baxter eyed the flag's enormity.

"So what are you going to do with it?" I wanted to know.

"Keep it. I don't know. Put it away."

Baxter's mother popped her head into the room just then and with a brief scan, immediately detected the flag. She looked to me and I shrugged.

"Baxter, where's the flag from?" she asked in a motherly tone; a tone only mothers know how to use, to transform questions into statements they already know the answers to.

"A friend gave it to me," Baxter said. I shook my head. A friend? Why not just say you found it, or better yet a green elf gave it to you. What a lame ass lie, I thought. Lars rolled his eyes. He seemed to agree with me. I was afraid for a moment Baxter might say he'd got it from me, but he didn't.

"Well make him bring it back to wherever he stole it from." His mom closed the door without another word.

Baxter pulled it back in the window, folded the flag up and stuffed it in a box in his closet. Then he sat down on his bed. I noticed something odd on one of his pillows. It was a white smudge, like clown make-up.

"What's that?" I asked.

"What?" said Baxter.

I pointed to the white spot on his black pillow case.

He looked at it, searched his thoughts for something to say, then shrugged. Edgea came to mind. I remembered the thick foundation she'd worn the first time we'd met. Then he turned back to us and noticed Lars and Ukala were wearing swimming suits that showed off most of their legs.

"What's up? Is there a gay pride parade today?" he said.

We went swimming, and I knew it would be over soon. Baxter was sick of me bringing people over to use his pool.

"My mom's been complaining that the pool's been dirty after you guys leave. Plus, the noise is bothering Mr. C." Baxter tried to sound casual, but I knew none of it was true. His mother didn't care if we were swimming. Ukala took a running start, leapt into the air with his arms outstretched, then pulled his body into a compact ball. He came crashing down in the shallow end of the pool and then immediately stood up to make sure he wasn't going to drown. Baxter's mother came out from the kitchen and told Baxter to do his homework.

Baxter rolled his eyes and turned back to look at me; he was agitated. I turned to the pool. Lars was doing a back stroke. Ukala's head was tilted to one side; he slapped the other side of it with his big beefy hand, trying to knock water out of his ear.

"Hey guys, it's time to go."

We dried off with towels, left them on the backs of the chairs, said goodbye to Baxter's mom in the kitchen and went back to my mother's house. Baxter came too.

"What about your homework?" asked Lars.

"I'll do it later," said Baxter, but he never did.

I had started to do better in school. Baxter was failing. I was dyslexic and he was normal. I worked hard and finished everything I started. Baxter didn't. For now he stayed in school to pacify his mother. But that wouldn't last long.

Over the following month, Baxter would go AWOL for weeks on end. His mom used every favor she had just to keep him in school. Punk shows became his newfound classroom and each band was a test. When The Exploited came to town on tour, Baxter vanished and submerged himself in a drinking binge with the band. My phone rang for days on end with his mother's calls of distress, but I didn't know where he was either. I began to worry.

By the time he showed up at home, his mother had already gotten his expulsion letter.

Cracked Out

YOUTH OF TODAY
"Break Down The Walls"
Look beyond the fashion or the crowd that they are in
Look beyond their riches or the color of their skin
Look beyond appearance and the truth you will find
Look beyond for what's inside before you make up your mind

On Friday night, the U.K. Subs were headlining a show with Warzone and Agnostic Front playing as their opening acts. Shows like those were the social center of our universe. Old timers and first time punks all came out for bands like these. W.U.S.T. Radio Music Hall was a large space built during the Big Band era of the 1930s and 1940s. Bands that performed there had been broadcast live to the rest of D.C. At its best, it had been glamorous, but by the time punk bands were doing shows there, it had become rundown and dark. Half the time we spent inside the show busting each other's bodies in a dance that was closer to a fight. The time in between bands consisted of curbside bullshitting, fighting, drinking and taking drugs. But I had another reason for being there. I had heard that Pierre was out. If he was, he would be at this show. Baxter had recently started dating Edgea. They walked around hand in hand and Lars came over and sat with me.

"Dude, what's up with that?" I said.
"She totally sleeps around," said Lars. "You didn't know that?"
"Like with who?"
"Everyone."
"Even Ukala?" The image made me a little sick.

"Okay, not everyone."

"Baxter is completely in love with her."

"Yeah, well maybe he loves the trouble. She's a fucked up girl. Her father used to molest her. Probably still does."

"Call the cops."

"If we did, she wouldn't admit to it. He's a city councilman for Georgetown and knows all the cops and judges. Once we were driving down M Street in Edgea's car and I saw this guy staring at me all crazy so I flipped him the bird. He walked over to the car and tapped on the window and I told Edgea to drive. She looked over at the guy and said that he was her dad. He made us get out of the car and got in with Edgea and started yelling at her. He's got a real bad temper."

"So that's her excuse for fucking a bunch of Baxter's friends?"

"I'm not saying that, just she's fucked up and her dad helped her get that way." Lars took a sip of his beer and finished his shot.

"Did she ever get tested for AIDS after she was raped?" I asked.

"Not at first. She was hoping she had it."

"What the fuck are you talking about?"

"She wanted to give it to her dad. But it turned out she didn't have it."

"Too bad." What a fucked up world, I thought.

I turned my attention to a familiar figure approaching. Pierre looked much bigger than the last time I'd seen him. He was still thin but had added more muscle. He wore a black bomber jacket with black slacks and ox-blood boots. His head was cleanly shaved, confirming what I had heard about him being a Skinhead. Pierre shook hands with Lars and Ukala, then turned and gave me a hug.

"I tried to write you but didn't know your address," he said. "When I called your house, I never got through."

"What happened to you?"

"I'll tell you later," he said.

I walked outside and found Baxter at Edgea's car. She was lying on the backseat and her other friends had vanished. She was paler and uglier than normal.

"She was mumbling and just passed out," said Baxter.

"What, is she drunk?" I asked. As I grabbed her chin, pulling her head forward, her eyes rolled backwards.

"No. One of the drug dealers from Dupont gave her something."

"What was it?"

"I don't know. I'm going to take her to the hospital."

"Okay, I'll drive the rest of them home. Call my machine and let me know if she's all right." I walked back into the show to tell the rest of the crew what was going on.

The show was over. Ukala, Pierre, Lars and I drove back to Mother's house. Ukala slept in the back seat next to Pierre. Lars sat up front with me.

"Do you think you could drive me to my parole interview tomorrow?" asked Pierre.

"You're on parole?"

"For what?" asked Lars. But we both knew it was for beating up a bus driver. What we didn't know was why.

In the rear view mirror I could see Pierre's eyes cloud over. He didn't want to talk about it, but knew if he didn't we would keep pestering him. "Yeah, I did time in juvie for aggravated assault."

"Yeah, I'll take you," I said. "What time is it?"

"8 am."

"Are you fucking serious?"

"Yes."

"Fine." I didn't want to get up. "How's your mother?" I asked.

"She's still mad at you."

"Why?"

"She thinks this is all your fault. You're a bad influence, you know?" He chuckled to himself.

We walked in the door and saw the new message light flashing. I pushed the button.

"Hey, I took her in to the hospital. They said she'd overdosed and if I had brought her in even a few minutes later, she would have died... I guess I'm the hero."

"Oh ferk," said Ukala. I told him to shut up.

"She's okay," Baxter continued. "The shot they gave her woke her up right away. I'll call you later."

There was no answer at Baxter's house. We sat on the back patio of Mother's. Ukala gave us each one Mickey's Big Mouth beer. Early in the morning, when the sky began to turn light blue, my phone rang; it was Baxter.

"She's okay?" I asked.

"Yeah, but she feels like shit. She said she can't deal with her dad right now." Baxter sounded tired. He told me that Edgea was in his bed, under his covers with the sheet wrapped close around her neck.

"You should have let me die," I overheard her say in the background.

Baxter hung up the phone. Later he told me that when he drove her home, her dad stood in the doorway and, without a word, stared at her and Baxter until she climbed out and limped up to the house with her head directed down at her boots and one short leg. Baxter had taken her to George Washington University's Emergency Room where they'd pumped out her stomach. Edgea's father knew someone on the hospital board. By the next morning, he had been notified of her situation.

On Monday, my phone rang in the morning just before I walked out the door. I was already leaving later than I should, meaning I was going to get to school fifteen minutes after the bell. I put down my bag and picked up the receiver.

"Hello," I said.

"Herr," said Ukala.

"What are you doing up so early?"

"The cops just came and got Pierre."

"For what?"

He said, "Parole violation. He failed his last piss test so they came and got him."

I told him I was late and had to go.

I got in my car and started to drive. I thought about the other day when I was dropping Pierre off at Dupont Circle. We had been alone in the car and he'd told me what had happened. Pierre had made friends with another skinhead at the shows. Taking the D.C. Metro was never a pleasure. It was "low class" and Washington was one of those cities, like Los Angeles, where everyone owned a car and only the poor took the bus. Stepping onto the bus, Pierre and his new friend had asked the driver to let them know when they had reached their stop. They had fallen asleep to the motor's hum. The bus had passed their stop and continued on to the bus depot in Friendship Heights.

The driver had put the bus in park and opened the doors, and then he'd noticed the two sleeping in the back.

"Come on, let's go. The bus is in the station. Hit the streets, you bums!"

Pierre had still been drunk and high and even the bus driver's yelling hadn't woken him. After waiting a few minutes, the driver had shaken the two, gotten them to their feet and pushed them towards the exit.

"Why didn't you tell us when we got to our stop?" Pierre had blinked his eyes open.

"Give us back our money, motherfucker!" his friend had demanded.

The driver had shaken his head, "I'm not giving you guys any money. I'm done. Go home."

The beating happened fast, but I only imagined a few isolated moments. The friend had drawn back his fist with muscles tensed, then released and struck the driver's chin. Then, Pierre had spun around the metal pole that riders hold for balance, and kicked the bus driver in his chest. They had stomped the driver until he stopped moving and ran. The battered man had crawled the length of his bus and pushed a silent alarm that all D.C. Metro buses had. Pierre and his friend had run between parked buses until they had come to a brick wall. Following the wall, they had searched for an opening as sirens had sounded overhead. Making their way to an exit, they had collided with waiting cops.

The bus driver had gone into a coma and they had been thrown into a juvenile correctional facility; a place that didn't correct, but perfected. Perhaps it should have been renamed "School for the Criminally Inclined". Pierre had studied the art of getting by without working and avoiding the authorities, and he had graduated with a degree in street fighting.

I pulled into the parking lot of school. I could see the top of Dash's blond hair through a window of the building.

"The principal wants to see you," said the teacher.

I was only fifteen minutes late. Why should I have to go to the office? And I thought of Pierre at that moment. Maybe some lady officer was taking him to see a judge. The teacher held the door open for me and I made my way to the front and followed her into the principal's office. The teacher left, closing the door behind her. I pictured a cell door closing behind Pierre and the both of us sitting in chairs.

Chelsea High School was set back in the middle of Jessup Blair Park. Silver Spring was half a town and half a city. It was a suburb of Washington with many of the city's elements bleeding into Maryland. The main road was Georgia Avenue, which had a Roy Roger's, D.C. Lotto and a Subway. I looked out the window across the field and at the avenue. Beams of morning sun crept across the field, casting long shadows from the trees. Older black men were walking the street and going into the Lotto building. I wondered what Pierre was seeing at that same moment. A gray wall, cops, other kids in handcuffs?

"We would like you to give a urine sample," said the principal, noticing my attention was out the window when he walked in. He was a small man who tried to make up for it by growing a long beard.

"What are you talking about?" I said, still looking out the window.

"We think you're on drugs," he said, and I turned to him.

"You're joking with me" I could feel the blood rising in my head. Was he trying to belittle me?

"No, we want you to take a urine test."

I nearly shouted. "I have the highest grades in the school."

"Yes, but you sleep in and between your classes. You seem dazed most days and we think it's best if you take a test."

"Okay, I'll take your fucking piss test, but I guarantee you that after this, I'll leave this fucking school!" I yelled. I had been doing well, but I wasn't sure what I was going to do after high school and not sure why I should care if I dropped out. Baxter didn't. None of my friends seemed to, with the exception of Charlie. He knew he wanted to go to college, but when I asked him why, he said "It's what you do after high school. Why not?" I'm a retard dyslexic, I thought. Why should I follow the norm off the cliff like a lemming? Punk rock had saved me in many ways, but it didn't have an answer either. I didn't want to be in a band. I didn't want to work at a record company. It couldn't provide me a future.

"Hold on a moment," said the principal.

"No, I won't hold on. I can't sleep and that's not your fucking business. Your job is to teach me. I'm not a drug addict. So go fuck yourself." He didn't say anything so I went on, "Let's go. Come on. I'm ready to take your piss test. Let's go!"

"That's okay. Go back to class… I'm sorry I mentioned anything."

"The next time you look tired, I'll be dragging you in for a test!" I said and I slammed the door behind me as an exclamation mark.

After school I was surprised to find Baxter waiting for me.
"What's up," I said.
"We have to go see Ronnie today."
"Why today?"
"Because there probably isn't going to be a tomorrow." I really wasn't in the mood. It was turning out to be a shitty day.

I followed Baxter's minivan to the hospital parking lot. When we walked into the room I wasn't ready to see how much he had deteriorated. Ronnie Motherfucking Collins was now a shrunken shell of his former self. He had tubes running in both directions. Machines were gathered around him like friends around the camp fire. A nurse was adjusting a tube. She gave him a tender pat on the shoulder and I knew he had charmed her, too.

"What's up, motherfuckers?" he said in a weak voice.
"Not much," said Baxter.
I shrugged. What could I say to a man dying of AIDS that would make him feel better?
"I know this motherfucking hospital is the place you motherfuckers don't want to be, but I wanted to enlighten you motherfuckers on some things." He reached out and took me by the wrist and pulled me closer. I leaned in so he wouldn't have to work so hard. "I hear you are the motherfucking man at school."
"What?"
"You're on the motherfucking honor roll."
"Yeah, so?"
"I was, too, motherfucker. Don't become a fuck up like me, motherfucker. I should have taken the scholarship at Saint John's, but instead I got too deep into the motherfucking scene and drugs. I was a motherfucking child prodigy."
"I won't fuck up," I said, but Ronnie didn't know about my dyslexia. He couldn't understand and I didn't want to explain it to a man about to die.

Baxter was next. He mumbled something in his ear. Twenty minutes later Ronnie was sleeping after having hit his button for morphine. He had spent his life chasing a high and now he had one at the touch of a button. As Baxter and I walked down the hall, I asked him what Ronnie had said.

"He told me to stop fooling around with drugs and get back to school."

"How does he know what we are up to?"

"Lars comes by and sees him just about every day."

"I didn't know that."

"Yeah, Ronnie just told me."

Little Sister

IGNITION
  "One Sided"
    When she tries to tell her story he never lets her get the words in

After the hospital I went home. Mother's house was quiet but I knew someone was there because the key wasn't exactly where Mother had left it. When it wasn't there, she got mad. I moved it back to where she expected to find it and went in.

"Hello."

"I'm in the kitchen," said Nicole. Nicole was Sister's best friend, so she was something like family to me. I had known her since she was small. She looked dark and little sitting by herself.

"Where is everyone else?"

"Your sister's with her boyfriend and I don't know where your mother is."

Boyfriend? Who's Sister's boyfriend? She'd assumed I'd known, but Sister hadn't mentioned it to me. I started to get a funny feeling. *Why would Sister keep a secret from me?*

"Where did they go?... my sister I mean. Did she leave a number?"

"You have Dash's number," said Nicole.

"Ah yeah... I got his number." *What the fuck?*

I was quiet for a few minutes. Nicole noticed.

"Did I just say something I wasn't supposed to?"

"No, its okay." I could feel my face turning red and my hands balling up in fists.

"Please don't tell her I told you. She gets mad at the smallest things."

"I'm not going to tell her," I said and went up to my room.

They had told me I had superior understanding of complex theories, so how did I miss this? Or did I know all the time. Sister had lied to me. We had had a pact. The Parents lied. We always told the truth to each other. I thought long and hard about how it had come about that she had lied to me. What had been the factors? What had been the path? Going backwards it had gone something like this. If I hadn't stopped Dash from making out with Maggie, maybe Dash and Maggie would have started dating. If I hadn't known Baxter, I wouldn't have met Maggie. I had met Baxter because I had been into punk rock. I had been into punk rock because it had been my salvation from being dyslexic. If I hadn't been dyslexic, I wouldn't have gone to boarding school. If I hadn't been in boarding school, Sister and Dash wouldn't have started hanging out. It all led back to that teacher in elementary school who had first figured out I was dyslexic. She had changed everything. But I could go back further. It had been my parents' bad genes that made me dyslexic. It had all been because I was dyslexic. I had just wanted to be normal. My dyslexia had probably put Pierre back in jail, too. I wouldn't have broken into the Lab School and started him on his path of crime. Then it turned back to Sister. I had lost the one person I could trust and there was no reason she couldn't tell me.

A few hours later Sister came home. I knocked at her door and she opened it.

"How could you lie to me?" I said.

"I didn't lie to you." Nicole must have warned her.

"Why? 'Cause you didn't tell me? You think that means you didn't lie to me? You're acting just like the Parents. They are supposed to lie to us. You and I tell each other the truth."

"You're the one who left me, remember? I was really sad and lonely and Dash was here to help me when you were at boarding school."

"So you lied to me?"

"I didn't want to make you upset."

"That's exactly what they would say! You fucking lied to me!" I slammed her door and went back into my room. If I had thought about it I would have known. Dash was showing up when I wasn't there and had came along for things like going down to the Lincoln Memorial to do our homework. Why hadn't I seen this before? I'd just assumed she would have told me. She'd made such a big deal out of things like Fluffball having been put to sleep by the Parents. I thought about her as a little kid, how she'd said she would never be like them. Now she was exactly like them. I would never trust her again and if I couldn't trust her, who could I trust? Then I understood. I was alone.

The Cloisters

Over the next few days, Sister stayed in her room and I stayed in mine. If by mistake we ran into each other, there was no eye contact. If she got too close to me, I told her, "Move out of the way, bitch."

Mother called us into the kitchen "What is going on with you two?"

Neither of us said anything. Mother had something to tell both of us and Sister and I were waiting for her to speak.

"Okay, well I think it's time to move," said Mother.

"Are you asking if we want to move?"

"No, I'm saying we're moving."

"But I have friends here," I said. But I really didn't. I didn't hang out with Ted anymore and the other kids in the neighborhood were all assholes. I avoided Fiona. I just didn't like change.

"Its not that far from here. It's just off of Reservoir Road. Your friends can still come over."

"When will this happen?" asked Sister. Her moon was out and orbiting her head.

"In two weeks."

"Well thanks for telling us," said Sister, but it sounded more like "fuck you." Sister got up and went back to her room, trailed by her moon.

Then Mother turned to me, "You'll make lots of new friends." I didn't really care. The new house would be closer to Baxter's and Georgetown.

We packed and the move wasn't that bad. In the new house, I took the first floor, which was the basement apartment.

"Why does he get the basement?" said Sister.

"He's older and he's a boy," said Mother, and I wasn't going to argue with her.

"That's not fair," said Sister, and stormed off to her new room on the third floor.

"Life isn't always fair," said Mother.

The Cloisters was halfway to a gated community. There was only two entrances. The neighborhood was a new development. All the townhouses were identical. The movers had just unloaded the last box and drove off. I went downstairs to unpack. The first box was marked "Punk stuff." I opened the top and pulled out my records and a few band flyers. I placed a one in the center of the wall: "King Face, Soul Side and Government Issue at 9:30 Club." The next flyer was the reggae show I was going to see the following week.

I'd stopped traveling half of the week between Father's and Mother's houses years before. One day when Sister was walking out the door, I hadn't followed her and neither parent had yelled at me. I hated Father's neighborhood. Mother's new house was better suited for my friends. A private entrance to my own apartment was one of the benefits of living in the basement. With a small patio just outside, it was easy to sneak in and out. I didn't have a curfew anymore. I liked the privacy.

I covered my room top to bottom with flyers and playbills from punk shows. A small fridge sat in the corner, sometimes filled with a six-pack of Milwaukee's Best and cans of Coca-Cola. Next to the TV were a stereo and a small collection of LPs, 45s and home-made mixed tapes of punk bands. The radio, which had never been used, was disconnected. A drum set, with a few busted heads left over from my ambitious preteens, sat untouched in one corner. My room was a great flop pad; its spare bed was used by Ukala, Pierre, Dash and Baxter. It would also be perfect to bring the girls there, though I didn't have any.

Busted

Baxter's minivan was full. I sat in the front and Dash sat next to Ukala and Lars in the last row of seats. Dash made no attempt to speak to me and didn't even look in my direction. The middle row held a few skinheads from Baltimore.

The show was at George Washington University, in their Student Union. The campus was downtown. I had just dyed my hair bright red and wanted to show it off. There were about twenty punks and skins there, mostly from D.C., with a few from Baltimore.

The show was mellow without anyone smoking weed. Campus Security walked among the audience, putting out joints as they were being lit up. The headlining act took the stage. From the front row I could smell the stink of weed rolling off of their clothes. SOULJA played their set and the show was over. Dash wanted to smoke weed, so he went outside And then started skating around in front of the student's union.

He was in the midst of tripping over his skateboard when a group of G.W.U. rugby students walked up.

"Only faggots ride skateboards," sneered one, while another shoved Dash.

"Is this a joke?" asked Dash, but he had forgotten the rule of "Why not?" There didn't have to be a reason for doing anything.

The doors opened. A crowd of drunk punks and skins spilled out onto the street between a neighboring Tower Records and the Student Union, just in time to catch the beginning of the fight. It didn't matter who Dash was, he was a punk and his attackers were jocks. Skinheads and punks hated jocks.

The two groups spotted each other. There was a heavy pause and then mayhem broke out. Yelling, punching, kicking and shoving was everywhere around me. A guy got my attention and lunged at me from between two parked cars. I clocked him square in the face, splitting his lip from the inside out. I didn't have time to think, but just reacted. I had a pair of brass knuckles, but chose to leave them resting comfortably at the bottom of my pocket; best reserved for a bigger threat than this. I only struck the guy once and he backed off, vanishing into the crowd of students. Campus Security showed up in their car and everyone started running when someone in the crowd pointed at me.

"That's him!" a guy yelled.

I didn't think they were talking about me. I had only hit one guy, and I doubted that anyone had seen it.

"The guy with the red hair, that's him!"

I am the only one with red hair. Goddamn it! When you're a punk you want to stick out like a peacock, but strutting my stuff also made me easy to identify. My feet and heart jumped with adrenalin; I ran as fast as I could.

Three Campus Security guards chased me block after block until I couldn't run anymore. It had to end. The drink churned in my belly, the leather jacket and the humidity were stifling. And besides, I was in no shape to be running. I slowed to a trot, then stopped and began to laugh. How embarrassing to be caught by two chubby women. Their supervisor was a moment behind them. White and obese, he was in no mood to be running.

"Get down!" he shouted.

I stood with my arms suspended above my head in mid-air as I'd seen hundreds of times on TV, but I hadn't gotten down on my knees. Hurrying over, he took the opportunity as an invitation to manhandle me into submission. Wrestled to the pavement, I avoided resistance and just started laughing. He cuffed me and we waited idly for the real cops to show. He presented me to them like a prize. I was turned over and handcuffs were exchanged. The student whose mouth I had busted shrieked at me like a little girl. He never left the safety of the wall of overweight campus security guards wearing cheap one-size-fits-all uniforms.

"You're going to jail, asshole! They're going to fuck you in the ass!"

"I'm going to 2D!" I yelled back, even though I knew I should keep quiet.

When dealing with police, it's always best to keep in mind that you shouldn't speak until spoken to, you should stay calm and most important, you should be polite. Officers spend a majority of their time dealing with domestic disputes, fist fights and other drunken behavior. Driving to a scene, they prepare themselves for an ensuing blathering tirade, but in truth, they're always seeking the path of least resistance. Or at least that's what Ronnie Motherfucking Collins had led me to believe.

"Yes sir. No sir. Take this path motherfucker and mister pig man will do right by you."

The funny thing about having previous experience with the police was that you weren't as frightened the second time around. I knew where I was going, and that my parents would come and pick me up. In the patrol car, I struggled to sit upright as it turned a corner. My hands were still cuffed behind my back. The cop struck up small talk, attempting to put me at ease.

"So what happened?" he asked.

Between my first and second major run-ins with the police, a small part of my brain had come to life. It lay somewhere between rational and irrational thought, and was in a constant state of scheming and plotting. The neurosurgeons had failed in discovering it when they'd tested me for dyslexia, but I knew it was there. I could feel it. As the cop chatted me up, it was speaking to me. *Be careful. Don't trust this motherfucker. All this motherfucker wants is for you to admit that you're motherfucking guilty.* It was Ronnie and his *Criminal Minded* way of thinking. I squinted and peered at the back of the officer's head, hoping I could see deep into his skin, past his skull, and into his brain, so that I would know what he was thinking.

"It's like what the bumper sticker says," the cop spoke as he looked through the rearview mirror at me.

"What's that?" I asked.

"Shit happens." He laughed, and I would've, too, if I hadn't suddenly found myself in such a serious mood.

"I know what you mean," I shook my head.

At the station, the other cells were empty. Father might be arriving in a mere twenty minutes, since Chevy Chase was close. I knew he'd be upset and I wasn't looking forward to that. He was so damn sensitive.

A few years before, a massive blizzard had rolled through the east coast dumping more than two feet of snow onto the city's streets. Mayor Marion Berry had been unreachable in the Bahamas. D.C. had shut down for weeks because they hadn't been able to release city funds without his permission. Dash had had a little gray hatchback equipped with snow tires that had no trouble maneuvering through the snowdrifts. When he'd picked me up from Father's house one afternoon, I had to promise Father that I'd be back soon for safety reasons. We drove through Georgetown, getting stuck in two snowdrifts and plowing down a snowman that had been made in the middle of the street, and then another that we had to drive up onto a lawn to mow over. By then it was well into the evening. On our drive back up to Father's house, I'd noticed a figure moving quickly through the snow, like some kind of hairless ape. As we got closer, I'd realized it was Father, coming out to greet us in an open bathrobe and bare feet, tears of anxiety running down his face.

"Where have you been? I've called the hospitals, the police and your mother. This is a real blizzard, and not even the metro buses are running. The city is closed. There's nowhere to go."

"Dad, go back inside, you're naked with no shoes on and it's cold," I'd said. And we'd all gone inside.

As I sat in jail, I knew this would be slightly harder for him to take than my getting lost in a blizzard. But the D.C. cop had taken pity on me, deciding not to charge me for the brass knuckles in my pocket.

"These will be recycled into manhole covers," he announced.

I'm sure they ended up in his private weapons collection. He handed me my driver's license, on which I had altered the date of birth with stencil and covered with lamination to help me drink in the bars. He told me, "The printed age is wrong and you need to get it fixed." In the police report he wrote favorably that I had been the sober one, and that the other guy had been drunk and belligerent. He was a good guy. His report kept me from probation, and Father wouldn't find out about the fake ID or the brass knuckles.

As I waited in a cell for Father to arrive, I wondered if this was like the one Pierre was in. Maybe he was picturing me at that moment. I pictured

Ronnie Motherfucking Collins. I knew what his cell looked like: it was a hospital bed. At 3 am, Father made it to 2D in record time, considering I had woken him up with my one phone call from jail. I would have called Mother, but I knew she was at her boyfriend's house. She wouldn't have been mad, as long as I had had a good reason. It wasn't like I'd wanted to fight. I just hadn't wanted to get hit, so I'd hit him first. Father walked in, looking pale and distressed. He wandered into the station looking confused, as he most often was. I was taking him away from sleep that he needed to work for Nixon. Fuck Nixon, I thought. Maybe that was the only good thing about getting arrested. It would take him away from Nixon at least for the moment.

"I'm here for my son," he said over and over.

Father still hadn't seen me. I didn't feel guilty for hitting the guy. But when I saw Father so dejected, I felt ashamed. I knew what Mother would have said. "If he was going to hurt you, he deserved to get bopped on the head." Mother and Father had opposing views on just about everything, with the exception of politics, where they were in line. If Mother had picked me up, I would have never said anything to Father about it. It was like a family tradition, keeping things from others in order to protect them. Back at his house, Father spoke with a trembling voice.

"How could this happen? Do you want to go to prison? Why couldn't you just walk away? Why do you do this to your mother and me?" One day he was hoping I would snap out of the punk rocker thing. The last thing I wanted to be was a lawyer. For a moment I pictured it. Me sitting behind a big desk, with a suit on, and a hot secretary like Stephanie taking notes. A few tattoos peeked out from under my cuffs. Then looking at the big picture, I knew that was all it would ever be, the same office, suit and secretary for eternity. Anyway, it didn't matter- it was too much reading.

"You are ruining your life," he said, tears rolling down his cheeks.

The only other time I had seen him cry was when he had told Sister and me about the divorce. Seeing him distraught worked more effectively than anything Mother could have said at top volume. I vowed to myself never to get caught again, to keep an eye out for the cops, to make sure I had an ample escape route before falling into trouble and never to loiter around afterwards.

Father arranged for one of his partners to represent me against the assault charge. Dash and I sat in the waiting room of the law firm. We had to give our depositions.

"Thanks for doing this," I said.

"You wouldn't have been fighting if you weren't trying to help me," he said.

"The guy was going to hit me."

"Yeah, but you don't remember. You were right next to me, yelling for me to back up. You weren't just standing there. You were trying to protect me. You are always trying to protect everyone."

"I don't remember. Everything kind of just happened fast and then I hit the guy."

Dash went into the office.

Later, I dyed my hair an even blond and cut it into a more normal style. The court date came, and I was dressed in my best suit and tie. Before seeing the judge for my arraignment, I was fingerprinted and photographed. I was the only white kid going through the system that day. All the black kids, lined up waiting to be fingerprinted, looked at me for a moment and then went back to worrying about their own problems. In the end, everything was dropped. The G.W. student never showed for the court date. The fight cost me more than $1000, and that meant I would be working it off as a secretarial assistant at Father's law firm for another summer.

Best Apple Ever

Pierre looked out onto the yard. There were no fences or guards. Leaning in the doorway of the living room, he borrowed a quarter from a friend.

"Pierre, going some place?" said the officer.

"Just outside to have a quick smoke."

"Okay, don't take too long." The officer went back to watching the movie with the rest of the juveniles.

It was a minimum-security detention center from what Pierre described on the phone. Pierre lit up his cigarette and looked back at the building to see if anyone was watching him, then he walked to the edge of the property and waited to see if anyone would call him back. No one came out. He walked up the road and called me from a payphone. Then I called Charlie.

"I need you to pick up Pierre," I said. I still felt responsible for everything he had done since we broke into the Lab School. If Charlie had been caught, that would have been my fault too.

"Where is he?" His voice betrayed his fear.

"Off the beltway. He just escaped from juvie."

"What? I don't want to pick him up! You pick him up!"

"I just got out of trouble for that fight. I've thought this through. Your father is a diplomat, right?"

"Yeah?"

"Well…That means you could get away with murder if you wanted to."

"It doesn't work that way."

"When I was a kid, a diplomat ran over a cop and killed him. He was drunk and nothing happened to him. If they catch you, say you were just picking up a hitchhiker. You're not going to get in trouble." I wasn't sure of that. For all I knew, there could've been a hundred cops, a Swat Team, and the National Guard surrounding Pierre as we spoke. There was silence on his end. I could picture Charlie. No doubt, he was recalling all the times Pierre had given him a hard time about getting caught beating off when we had been younger. That had been the reason Charlie had joined our gang, and now I was going to send him off in the darkness to rescue his tormenter/friend. But if Charlie picked him up, Pierre would never call him jerk-off again. "Come on, Charlie, don't be a pussy. Besides, it's Punk Rock."

A few hours later, Pierre was at Mother's house and Charlie headed back to his.

"This is the best apple I've ever had," Pierre said through his bites.

He sat across from me on Sister's bed, looking at the apple as though he'd never seen one before. Among the furniture in Sister's room was a pair of white end tables and a lamp with a pink and white rose-patterned stand and shade. The room was very feminine in design, because of Mother. Sister had trouble stomaching it and often left it vacant. Pierre was out of place, but he was perfectly relaxed, with a big grin on his face and an apple in his hand.

"I haven't had an apple in a long time." He devoured it down to its core.

"It's pretty bad in there, huh?" I said as I searched in her closet for any of my missing records that she may have borrowed. I flipped through: They Might Be Giants, The Dead Milkmen, The Nails, Bad Manners, The Residents, Adam Ant. Her whole record collection was made up of my throwaways, music that was New Wave or too soft.

"I don't feel like I'm being punished. It's more like summer camp where I can read and play chess. It's boring, that's all." Maybe prison was helping his dyslexia. Maybe it made him focus on reading. I pictured myself there, trying to read. I didn't like the idea much. But later I realized he hadn't learned how to read better, but how to be a con-man. They taught him that there was little value in working hard. Why did he need college? He talked like an educated man and had become well read. With a quick wit and the capability to learn things fast, he lacked the drive to further himself. He worked hard to be lazy. Most of his time was spent mooching off his friends or girlfriends, and sometimes even his girlfriend's friends.

The similarities that Pierre's women shared was an element of damage, often in mental terms but sometimes physical. Another prerequisite Pierre was insistent upon was a Chelsea haircut, which is a head that's been shaved except for a loose cluster of bangs left hanging in front, like a backwards mullet. It was a skinhead girl hair cut. If the girls didn't already have a Chelsea, Pierre made sure they got one soon. Since they all had the same haircut, it was difficult for me to identify the old from the new. Calling them by the wrong name often resulted in a quick blow to my tender belly.

The latest girl had a problematic spine that didn't measure up to the rest of her limbs. She'd hobble along, aided by a cane. Pierre was seeing a second girl and his bouncing between the two was causing friction.

"Fucking cunt! Dirty fucking whore!" screamed the gimp when she saw the other girl.

"Oh, this is going to be great," said Lars and he moved into a better position to see the fight. It was a Friday night outside D.C. Space. An Emo band played inside, but the show outside was more entertaining. It was only a few weeks since Pierre had escaped juvie and already he had two girls fighting over him. *Why the hell was I alone?*

"Aren't you going to break this up?" I said to Pierre, but he seemed as interested in seeing the fight as the rest of us. The gimp swung her head to the side and ducked a punch from the other girl. Then they both fell to the ground scratching, bodies intertwining and rolling back and forth, punching and pulling hair. The other girl started to cry when the gimp had her around the neck. Ukala picked up the gimp and held her over our heads.

"Let me go, you fucking monster!"

"Cerrm derrrn," he said.

The loser got up and walked off with her friends.

"I said put me the fuck down! Right now, goddamn it!" She was moving like a snake held at its middle. Ukala waited until the loser was out of sight, then turned his attention back to what he was holding and made a face of disgust before dropping her.

The crippled girl went to brag to her friends about the fight, claiming what was rightfully hers. And why not? God had already denied her a normal body. Pierre was leaning against a car.

"So what's it like having sex with a crippled girl?" Lars was smiling under his wilted mohawk when he asked.

"Dernt you all have sex with Edgea?" said Ukala. "She's der cripple."

Baxter said nothing and walked away. He was sensitive about anything that concerned Edgea.

"You mean what's it like to have sex with a girl instead of your hand, bitch!" said Pierre and he smiled.

The gimp walked back over. Her upper body rolled from side to side as if it were attached to a spring as her knees swung in large ovals underneath her. She stopped in front of Pierre and he had to bend to half his height to lean down and kiss her.

"Baby, can I have a few bucks?" he said, and I couldn't help but smile.

"Sweetie, I'm all tapped out," she said, not realizing she had just ended the relationship. She walked off with her friends again.

"What are you going to do for money?" said Lars.

"I guess I'll have to get a job," said Pierre. "Or maybe a new girl?"

"Hey man, if some guy calls you and asks about me working for you, just say I did a great job and all that." Pierre was talking to me but playing the video game on my TV. It was twenty-four hours later; he'd dumped the crippled girl and thought he would try getting a job. I looked out the window and wondered if there were cops out there looking for him.

"Okay."

"They're not going to call, but if they do just tell them I'm a great guy."

"What do I say if they ask about the jail time?"

"Man, I don't tell them about the jail time. I was at college. Maryland State or some other bullshit."

Why should I bother with college? I thought. He was doing fine lying about it.

A few days later, Pierre found a desk job in the mailroom of a local company. The night before his first day of work, we went to a party.

At about 3 am, Pierre was off in a far corner sleeping and still wearing his black sunglasses, a black pork pie hat and a black bomber jacket. Ukala was holding a Mickey's Big Mouth and pointing it at Pierre, gesturing for me to mess with him. I lightly touched his nose. Snapping out his arm and jumping to his feet, he toppled me with fingers clenched into a tight fist. His sunglasses fell off and I could see a dark light coming from his eyes. It was cold and uncaring. But Pierre caught himself, then broke into uncomfortable laughter once he recognized it was me. It was frightening. I wondered if that's what the bus driver had seen before being beat.

"Just playing with you, man," he said.

But I could see his weaker moments. Jail wasn't as easygoing as he'd made it out to be, and I felt sorry for him.

It was after 4 pm when Pierre called me the next day.

"Aren't you supposed to be at work?" The background noise didn't sound like an office. I could hear a TV and what I thought were the sounds of a soap opera.

"I didn't feel like going in. Maybe tomorrow. What are you doing? Come get me."

"I'm beat. I only slept an hour and went to school all day."

"You're not going to sleep."

"I want to."

"Sleep later."

I picked him up from the house where he had crashed the night before, and we drove over to Stephanie's house. Her car had broken down again and I said I would drive her. I would have said yes to anything she'd asked me.

"I wonder what Stephanie would look like in a Chelsea cut?" said Pierre. No doubt he was picturing her with some kind of disfigurement, too.

We both had a crush on her. Everyone in the scene did, even some of the girls. As we drove, I compiled a list of things Pierre hated in my head: being snuck up on while he slept, Nazi skinheads and domesticated cats.

From outside Stephanie's house, I could hear the hairdryer blasting as she yanked and sprayed her mane into stiff spikes with Aqua Net. I had a deep desire to walk in there and kiss her.

A longhaired cat, white with hints of yellow, jumped from the porch next door. As Pierre and I waited, it snaked its body between my boots and I dropped my hand so it could brush its face against the back of it. It walked over to Pierre seeking more affection. Pierre looked at the cat like it was an insect. He drew his leg back and sent the cat howling through space. It landed feet-first, and like a bullet, it was gone. The door opened.

"Did you guys hear something?" Her eyes swept over the scene. "Have you guys seen my cat?"

"White and fluffy?" I described.

"Yes." She smiled.

"No…" I shrugged my shoulders for effect.

Lost and Found

RITES OF SPRING
"*Patience*"
Hearts that won't just beat on their own
Because every beat without purpose or thought
You know..
Makes me feel more alone

After the show we dropped Stephanie off. As she walked up her steps, I watched her ass move under her short skirt and pictured her in cotton underwear, each cheek perfectly round and moving like the parts of a cotton candy machine, spinning its web of sugar. Pierre turned to me saying;

"She's hot." I nodded. "Can I crash at your place?" he said, and we drove back to Mother's house. On the door were taped copies of the phone bill with large segments highlighted in yellow and a note reading, "Who is responsible for these calls?" I looked at Pierre, who ducked by me and sat in front of the TV, getting the video games ready to play. I looked at the numbers and didn't recognize any of them so I picked up the phone and called the first one. It was a recording of a woman's voice. She sounded tired and sexy, and then the recording warned me that someone live would be on in a few seconds if I didn't hang up, so I hung up. I looked at the balance of six hundred dollars.

"These are 970 sex calls. Why did you make these?" I said to Pierre.

"I didn't make any calls."

"Look at the dates. Every call was a day you were here," I said and waved the bill under his eyes.

"Maybe someone else in the house made the calls?"

"Who? My mother? Maybe my sister? I know I didn't make the calls... and look, they're at 5 am. None of us were even awake."

"See what I mean. How could I make the calls if I was sleeping?"

"I mean my mom and sister were asleep. You! I know you were up." He took a closer look at the numbers.

"Oh, I do remember some of these, but the first thirty minutes are free," he said.

"It's the first thirty seconds," I grumbled back.

I dropped Pierre off at the Foggy Bottom subway stop to meet up with his friend. Mother said he couldn't stay with me any more after the phone bill showed up. He introduced me to the taller black guy, who looked like he had never smiled in his life.

"This is Cross," said Pierre. My mind flipped through its giant Rolodex of every name I had ever heard and it came to an abrupt stop.

Cross.

Drug Dealer.

Glover Park.

Wants to kill you over your gang infringing on his territory.

I hesitated and then we shook hands. I wondered if he recognized my name from Glover Park and I started to sweat.

"You keeping all the little bitches tight?" he said.

And I said yes, even though I had no idea what he meant. It was the first time I had seen Cross. Before, he had been just a name Stephanie had mentioned. He was big and had flat knuckles and ears of cauliflower. Walking back to my car, I could feel him watching me.

"Yo, man, that officer Franklin was looking for you," said Cross to Pierre.

"Oh, yeah," said Pierre just as I was out of earshot.

The next time I saw Pierre he told me that right after I left, Cross robbed a white guy. Cross called it *picking up money from the ATM.*

"Listen to this!" Baxter pulled out a rare vinyl from its sleeve and dropped it onto the turntable. The raspy voice squeezed its way out of the speakers - The Jam, The Red Skins, and Angelic Upstarts. The clock read 10:55 pm and the bars would be closed by 2 am on Sunday. We were in Baxter's room. Nothing had changed since he'd dropped out of high school. It was just another reason not to go to college.

"Baxter, let's go." I knew it would be another half hour until we made it to Poser's.

Poser's, a bar on M street, held a "Punk Rock Night." Popular with the scenesters, it wasn't hard to get into without an ID if you knew the right people, and someone always knew them. It was our weekly ritual. I'd walked over to Baxter's house at about 9 o'clock. Ukala was still there from the previous night, since he didn't own a car and Baxter had refused to drive him home. Old milk crates filled with records lay on the bedroom floor. On the unmade bed lay a white "Flying V" Gibson guitar, and a dozen dirty shirts lay piled in one corner waiting for his mother to pick them up.

"You should gerrt CD," said Ukala, wiping away the globules of sweat that beaded his extended forehead. "They arrt better than old records."

"That's not true," said Baxter. "They don't have full sound."

"Burrt they say they never will scratch."

"I don't trust that. How could they not scratch?"

"It uses a red lazar."

"Red lazer? What, like in Star Wars? Fuck that! The record player is more than a hundred years old. It's tried and true technology. I'm not going to put my whole collection on CD and then a year later it goes bust, like the eight track tape or betamax. There will always be records."

"Come on!" I said.

"Why are you in a rush?" Baxter looked up at me from the floor as he found an old shirt to wear.

"I don't want to miss anything."

"What are you going to miss?"

"I don't know, whatever happens." *Stephanie, Maggie, new hot girls I haven't met yet.*

Finally, we piled into the minivan and drove to Prospect Street where we parked and then walked the two remaining blocks to M Street. Poser's was painted black and lit with a few black lights. It reeked of old beer and bar funk. Booths lined one of its walls and televisions were spread out over some of the tables, the bar and the front entrance. I recognized the DJ. It was Tyler from the Lab School, but now he wore all black and had a tall mohawk. He looked older, chubbier, and unhappy. I walked over to his booth.

"What's up, man?" I said, putting out my hand to shake.

He took a moment, then shook my hand. "Last I heard, you broke into the Lab School and got sent away."

"Nah. I had to work off the damages then see a shrink, but the shrink was cool and got me out of having to see him."

"Those your friends?" Tyler motioned towards Ukala and Baxter with his shoulder, still holding the headphones to one of his ears.

"Yeah," I said. I could tell from the stink expression on his face that he didn't approve.

"Okay, Tyler. Good to see ya."

"Hey man, call me mohawk Tyler," he said. He was trying to reinvent himself. Rev's friend Blitz used to be called the Geek. Then he became tough. I guess it was part of being punk rock. Pierre, Paul, Baxter and even I had all wanted to be someone else. You take on a new identity, depending on how you cut your hair, dress, and also on the music you listen to. If I'd wanted to be a skinhead, all I would have had to do was shave my head, put on a bomber jacket and listen to Oi music. I could have been a completely new person just by changing costumes.

"Are you serious? I mean, can't everyone see that you have a mohawk?"

"Yeah, it's my DJ name."

"Fine." I made the same stink face back to him and walked over to Baxter and Ukala as Tyler changed the videos that played on the screens. I had compiled a list of my favorite music videos: The Specials, Bad Brains, Cro-Mags, and Madness were a few of the bands. The other DJ's did the same thing Tyler was trying to do that night, which was not play my requests. I still requested the Bad Brains songs, even though Tyler had made a large sign and hung it over the side of his DJ booth that read "ABSOLUTELY NO FUCKING REQUESTS." Maybe he hated me? But more likely he didn't approve of my new friends or what we had turned into. There were dozens of different factions in the scene and it was clear Tyler was a New Waver. New Wave music was soft and only girls listened to it; it was also part of the mainstream and mainstream wasn't punk. That's why I gave all my New Wave records to Sister. After an hour I realized that all he wanted to do was play Ministry, The Smiths, The Cult or

The Cure. But Tyler was new and this was our night. He would have to learn. I devised a plan to deal with Tyler and his sign. First, I asked again for the video; he pointed to the sign. Then, I sent Baxter to ask for the same video. Tyler's face pinched up and he said nothing. After eight or nine times asking for the same video, he broke down and played it, just so we'd stop bothering him. We had a few more beers. About two dozen people showed up. Paul, Dash, Lars, Edgea, and even Sister stopped by, but she looked at the crowd and her moon came out. Sister left a few minutes later. It was fun, like a party. Maggie showed up. She looked hot. Her hair was in two long braids and it made her look like Pocahontas. I stole glances at her whenever Baxter wasn't watching. Paul came out of the bathroom with that look of his that meant he had just done something bad. At the shows he'd started fucking up the bathrooms, shitting on the floors, smearing it on the walls, toilet, and everything in reach. The others guys in the scene didn't know who was doing it, but I knew it was Paul. Maggie was walking by me and I wanted to talk to her. I didn't care about what as long as she paid attention to me for at least a moment.

"Won't your mother be mad that you are out so late on a Sunday?" I asked Maggie.

Her face wreathed with a smile, she pressed her finger to her lips, signaling for me to be quiet.

"No new boyfriends?"

"No. Why, you interested?" God, her brother did that kind of thing to me all the time. I had to be careful of what I said or she would figure everything out. Baxter sat on the other side of me. My face flushed. If Maggie hadn't known before, she sure did now. I needed an escape, a distraction.

"Go dance, Baxter," I'd tried to push him out of the booth, but he didn't move. He had only done it a few times, but it was so funny. I asked him every Sunday. I went to the bar and bought beers and shots of whiskey for us. Maggie went out on the dance floor first with Dash. I felt a bit jealous.

My gaze fell on Baxter. "Come on, will you dance now?"

"When the right song comes on," he said.

Tyler went into his dance set with "Off the Wall." Baxter downed the shot, stood up with purpose and determination, walked out on the dance floor, pointed one finger to the heavens and the other to hell. His head was down as the song slowly rose in volume. We climbed out of the booth and gathered around Baxter, clapping and shouting. He looked like a lightning bolt frozen, then he broke into a moonwalk, ending in a spin. Eventually the song faded out. Pierre and Cross walked in and joined the circle. Ukala elbowed me in the ribs and pointed out two girls at the bar.

They were older punk girls from Virginia, done up like sluts with colored hair, tight clothes, leather and vinyl. Edgea hated them because she knew we would never look at her the same way.

"Weekend punks. Stupid bitches. You guys only want to fuck 'em, but you know what, they won't fuck you. So give it up," she grumbled and walked over to Baxter. Lars was drinking every leftover beer in the bar. When I saw him stealing the bartender's tips, I stopped him and bought him a cheap shot of whiskey out of pity.

Cross looked out of place, dressed like the GoGos from South East, wearing Gucci, Timberland boots, a puffy black North Face jacket, and a black knit hat that sat off to one side of his head. Suddenly, cops walked into the bar looking for someone. They made the room look funny, like a cheap episode of CHIPS. I stood behind Baxter and could see a hand moving around to his side, and it wasn't taking his wallet but trying to give him something. It was Cross. I could see the butt of a gun sticking out of Baxter's pocket.

"Hold this for me, cracker man," Cross said in a low voice and turned his back to Baxter.

The cops walked around the bar once. Casually they looked people over, not stopping anyone or asking any questions. They could have had a major bust if they had asked one of us for ID.

Charlie showed up at the door and, even though he had a fake ID, the doorman wouldn't let him in. Charlie looked the same age as when I'd first met him at the Lab School. It was funny how some kids developed and others didn't.

"Thanks," said the cops. They strolled out onto M Street. Cross stuck his hand back into Baxter's pocket and retrieved his gun. The doorman finally let Charlie in with a non-drinking stamp on the back of his hand. It was a giant X.

"What did I miss?" asked Charlie.

It was Monday after school. I just wanted to take a nap. I could faintly smell Fiona's perfume on me. She had hugged me at school and now I carried her scent. My phone rang. I thought it might be her. It was never a girl on the other end, but I hadn't given up hope just yet, so I answered.

"Hello, it's Officer Franklin. Have you seen Pierre?"

I was looking right at Pierre, who was playing ColecoVision, a space invader video game. He hadn't even looked up when the phone had rung. He wasn't allowed to stay the night and we were only stopping at my place so I could get a few dollars from Mother.

"Officer Franklin," I said.

Pierre's ears perked up, but his attention was still focused on the TV screen.

"Tell him I moved to Spain," Pierre snickered quietly.

"No, I haven't seen him."

"Well, let him know I'm looking for him."

"I'm sure he knows," I replied.

"So you guys still hang out in Tenleytown?" he asked.

"Isn't Pierre in Juvie?"

"He was."

"Well, where is he now?"

"I would like to know. Alright then, I'll see you later." He hung up.

Pierre concentrated on a difficult maneuver, firing on alien invaders, and then he said, "I thought they had forgotten me."

Tenley Circle featured a twenty-four hour mini-mart, a Roy Rogers, a movie theater and an arcade, though the arcade didn't last long. Too many parents were against the idea of loitering kids.

Behind the Roy Rogers was a park that formed one side of a valley. On weekend nights, kids congregated there. Pierre was usually already fighting when I showed up. Each week it was someone new, but it was never serious, more of a scuffle leaving behind bruised egos. It was how he built his reputation.

Walking into the parking lot on Friday night, I saw Lars first. He was past drunk. His mohawk stood up straight from his scalp.

"What are you looking at? Fucking motherfucker!" Lars attempted to lift his butt from the curb, but his pants must've been filled with lead. His arms strained for a moment as the lower half of his body came crashing down in the same spot.

"Give me your money, yuppie scum bag!" The couple getting into their black BMW parked two spots away didn't notice him.

Ukala had just gotten back from the Tenleytown mini-mart and was carrying two six packs under each arm, an entire case in all.

"Don't even think about it. If you didn't put any cash in, then fuck off," Ukala spat in his own mumbling way. I reminded him that he was crashing on my floor and he promptly handed me a beer. I was thanking him when I noticed someone walking out of the woods and cutting through the parking lot. I knew who it was from the strut. Pierre made his way towards us, and Baxter trailed behind. I could see Pierre's smile and hear a chuckle. Ukala drank from a Mickey's Big Mouth beer as Baxter recounted the details of that night's fight between Pierre and Robbie. I knew Robbie from The Lab School. Younger and smaller than me, he couldn't have been much of a challenge for Pierre.

I didn't think of Pierre as a bully. To me he wasn't threatening. I had my own bullies to be scared of. But I guess it was a matter of perspective.

After school the following Monday, I drove up Western Avenue to Friendship Heights, where there was a theater at the Mazza Gallery Mall and a McDonald's in the basement. National Cathedral School girls hung out there after class, which delighted me to no end. Mother's new house in Georgetown on Winfield Lane was next to the lawn where the Catholic girls played field hockey. Wearing plaid skirts, they ran, jumped and screamed during the game and I loved watching every second of it. I'd yell "Hello!" and they'd respond by giving me the finger and screaming, "Fuck off, punk!" But that just made me like them more.

I met Pierre. He went into a record store in search of a Madness pin for his bomber jacket. I was waiting on one of the benches inside the mall, looking at girls, when Officer Franklin spotted me. In his forties, white with dark hair and a flat face, he really looked like a cop.

"Pierre's friend, right? Have you seen Pierre?" His eye started at my feet and worked up to my face. The clothes I had on were old and beaten. The Doc Martens were falling apart. He was trying to figure out if I was a runaway or might end up as one of his parolees some day.

"No, I haven't seen him." I put my hands in my pockets and a finger poked out a hole.

"Alright, then," he said, as if he knew I was lying. I had stepped in front of the officer so he'd have to face away from the record store. I saw the fugitive appear in the store's doorway and locked eye contact with the cop, knowing if I broke it he would turn to see what I was looking at.

"You ever fire that?" I pointed to the gun that rested on his hip.

"Only at the range."

Pierre stepped out of the record store. Looking down, he affixed the Madness button onto his lapel, then glanced up. Recognizing the back of his parole officer's head and the gun on his hip, he spun around and ducked back into the record store behind a row of 45s.

"I'll catch you later." The officer smiled at me and walked away. I waited until he was gone and went into the store to find Pierre.

"Why am I always doing your dirty work?"

He smiled at me just like the officer had.

"I'm going to get something to eat."

At McDonald's, Pierre was in line with a few bucks he'd bummed from me that I'd bummed earlier from Mother. John Highwater from my school came walking in. I saw him first. I was still scared of Highwater, even after Paul had fixed things. He was big and must have spent a lot of time in the gym.

"Have you seen Pierre?" he said.

"He's a very popular fellow today. What do you want?" I stared into his eyes without blinking or breaking contact. I wouldn't let him know I was afraid.

"I'm gonna fuck him up," he said, puffing out his chest some. "You gonna back me up?"

"I'm here with Pierre, so... no."

Pierre strolled up and handed me a cheeseburger. He had eaten half of the other one.

"So, John, you're going to beat Pierre's ass? You sure about that?"

Pierre looked at Highwater, and Highwater lowered his eyes and let the air out, sagging in his middle.

"Well I'm supposed to. Robbie's father gave me $200 to do it." He didn't want to fight. In his heart, Highwater was a coward.

"No shit? $200 just to fight me. Maybe we can work something out," said Pierre as he led John to a table.

Highwater paid Pierre a hundred bucks. John reported back to Robbie's father that he'd done his job. The hundred dollars was gone within a few days, spent on beer.

We were in the kitchen at Mother's. I was making a tuna fish sandwich, and drinking a can of Coke. I made Pierre one, too, and a glass of milk. We were eating at the wooden table Mother had brought from Rhode Island when she walked in.

"You boys look right at home." She had just come back from jogging and her face was flushed. "It's a great day. You two should go out."

"I have to look for work," said Pierre.

"What kind of work are you looking for?"

"Anything that pays," he said.

If someone fell in favor with Mother, she'd go out of her way to help them, supplying odd jobs and dispensing advice, legal as well as personal. She'd even give you a scolding if you needed one. My friends could rely on her if they had a problem and she would do her best to provide support. Pierre was well spoken and for the most part, a gentleman, or at least he was in front of Mother. And to her, that made all the difference. In her words, Pierre was "a bright young man." She thought the phone sex calls were made by accident. I didn't know how you could make six hundred dollars in accidental phone calls, but Mother figured it out. She had known him since he was a little boy so she couldn't see him as a dirty phone pervert. But she banned Pierre from staying the night just in case she was wrong. Just like me, Mother didn't fully trust anyone.

"There are jobs opening up at the bank. You could be a teller." She took a bite of my sandwich as I tried to catch Pierre's attention with a direct and agitated stare. She was a senior executive at the bank, specifically in charge of legal and security matters.

"I'll make some calls tomorrow and pass on the information to my son." She ran upstairs to her room.

"Are you fucking crazy? You're wanted for escaping juvie! And unlike at your other jobs, they're gonna check your references and run your name. When they find out that you are wanted, they'll throw your ass right back in jail! Besides, how's it gonna look for my mom to hire a wanted criminal? And what do you think she's gonna do when she finds out? Who is she going to blame?" I waited for him to answer my questions. "Me, she will blame me!" I was yelling, but trying to keep my voice down at the same time. "She might be upstairs right now calling your mother and if your mother finds out you're here that won't be good."

"Yeah, you're right," Pierre sulked. He never brought it up again. Work wasn't a necessity; it was an inconvenience that he occasionally suffered. As it turned out, he had his eye on a girl. She had money, so he wouldn't have to get a job from Mother.

It's Always Safe in the Minivan

GOVERNMENT ISSUE
"Teenager in a Box"
   Doing drugs and booze everyday
   Driving your car in a psychotic rage
   You don't hear what anyone says
   I'll read about you in the obituary page

Baxter ceremoniously dyed his hair a vibrant green with Manic Panic dye imported from New York City. He was the envy of the punks who, at their core, were repressed hairdressers. The green was a shoo-in for someone without an ID at the bars on St. Patrick's Day, but he wanted to go to a party in Virginia.

The minivan was crammed to the brim with the usual cast of characters. We slipped through D.C.'s border and floated out into the Virginia wilds to a party in Old Town, Alexandria. Lars, Ukala, Pierre, Dash, Paul, Charlie, Stephanie and Edgea were already there. Rev and Blitz sat in a corner and most of the Georgetown Day senior class were there too. The only senior from G.D.S. that we liked was Rankin. We called him Skankin' Rankin. He had moved to D.C. from New Zealand three years earlier. He was a Mod, and he could drink more than any of us, so we accepted him.

The house was average for Old Town and so was the party. Paul upper decked the toilet, then when it was obvious I had no clue what it meant, said, "I took a shit in the tank and put the lid back on."

"Why do that?" I was annoyed. Didn't he get it? That was half the reason these GDS kids thought we were retarded. I felt a tap on the shoulder. I swung around and was disarmed by Maggie's beautiful smile. She planted a sloppy kiss on my face, which completely took me by surprise.

"How's it going?" said Maggie.

"Fine. You're not going to make out with any of his friends, are you?" I pointed at Baxter. Lars was playing the hand slapping game with him.

"Not unless you want to make out?" She batted her eyes at me.

"Don't be funny."

"You think it's funny?"

In a few years she would be super hot, maybe a model. I looked over at Dash and remembered how mad I'd been at him for fooling around with Sister. But then again my anger had faded. Maggie grabbed me around the waist and hugged me tight. I wanted to kiss her. Instead I pushed her off of me before she could feel the erection building.

"You'll regret it," she said.

"I know."

I found Baxter. Standing next to him made it hard to want to go find Maggie.

"Nice hat," he said.

I was wearing my favorite Cro-Mags baseball cap. The big thing about baseball caps was bending the brim just right. You could tell where a boy was from by his brim. In California they left the brims flat. On the east coast, up north, there was a slight curve and the further south you went, the tighter the curve got. Everyone had their own tricks: wetting the brim and rubber banding it, wrapping the brim around a baseball and rubber banding them together, or just curling it in your hand.

"Ronnie died tonight," Baxter said.

"Tonight?"

"Lars just told me."

"He was sick for a long time." Thinking about Ronnie Motherfucking Collins bummed me out. I just wanted to go home. "Why didn't Lars tell me this before?"

"He knew it would bum you out and you would stay home."

Over Baxter's shoulder, I could see Stephanie in a friendly conversation with Rev and Blitz. Rev actually looked bashful. I didn't want to think about them dating. I wanted to go home. This party was getting on my nerves.

It wouldn't be long before the beer was gone and we'd have to leave. If you wanted to have a good party, you had to have more booze than the next guy. The high school parties ran out fast and that was why you had to keep a six-pack in the car for the ride home, or know where the next party was being held. Dash said he knew of a party in Maryland. He gave Baxter the address.

After the two kegs were spent, we steered our clown car back to the Capitol Diamond. With Baxter behind the wheel, driving drunk, I belted myself into a seat and awaited my opportunity to bail out. Baxter, sensing this, rarely stopped long enough for me to slide open the side door. Keeping his speed up, he exceeded the limit by more than twenty miles per hour. Baxter glanced up into the rearview mirror and noticed that we were being followed.

"Is that a cop?" Baxter tried to sound calm, but I could hear the panic.

"The headlights are square," replied Rankin.

"They must be rednecks out for kicks," said Baxter, and then he slowed to a whimper before tearing off. Our car weaved across both lanes, the other car was in tow. Baxter accelerated the minivan's speed and we pulled away for a moment. The other car caught up and put on its lights. I wasn't surprised when it turned out to be the Virginia State Police. The red and blue that illuminated the back of Baxter's head mixed into a purple hue, thanks to the green Manic Panic.

"We're all going to jail," I said with a twisted smile.

"Why are you happy about that?" said Ukala.

"Maybe he likes jail," said Pierre who was sitting next to Ukala. Pierre, all in black with a shiny clean shaven head, was hidden behind Ukala's greasy mass of leather and hair.

"Shut up," Baxter said.

I thought of every time I had warned him not to drive drunk. Each lecture ended with him saying "But I drive better drunk" or "You're always safe in the minivan." The first day I had met him, he'd driven me while drunk. It had set the precedent.

The trooper stood next to the car and listened as Baxter declared that he didn't have insurance or a driver's license on him.

"No driver's license or insurance. You've broken every rule in the book," contemplated the trooper. I could barely see his eyes. The brim of his hat tilted so far forward that he was partially hidden. Baxter listened with a serious expression on his face.

"Here it comes," I thought gleefully. The corners of my mouth broke into the smallest of smiles and I tried hard to suppress it. I didn't want to seem insensitive to Baxter's predicament, but he always did things with a disregard for the consequence.

"It would take me all night to charge you boys with these offenses and we're just about done with our shift…" the trooper trailed off in thought.

Drunken laughter erupted from the back seat. Ukala and Rankin were still sipping from their cans. Pierre was silent, not wanting to be noticed, since he was wanted.

"Keep the speed down and get the hell out of here," the trooper sighed. He turned on his heel and was back in his car and gone in a flash.

"I can't fucking believe it, lucky bastard!" I said, my smile vanishing, even though I was glad not to be going to a Virginian jail.

Baxter went back to half stops and twenty miles over the speed limit as I plotted my escape from the drunken minivan. In that one moment where he'd have to stop at a crosswalk or when the van slowed to a crawl, I'd make my escape. Besides, Maggie was drunk and had nuzzled into me during the ride. Her mouth was creeping up towards my lips. I was fighting off a constant erection. I'm not going to make out with Maggie, not here, not while Baxter is right in front of me driving, not ever. Fuck, I had to get out of this minivan. In Virginia's inlaid barren wasteland of country roads, there would be little chance of me finding a ride back, but in the city I knew it was no more than a few blocks walk back home.

Crossing Key Bridge, we rolled to a full stop in Georgetown. Maggie reached around my waist and hugged me. It was too much. *I have to get out now!* Three cars sat in front of us and with cars behind, we were trapped. I seized the opportunity.

"No! Wait a second!" bellowed the green-haired driver as I bolted down the street.

I was in my own neighborhood, a fifteen-minute walk from home. I made it to the corner and turned down Prospect Street. That evening, Edgea had given me a copy of *Helter Skelter*, the book on Charles Manson's murders. As I walked my face was buried in its pages, not reading, but looking at the gruesome photos of the crime scenes. I was trying to get rid of my erection as fast as I could, when a guy strutting by called me back into the realm of reality, interrupting my thoughts.

"What's up?" he asked.

"Not much," I said with all earnestness, looking up from the book. He was a black guy in his twenties. I searched my mind, but didn't recognize him. He squinted at me as if looking into a dazzling light. Then I noticed he had friends. I shrunk back instinctively.

Seven big black guys encircled me. The rest of the street lay empty. The wind had grown stronger. I felt a chill. I flipped through scenarios of strategic escapes. I could feel my pocket being weighed down by my new pair of brass knuckles. I could punch one guy in the face, possibly doing damage, then take a heavy beating from the rest. The "What's up guy" threw a punch that skimmed off my arm.

I lurched forward, breaking through their ranks and exploded ahead. I was the runner sprinting through the woods, the Olympian at the first hundred yards of a dash. My feet bashed the sidewalks. I pushed until I felt I was at top speed, only going faster as I heard them coming closer behind me, their feet slapping the ground with sneakers and Timberland boots. The closest one reached for me, but caught nothing, just air. I thought of being at home in bed under the covers while the air hit my face. I kept running.

"Get that motherfucker!" I heard one scream from behind. The last time I ran like this was from the cops, and I was drunk. I also wasn't afraid of them. For the most part I was sober this time and the fear of being murdered had all the adrenaline I could muster pumping through me. You could have strapped Ukala on my back and I still would have made good time.

I sprinted four blocks before the sounds of their huffing and puffing faded away. My favorite Cro-Mags hat had slid off at some point in the chase. I slowed my pace and took in the extra breath of air before my lungs quit.

No reason to stop now. I'm almost home. Besides, what if there's an athlete in the group and I just can't hear him? I reasoned with myself and continued to run, but not as fast. *How had this happened?* I traced it back. Baxter had been drunk, and Maggie had given me an erection. My parents had almost been killed by a drunk driver so I hadn't wanted to be in the car. Maggie was Baxter's sister so I hadn't wanted to fool around with her. It had all led to me almost getting jumped.

I burst into the house, ran up to the third floor and woke Mother. I had lost my erection during the chase. It was some time after two in the morning.

"These guys just tried to jump me and I got away!" I gasped, out of breath.

"What was that?" she asked. Being from Rhode Island, Mother didn't understand what the phrase "got jumped" entailed.

"I was almost mugged," I translated for her.

"Are you okay?" she asked, slowly blinking her eyes open.

"Yeah, but I have to go back. I lost my hat," I said, still high off of my own adrenaline.

"Don't go back. What if they're waiting for you?" she said. Her accent was extra thick, as though I'd woken her up from a dream of her childhood and she hadn't shaken off the past for the present reality.

"They're not going to wait for me. That wouldn't be smart." I scoffed.

I could hear his voice in my mind. It was like Ronnie Motherfucking Collins was talking to me from the grave with his *Criminal Minded* way of thinking. "If they be calling the motherfucking pigs on you, man, you've got to be getting your motherfucking ass outta there. Go change your clothes, man, them motherfuckers will be looking for some motherfucking fool with a hat and sweatshirt on. Besides, why you want to be waiting around after you just got in some motherfucking fight? Either you get your motherfucking ass beat or you beat some poor motherfucker. Waiting around you be taking a chance, motherfucker. That motherfucker may be going to get his gun or a bunch of his motherfucking friends." But I also knew that black guys in D.C. always assumed that white boys called the cops after getting jumped. They wouldn't be there.

I was sitting next to Mother in her red LeBaron convertible. She was in her bathrobe and slippers. I wondered if she knew about the things I did, like kicking over trashcans and fighting. Most likely she was thinking about what had happened to her comfy bed and dreams of Rhode Island.

Mother drove me back to the scene of the attack. At three in the morning, Prospect Street was empty. I couldn't find my hat. Searching the street, I considered that it might have been carried off as a prize. I pictured one of the seven from the gang wearing it, hoisted onto the shoulders of his comrades as they marched off triumphantly down the deserted street. In reality, they probably just tossed it beneath some random car. I opened the door of the LeBaron and climbed back into my seat.

"No hat?" said Mother.

"No, it's okay. I'll get another one. I'm glad this happened," I muttered.

Mother looked puzzled by my statement.

"I mean I wasn't hurt. I outran seven guys." It was like I'd defied death. I had always been so scared of it.

"You don't need any more adventures like that," was her motherly advice.

The image of Maggie nuzzling me plagued my thoughts. I had to do something, so I beat off thinking of her for the first time. It would become my new bedtime routine. Maggie in a school girl uniform, in all kinds of compromising situations. When I was finished, I felt guilty for dragging such a nice girl into those dark corners of my mind. Baxter would have killed me if he'd known. Ready for sleep, I had the sheets wrapped around me, and a pillow over my face to keep out the daylight. I thought about the seven guys who'd wanted to jump me. It wasn't personal. We'd never met. It had just been another senseless act of violence.

The next day I told Baxter what had happened, leaving out the wild fantasies I had had about his sister. He simply said, "See, never get out of the minivan! It's always safe in the minivan."

Even if He Blinks, Don't Think He Didn't See

IRON CROSS
 "Crucified For Your Sins"
  I find myself nailed to a cross
  For something that I didn't do
  It's your fault you've ruined our lives
  And we're the ones you crucify
  You're the ones who commit the crimes
  But it's always us who do the time.

Inside the 9:30 Club, the bodies fell to the ground. There was pushing, and I pulled on the guy next to me to get back to my feet. A fight had broken out and the crowd had scrambled out of the way. Kids were backing up into a circle. The row behind them was peeking overhead to get a better look. An arm covered in tattoos swung down on a body underneath. Its owner stood up and I could see that the tattoos flowed up to his neck. His head was a triangular wedge between his shoulders. He punched down, and the guy under him fought back, but was no match. Government Issue was on stage and stopped playing when they noticed the attention averting to the circle.

"Hey, if you guys don't cut it out, we're not going to play," said the singer.

"Blitz is fighting again," said a fat punk next to me.

Baxter was the type who took in strays. The undesirables crashed at his house. My house had a higher standard. No bums or psychopaths allowed, and if they showed up, I had a policy of no vacancy. Mother had already banned Ronnie Motherfucking Collins and Pierre. When Baxter had brought Blitz to my house, I had been forced to play the cordial host, even after Blitz had spilled a can of Guinness on my beloved Cro-Mags CD and ruined it. Had it been Ukala or anyone else, I would have thrown them a beating, but instead, since it had been Blitz, I had smiled and decided to be quiet and keep my teeth. It took time, hours, but Blitz had left to go get some weed.

"What, are you fucking out of your mind?" I had said to Baxter.

"What did I do?" he'd said as he'd shrugged, pretending not to know.

"Don't bring him here. He always wants to stay, and I can only bullshit him for so long."

"Well I don't want him staying at my house either."

"He always stays at your place."

"Yeah, I know that," he had said and I'd got his point.

"Well, next time take him to Ukala's."

"I already tried that. He didn't open the door." *Why hadn't I thought of that?*

It was two days later when I heard knocking at my back door. It was Blitz and he had already seen me so I couldn't pretend I wasn't there. Before I opened the door I looked down and saw that he had brought along his two pit bulls. They were both big, but the white one was huge. I had never seen a pit that big. It was smiling at me through my door as if it knew something I didn't.

"Do me a favor and watch my dogs. I have to see my probation officer. I'll be back in an hour," he called out, vanishing through the door, and then I knew what the white dog was laughing at. The big one was a boy. He walked over to me and dropped his head in my lap, looking up at me. I patted his head, and could feel the muscles that gripped his jaws. Then the girl came over and nudged my leg with her head and I patted her, too.

An hour passed. It was hot out so I gave them water and went back inside to watch TV. Blitz didn't come back, and that night I didn't sleep well. Late in the afternoon, I woke up with a note on my door "Whose dogs are those?" in Mother's handwriting. I had forgotten and went to check on them. As I opened the door, they looked up at me. My stomach was growling and I realized they were hungry, too. They hadn't eaten in more than a day. I called Dash and asked if he had seen Blitz. Sometimes they hung out since they both smoked a lot of weed.

"No, but I can bring over some dog food," he said. Dash had eight pugs. They were like a gang of old men snorting at each other. An hour passed before Dash came crashing through my back gate with a plastic bag from the grocery store filled with dog food.

I handed Dash one of Mother's bowls for the food and went back inside for more water. Dash balanced his cigarette on the edge of the windowsill and poured the entire bag into the bowl. Both dogs scrambled to their feet and raced to the food, knocking heads on the way. They gulped down mouthfuls of the food without chewing, snorting at each other as the friction built between them. I refilled their water, hoping it might calm them down.

"Do you think it's a good idea to feed them together?" I said to Dash. I had had dogs before and I'd fed them separately. I thought of my first dog, biting my arm. I didn't want to get bitten again.

"Yeah, why not? I feed my dogs like that all the time."

"Well, these are big dogs and..." I was interrupted by the female bearing her teeth and growling at the male. He continued eating. She bit him on the cheek and snarled. The sounds of half barks started, bouncing off the wooden slates of my backyard fence. Dash and I were on top of the two, trying to grab some of their skin and fur because they had no collars.

"I don't think I should have fed the dogs together!" he said.

"No shit!"

The male dog had a hold of the female and wasn't letting go. They were both bleeding.

"We need something to pry his mouth open!" yelled Dash over the female's yelping. There wasn't anything around that we could grab.

Dash wrapped his arm around the female's waist and pulled the skin around her neck with his other hand. The male bit hard on her ear and the meat attached to it. She emitted screams, human-sounding screams as if she were being murdered. I grabbed the male at his neck, but he wouldn't let go. I punched him on the head, but he didn't notice. Dash let go of the female and picked up his cigarette, and started smoking fast.

"Dash, what the hell are you doing? I need help! This is no time for a smoking break!"

Dash pinched the cigarette by the end and blew on its cinders, making it hot as fire itself before bringing it down on the male's nose. The dog's eyes were fierce but the look changed to panic and pain as Dash pushed the hot cherry into tender flesh. With a yelp, the dog let go of the female. The struggle was over and Dash, the dogs, and I were splattered in blood. They separated and cowered in different corners as if I were going to beat them for fighting.

"Oh man, Blitz is going to kill you" said Dash.

"You're the one who fed them together."

"Yeah, but I'm going home."

"Fuck. He's is going to kill me." Dash headed out the back gate.

I cleaned the dogs up. The boy dropped his head in my lap and I patted him gently. His fur was light pink in patches from the blood that I couldn't get out. The back gate opened. It was Blitz. He looked at me, then at his dogs. He put on their leashes. I was ready to take my beating, and wondered how it would start. The muscles in my face tightened, my heart stepped up its pace, and the sweat came.

"Thanks," he said and they left. I watched him walk out the back gate and I let out a sigh.

Immortal was Washington's only skinhead band at that time. The music was reminiscent of New York Hardcore: fast, hard, attacking vocals with a beat to march to. It was something for the angry youth; it often led to violence. The front man, Max, was a 5' 2" stocky white guy, and his most dominant features were his large nose and small ears. He dressed traditional in laced-up boots, a tucked-in Ben Sherman shirt, thin suspenders and pants with the cuffs rolled up. He was known to carry an eight ball in a sock as a weapon and once hit a guy over the head with it so hard that the ball tore through the sock and was almost lost.

I had seen his band a dozen times. Since there was nothing better to do that night, Baxter drove Pierre, Dash, Ukala and me over to Northeast to a church where they were playing. The show itself was uneventful. The crowd climbed the steps from the basement and out to the street in front of the church. The scene was being made on the street in front.

Pierre was telling a bad joke. It didn't matter which one; all his jokes were bad.

"What do you call two onions that love each other?" He waited for someone to guess, but no one did. "Lesbi-onions!" The funniest thing about his jokes was the fact that Pierre was the first to laugh, so I never minded hearing one. Ukala walked back to the minivan to get a six-pack of Mickey's Big Mouth beers that he'd bought at Habib's, a mini market in Dupont Circle. Dash stood off to the side talking with Stephanie, whilst holding the flame of his lighter below a quarter to make it nice and hot. Stephanie caught me staring at her. I turned and saw Blitz walking up to Max with an attitude in his step that I'd seen before all of Blitz' fights.

"So you're a skinhead, right?" Max was puzzled by this question.

"Yes." His voice was deep and lacking confidence.

"What's the matter with you? Your vagina wet?" said Blitz tilting his head slightly to the left without breaking eye contact with Max.

"What?"

"You need moisturizer for your pussy?"

"I don't understand what you want," said Max.

"If you're a bad ass tough skinhead, then fight me," Blitz demanded.

"I don't want to fight you."

Blitz struck Max with an open hand across the face. Max turned away. Dash was watching the action as the quarter became red hot. With a howl he dropped it. Blitz was slapping Max like a little girl.

"Stop, Blitz! Leave me alone!" Max screeched, doing his best to escape Blitz' reach.

"You're a fucking pussy," said Blitz as he kicked Max in the ass.

It was embarrassing to watch them. Blitz made his point. Max's shining example of skinheadism was destroyed. This was the part of the scene I hated. It wasn't any different than high school. Blitz could have been Sermon, or Highwater or any of those kids who had called me retard. The scene was supposed to be a place to get away from that, but in many ways it mirrored high school. Everything was about cliques. Rev, Blitz and the students from Master Woo's were like the jocks; even though they fought with the jocks all the time, they were the same.

Max ran off. Dash turned his attention to the quarter lying on the sidewalk as a Punk Rock kid stopped in front of it. Dash nudged Stephanie, saying, "Check out this kid about to get burned." The punk picked up the quarter, flipped it in his hand, put it in his pocket and walked away. Dash frowned.

"He's no skinhead," Blitz told us later that night at the gazebo, just off R Street in Georgetown.

The gazebo was across the street from Baxter's house, just far enough away to escape the Parents, but close enough to walk home drunk. It was a serene setting, as a slight breeze blew our way. The humidity had let up enough that we could sit comfortably without breaking a sweat. In the dark, Baxter was drinking a Tall Boy and Pierre was rocking back and forth on a swing in the playground. The tennis court next to the gazebo was empty. I imagined the ghosts of that afternoon's players in white shorts and white mini-skirts chasing the ball. I wondered if Maggie ever played there? I should come back in the daytime to watch the girls play, I thought to myself. Blitz was holding his Guinness. I didn't have a drop to drink, even though I wasn't driving. I didn't want to be drunk around Blitz.

"If someone runs from me in a fight, well then every time I see him I'll beat his ass," Blitz suddenly interrupted the silence. His triangular head in silhouette was like a yield sign you walk by in the dark.

"I can't wait for the next Immortal show," he went on.

If Blitz ever started with me, I would have to fight back and hope I didn't get murdered. He wasn't much bigger than me, but was a hundred times crazier. And that's the deciding factor in a fight, Ronnie Motherfucking Collins had once told me. The only other option was to evaporate, I thought.

We stayed there drinking. I wanted to leave, but was afraid of making Blitz angry. If I went home he would ask to stay at my house, so I waited for Baxter to leave first. At 2:30, Baxter decided to go home.

"Hey, I'm crashing at your house." Blitz wasn't asking, he was telling him. Pierre went with Ukala. They left and I started walking the four blocks home. It was dark, and I could hear the crickets and the breeze through the trees. I could smell fresh cut grass. Spring was right around the corner. A few cars drove past and I watched and wondered what the drivers were doing up at 3 am. Most of the lights were out in the houses I passed, except for one. The blue light from the TV flickered and bounced off the walls, much like the way the light of a fireplace might. I stopped and peered in. I liked looking into houses. Walking the same streets, I'd think about how many houses or buildings I'd been in, mapping them out in my mind. I turned onto Reservoir Road, then onto Winfield Lane. I passed my neighbor's backyard, where, hidden by the high wooden fence, there was a giant bear carved out of wood with a large erection. I felt like that bear a lot, especially around Maggie. From the street you could only see the top of its head just over the fence.

I opened the back gate and sat in the lawn chair. The bowl of water for the dogs was still there.

"The last weeks of school are a total waste of time," said Dash as he searched for something in his pocket. "They should just cut off the last week. No finals, nothing, that's it." He produced a lighter from his gas station jacket and lit a cigarette.

"The next year you would say the same thing and then every year it would get shorter by one week until there was no school left at all," I added.

"That's the best plan. No school."

"I'm going to get something to eat. You coming?" I said, but I knew he was planning to sneak off and smoke weed.

Walking over to Roy Rogers, I saw Blitz, Ukala, Pierre and Rev standing in the parking lot, watching the students make their way across the street. I was happy for a break from the usual monotony of the school day, but knew it meant trouble.

"What are you guys doing here? I don't get out 'til three." I said, looking at Ukala and Pierre and knowing that they obviously weren't there to pick me up.

"Rev's going to kick the shit out of Paul." As Pierre spoke, he turned to the stream of students, looking for the novice skin. Blitz looked stoned and didn't say anything at all.

"Why?" But I knew the answer, why not?

"Because he has been going around saying he's a skinhead," said Rev.

"You can't do it here!" I protested.

'Why not?" Rev wondered distractedly, still searching.

"The teachers will call the cops right away," I said, almost pleading. Then I singled Pierre out. "What, do you want me to get kicked out? Besides, you know you'll see him again. Why not get him at a show or party?" I suggested. A cop car pulled into the parking lot and I made it obvious that it was there by staring. Pierre turned first, then Ukala and Rev. Pierre gestured to Blitz in the direction of the patrol car, but he didn't get it. I pointed, "The police", and he understood.

They left. Even if they did beat up Paul, it was unlikely that I would have been kicked out of school, but I felt like I had done a good thing. Paul had kept Highwater from bullying me and now I had paid him back. Paul wasn't a bad guy; he just did stupid things. Besides, Pierre had known Paul as long as I had. *What the hell is his problem*, I thought. It was like he was a traitor to his own dyslexic family. Or maybe it was Ukala? He was still trying to make peace with Rev for hitting one of his fellow martial arts students. Why else would they have brought Rev? Maybe Rev was there just to watch? None of it had made sense, but then the scene never made sense. It was unpredictable. That was part of its appeal. I wasn't bored. I pictured what my life would be like without it. No music, no shows, no parties, no clothes, no friends, nothing to talk about, nothing to distract me.

Dash wandered up, smelling strongly of marijuana. How could the teachers not know he was stoned?

"I just saved Paul from getting his ass beat."

"Why did you do that?" asked Dash.

"Forget it." I walked back to school and took my last exam.

A Pretty Yellow Dress in Texas

THE MEATMEN
  "1 Down 3 to Go"
    Lennon's dead hip hip hooray
    All his dues he now must pay
    George, Paul, Ringo any day
    Will be dead we all must pray

At Fort Reno, a crappy band banged away on their instruments as I searched the field for cute girls to watch. The sun was ready to go into hiding for the rest of the day and relieve us of its heat. There was more drama happening in the parking lot than onstage that night. Plenty of people were milling around. That was the best thing about it if you were in a band. A crowd of kids was always present unless it rained.

"You know, if you would just stop talking, I would explain the entire thing to you!" said Fiona. I don't know how we'd started talking about it. I'd ignored her at school but somehow she'd cornered me in the park. She'd wanted to talk about why we'd broken up years before and why I was still mad at her.

"Now you're not even listening to me!" She was yelling, and she was right. I wasn't listening to her. I could see Maggie walking over to the parking lot, on the arm of some boy I didn't know. It was as if something inside me began to crumble. Then Fiona punched me hard in the stomach, knocking the wind out of me. It was unexpected. I dropped to the ground, trying to pull air but laughing, too. What a joke, I thought. One girl I hate hits me while the one I like goes off to the parking lot to make out with a boy. Fiona stood defiantly over me with her hands on her hips and feet firmly planted. I looked to see if Maggie had seen, and Fiona noticed my stare and followed it to where Maggie was crossing the street. Fiona gave Maggie a look of pure loathing, then turned back to me. I could smell Fiona's perfume. It was overwhelming, as if she was trying to cover something up.

"I'm so much hotter than her," she said.

I shook my head.

"She won't fuck you, anyway!"

I shrugged.

"Why are you laughing at me?" said Fiona.

"You're kind of a joke, aren't you?"

I got up. I brushed the dirt from my pants and could see she felt bad for hitting me. Ukala came over and handed me a beer without me having to ask for one.

"I didn't cheat on you," she said, whining.

"Whatever," I said in a sarcastic tone. I started walking towards the parking lot against the light. A motorcyclist screeched to a halt to avoid running me over. I stopped in my tracks and turned towards the driver, as an impulse struck me (or maybe it was the drink mixed with the residuals of the fight, or seeing Maggie walk off with that boy). I slapped the biker with an open palm on the side of his helmet. This was not a brilliant move on my part; he could have let the clutch go, releasing his bike to finish me off. Instead, he dismounted. I realized I couldn't punch him in the face, which was my favorite target. He had his helmet on. Men are as vain as women and don't fancy carrying the scars from a fight - black eyes, fat lips, cuts and scrapes. Victories are determined by how bad the person looks the next day. Your opponent may have run away from you, but if you looked like the one who got the beating, then you lost. Always strike at the face first. The biker put up his fists. *Shit! What can I do? Run!* I was moving fast. Pierre jumped in the biker's path, giving me a few seconds to create some distance between us. Baxter and Ukala looked on.

"How about a little help here!" I shouted at them as I ran past.

They continued to stand there and watch, still in the works of figuring out what exactly was happening and why a guy in black leather and a helmet was chasing me. With Ukala's brain, it would have taken more than half an hour to dissect the situation. I ran back and forth, making wide and small circles, with no plan or pattern, just leading and being followed. I wasn't frightened, but giggling. I had no intention of fighting now.

Lars tried to grab the mad biker as I flew past him, but the leather was slippery. I tossed a metal drum that was used as a park trashcan behind me, and the pursuer fell over it, crashing in the dirt, but his leather outfit protected his fall. I couldn't help myself; I had to laugh and laugh loud. Baxter and Ukala's brains finally came to speed and blocked the motorcyclist as I chuckled and made my way across the street to Wilson High School. *I'm such a dick.* The motorcyclist lost me in the crowd of kids. Edgea's car was parked and I saw smoke billowing out of the windows that weren't rolled all the way up. I threw the door open and hopped in, frightening all inside. I turned to my left and sitting next to me was a kid I had never seen before. His hair was a bright blue and stuck out in all directions, like the rays of the sun.

"This is Dillon. He's from Texas," said Edgea, slurring her words from the alcohol. The motorcyclist stormed past, searching for me. I pretended to see something on the floor and ducked down until he passed.

Dillon was an oddity. He swept into town, hitching rides up the East Coast. He had more than a few tattoos placed randomly across his body, like the Misfits skull in bright day-glo colors on his bicep. His appearance coordinated with his mental state: crazy. Dillon was the drummer for a band. They played the local clubs in Texas but had once been banned from playing the largest of the clubs, Emo's. The only logical thing they could do for revenge was name the band "Fuck Emo's." The club loved it and put out a record.

"What do you do for fun down in Texas?" I said, sinking deep into the seat to hide.

Outside of Edgea's car the motorcyclist walked past again but didn't see me in the back seat. My eyes followed the black helmet as it left the parking lot.

"For fun, I hitch rides out to the hick towns, outside of Dallas," said Dillon. "Then I put on my best Sunday dress. It's a canary yellow blouse with puffy sleeves, an ankle-length skirt and a bow around the midsection. You know, like the old black ladies do when they get all done up. Then I take a fist full of acid, walk out to the nearest crossroads and freak out."

"Freak out and do what?" said Edgea. I thought she was asleep since her eyes were closed.

"Spin around, mumble, attack the good citizens," he said.

"Aren't you afraid they'll arrest you?" I asked.

"I want to get arrested. The town's sheriff will pick me up and throw me in the cell for the rest of the weekend. Not like a big city jail. That's why I go to the small towns, places my friends get arrested, and recommend to me. The food is pretty good, too. And I always meet good people in there. By Monday, the sheriff tosses me out with the same 'Don't come back' speech. I leave that town with a new legend."

"Sounds like fun," said Edgea. Her arm dangled out the window with a lit cigarette that looked as if it were about to drop, but it never did. From Edgea's car I could see into the car across from us. Maggie was passionately making out with that boy. His hands moved down her front and seemed to disappear between her legs. I felt sick.

"I'm taking Dillon to get a tattoo from Running Bear," said Edgea. "Want to come?"

"Na, I'll see you guys later." I left the car and walked up the hill to where Baxter and Ukala were standing. I just wanted to be with my friends.

"He's gone," said Baxter.

"That was fun," I said. I wished he'd come back. At the moment I would have welcomed a punch in the nose, anything to make me not think of Maggie.

Blitz walked up. I could see his knuckles were red and sore, but not from fighting. He had a fresh tattoo from Running Bear. Rings that wrapped around his knuckles, ornate and fine-lined, a design that was meant to emulate the rings that punks wore at the time. I thought they looked cool and wanted some, but knew Mother would kill me if I got them. "How are you going to get a job with those on your hands?" Mother would say.

The next day, Baxter and I met up with Dillon and Edgea at the aqueduct by the canal in Georgetown. The late afternoon sun crashed through the overhead branches and tossed patterns over the yellow sand path and slowly moving water. The air smelled of rotting vegetation from the canal. Baxter carried a six-pack that we had made Ukala buy for us. Sitting next to Dillon, I asked to see his new tattoo. He showed me his hands that were bandaged up between the knuckles. I had a sinking feeling in my belly.

"Rings?" I said.

"Yeah, how did you know?" he asked.

"I saw some earlier."

"I didn't know what I wanted, and Running Bear said he had something already drawn up. He showed me this drawing of rings. I liked them and so got them." He started pulling off the bandages.

"Aren't you supposed to leave those on for a few days?" I said, thinking of the possibility of infection or Blitz walking up unexpected.

"Yeah, but I never leave them on," said Dillon.

Baxter drank his beer. When he noticed Dillon's new tattoos, he choked and said "Oh shit, that's the same tattoo Blitz got."

"That's not the exact same as Blitz," said Edgea, defending her friend Running Bear. Most guys in the punk scene wanted one-of-a-kind art.

"It's the exact same," Baxter said. "Blitz is going to be pissed."

"Who is Blitz?" asked Dillon.

Walking up to the party that night, I didn't see Blitz through the window, which didn't mean a thing. He might show up later. *Whose party is this?* I couldn't remember; they all started to blend into each other. No one seemed in charge. Dash, the party master, had told us about it, so for all I knew it could have been borrowed while it's owners were out of town. Go Go music blasted from a stereo in the living room. Ukala talked with Dillon. Dillon seemed to understand what Ukala was saying, even though Edgea, who had known Ukala for years, kept interrupting the conversation with "What the hell did you say?" Dillon translated Ukala into English. I had a beer and walked around the house, looking for girls or anyone new to talk with. Blitz and Rev walked in.

Ukala pointed at Blitz, telling Dillon, "Darts herm."

Blitz was high. He had heard about Dillon and his new tattoo. Recognizing that look of fear in Dillon's face, Blitz walked over to him as Dillon started to get up, throwing his duffel bag over his shoulder. Blitz raised his fist, and Dillon swung around, hitting Blitz with his duffel bag and knocking him onto Ukala's lap.

"Arrag, Grawrt Erff me," said Ukala as Blitz grabbed at the air and anything that might help him right himself. Dillon was out the door whilst Rev watched, laughing at Blitz. Dillon hitched a ride and was back on the road, heading up 95 to Boston.

"That was fun," Edgea said to Ukala, but it looked like she had directed her comment at Blitz' ass as he was getting out of Ukala's lap.

I never saw Dillon again. But after meeting him I realized that the scene was much larger than I thought. It was in every major city, every suburb and anywhere you could hear music. It was carried on the backs of punks who criss-crossed this country, the bands who went on tour, and the records in the shops. I was a part of something larger than just my neighborhood, town and city. There was something else about Dillon; he didn't think like any of the punks I knew. The more I broke it down, the more I realized that the punk scene was conformist. We listened to the same music, wore the same clothes and had the same hair styles. Dillon was more punk rock than any of us. Taking acid, wearing his Sunday dress, and getting arrested were his holiday. It was crazy and beautiful at the same time. But here was the problem: why should any of it matter if we are all just copies of each other? It was the first tiny fracture in what I had put so much faith in. Over time that fracture would grow.

Doing Penance for Pennies

CRO-MAGS
 "Hard Times"
  Hard times are coming your way
  You're gonna have to rise above it some day
  Organize your life and figure it out
  Or you'll go under without a doubt

"What's Ukala's real name? I may have some work for him," said Mother.

"I don't know."

"How could you not know?"

"I never asked."

"How can you really be friends with someone if you don't know their name?"

After Mother's comment, I started asking my friends their last names, their real names. It was an issue of trust and I needed to know they trusted me.

When I had first started to hang out in the scene, I had discovered real names were rarely given and I had learned not to ask. Nicknames were most often used instead. I had been calling Blitz, Tiny, and Ukala by their nicknames for so long I had forgotten that they had other names. It might seem odd to outsiders, but most of the kids in the scene just felt safer keeping those things secret. Nicknames were based on common sense. If there were two Dashes, one became Little Dash, or if a girl constantly wore a jacket covered in safety pins, she became Safety Pin. Rev's real name was Iranian and Rev was just easier to pronounce then his real name. Edgea was really Aegean, but somehow it ended up as Edgea, like she was on the edge.

Pierre was playing video games. I knew his last name, but wouldn't tell anyone else. It wasn't my place. Ukala gave me a side-glance when I asked his last name.

"You already know it," he said in his own muddled language.

"Oh yeah," but I had forgotten it. It was something normal like Smith or Jones.

I walked upstairs to the third floor where Mother's room was. She was riding her stationary bike, sweating and breathing hard.

"You're always working out."

"My mother died at 56. If I don't take care of myself, I won't make it past that," she said and drank some water that was resting on her television. She was afraid of dying too.

"Can Pierre stay over? I know he's not supposed to after the phone sex calls and all."

"He won't be able to make those calls again. I blocked the phone. I like Pierre, so sure."

"Thanks." I walked downstairs.

"Is it cool?" asked Pierre.

"Yeah. Why don't you get an apartment?"

"I'm still a wanted man and why pay rent when there is an empty couch or piece of floor?"

My parents had no clue if my friends were degenerates, sociopaths, wanted criminals, or choirboys donning mohawks and leather jackets. They trusted me. I, in turn, trusted my friends, even the criminals. All the Parents knew was that my guests might stay over for a night or a month. Mother had grown accustomed to my friends staying over for as long as they needed. Baxter only stayed over a single night at a time. Ukala would stay two, maybe three days at the most. He lived with his parents and could go home anytime he wanted. However, Pierre had nowhere to go. His mother lived above the zoo. It would be the first place the cops would look for him. At my house, Pierre could eat and sleep in one of the guest beds. Friends were treated like family here.

"It's Sunday. We should get some beer and acid and go to Ocean City." Baxter sipped on a can. I only had a few days left before I had to start work again so I could pay my legal bill for the fight.

I saw subtitles as Ukala spoke: "Crass Kerry has a house down there, but you'd probably have to fuck her to stay there and you know she's got crabs." Ukala then chuckled to himself.

Lars puffed on a cigarette. He held it as though he hadn't had one in a long time. His mohawk was pasted behind his ear. Already stoned and drunk, Lars looked like he was going to fall off his patio chair at any moment.

"Look, man, why don't we go to that show?" He was slurring but we could all understand the words spilling out of his mouth.

The intercom interrupted with a rumble of static, as if to clear the air before it spoke.

"You are keeping me up! Now be quiet!" it demanded and fell silent.

I didn't have to explain anything; they all knew it was Mother. They heard the same message every night. It was time to go.

Mother was a light sleeper, an insomniac. Three floors above the fenced-in patio, she'd sleep under sheets while the hum of the central air conditioner did next to nothing to muffle our voices. I believed she could hear us but was unable to make out exactly what we were saying. She might have used the intercom right next to her bed to listen to us chattering candidly about drugs, sex and criminal intentions. This might have been her window into all the dirty little details of my secret life. Years later when I asked her, she would deny it, saying "I actually didn't use the intercom for that purpose. I did use the security system – which beeped when a door was opened or closed – to know when everyone was in the house at night and accounted for. I was never much for spying – too much work and what do you do with the information once you have it – and how do you explain how you got it if it wasn't through spying

– and then wouldn't that undermine my message to you that I trusted you?" But who really trusts their kids?

A few days later, The Fall were playing. I'd never heard of them, but had nowhere else to go. I grabbed my favorite T-shirt of the moment, Slap Shot. It was old and beaten up but I liked it because it reminded me of Boston. I grabbed my boots and drove over to Ukala's house to pick up Pierre and him.

I couldn't tell you who the local Congressmen were for Maryland or Virginia, but I could name off all of the prominent scenesters who made it to the show or simply loitered out front. Never getting my fill of socializing, I would ultimately be one of the last to go home. It was a mixed crowd. Rev and Blitz were there with two new students from the martial arts studio, and Dash. Dash had just started going to Mr. Woo's. When I asked him about it, Dash said, "Look, if I go there then we all have a connection to Rev and Blitz and, if something happens to me, they will back me up." Besides Ukala, Lars, Pierre and me, a dozen of the other regulars were there. A new gang was on the scene, out of Virginia. They sported dyed blond hair and called themselves the "Blond Gods." What a joke, I thought. Didn't they know they lived outside the city? They would never be taken seriously.

The 9:30 Club was centrally located downtown. When Martin Luther King, Jr. was assassinated, much of this section of the city was destroyed by the fire and riots. The National Guard moved in and tanks patrolled the streets. Many of the buildings remained abandoned. D.C. Space, another small club, was only a few blocks away. I could find just about anybody I knew at one of these two venues. I would make repeated trips between both places. Behind the 9:30 Club was an alley where punk rock bands, such as Bad Brains, Minor Threat and a thousand others, would load in and load out. It was the same alley where the cops harassed me for urinating in public, where the punk rock graffiti dated back as far as the 70s. This was the same alley that John Wilkes Booth hobbled down and fled on horseback after shooting President Lincoln in the head.

It was a humid night. I felt like I'd just stepped out of the shower, but was just covered in my own sweat. There were no assassins lurking, just a few pimpled punks. Rev had come down to the show with Stephanie. He was leaning against her car with the two students. Rev was shy and reserved. I could tell he liked Stephanie. I think she liked him back. I made my way back to Ukala and Pierre. A garbage truck rumbled down F Street. As it passed the club and the alley next to it, I noticed a circle of Blond Gods. They had staked out a small piece of the street. Two kids, with spiked and colored hair and dressed in the finest of punk fashions, entered the half circle. The Criminal Minded knows "Never to walk in no motherfucking circle. Stand on the outside and watch the motherfuckers. Watch the bullfight, but don't become the motherfucking bull," One of the Virginia gang started in on the two spike-haired kids with a verbal assault. "What the fuck are you looking at, faggot!"

Curiosity aroused, I wandered over to see what the commotion was about, keeping in mind Ronnie's words and standing on the outside. The two punks in the circle were being pushed around. They weren't fighting back. I didn't want to get into a fight, but I also knew that what was going on wasn't right. Someone ran up behind me. I thought it was just another spectator, but then I was sucker-punched in the back of the head. And, just like Lincoln, I didn't see it coming.

Throughout my life, whenever I've been struck in the head, a flash of white follows. Filled with rage, I lose all control of my senses. After regaining my faculties, I find myself in the midst of throwing loads of punches, attempting to kill whoever is close enough to grab. Victor Da Skin had once taunted me because I'd refused to give him a bite of a tuna sandwich I'd bought at the Tenleytown Mini-mart. He had kept slapping me in the face. I had been a sixteen-year-old punk at the time; he had been a thirty-plus year-old who'd been bullying me for months. He had finally slapped me too hard. I'd snapped. A flash of white had rushed over me and, before I'd realized, I'd punched him dead center in the face, dropping him to the ground, I'd straddled him and had gone to work. Dash had pulled me off Victor, whose nose and mouth were bloodied. That had been the last time Victor harassed me.

After being struck outside of the 9:30, my expression turned fearsome. The kid knew he was in for it and retreated. The chase was on. Adrenaline surging, I still couldn't catch him, ranting and raving, foaming at the mouth. Everything was circular. Just a few weeks before, I had slapped that guy in the helmet and he had chased me around Fort Reno; now I was the one chasing some kid. Ukala caught him across the street. They both spun around and the kid dropped to the ground. The kid got up, pulled free from Ukala and ran straight into Dash, knocking him over.

From where Rev was, it must have looked like the kid had attacked Dash. Rev was on top of him with a burst of punches, as another one of the Blond Gods came over and attempted to topple Rev. The kid under Rev was knocked out. Rev turned to see who was attacking him from his side. It was their heavy, their biggest guy. Rev took both the heavy guy's arms and folded them quickly behind his back, head-butting the kid as his legs buckled under. Rev, sitting on top, was trying to bite his nose. Blitz came flying through the air, leg extended, kicking another kid square in the head. His form was perfect, right out of a martial arts movie. The Blond Gods were being beaten; they never really had a chance. They were from Virginia, after all. Pierre walked by one, then turned around and punched him in the face. One of the Woo students kicked another in the head with a roundhouse and then gave him a right hook to the jaw. Blitz found the second largest Blond Goddess and was kicking and punching him. The kid did his best to cover up and protect his face, before running away from Blitz. Rev let go of his victim, who ran off crying, cradling his nose. Ukala and Pierre had captured the one who originally had hit me.

"I'm sorry man. I'm sorry man." He begged for mercy.

"Sorry?" I raved, "What is 'sorry' supposed to mean to me? I'm not your friend! Even-up."

"What?" he asked with a confused look. I punched him in the face. His head sprang back as if it were elastic.

"We're even now," I said.

"So we're cool, right? Everything's cool, right? No problem?"

"We're even. That's all," I said.

Ukala let go of his collar and we walked back to my Oldsmobile.

"So you're down with Rev?" asked Pierre.

"Not me. Dash is." Something had happened and Dash's status within the scene had moved up a bit, so in a way ours had too. After the fight, the scene considered Dash and me associates of Rev and if anyone messed with me, they might be messing with Rev. Or at least that's what they thought. I sat in my car, rubbing the back of my head and then the knuckles that had made contact with the kid's face. As I watched, Rev, Blitz and Dash climbed into Stephanie's white Pinto and headed back to Bethesda, where Rev lived.

Party On

COCK SPARRER
"Where Are They Now"
Was it ever worth it
Causing all the fuss
You know, I believed in them
Don't you believe in us

I put the suit back on. My hair was so blond that it was almost white. Monday was the first day of work. They put me in the mailroom right next to the fax machine.

"So what exactly am I supposed to do?" I asked.

"You're a secretarial assistant," said the office manager. "You do whatever they need help with."

"Sounds like a made-up job."

"It is. But there will be plenty for you to do, running packages and faxes to all the secretaries."

The fax machine started buzzing and beeping, then paper slowly spit out its side.

"Here you go." The manager handed me the paper and told me where to bring it. I rode the elevator up to Father's floor and dropped the fax off at the right desk after asking twice where it was. Passing Father's office, I could see him talking into a tiny recorder and walking aimlessly about the room. He was lost to Nixon again. On the far wall was a photo of him with the ex-president. They were smiling and shaking hands.

"How's it going?" said Father's secretary.

"Fine."

"Back for the summer?"

"Paying off a debt for a fight."
"Well, you shouldn't be fighting."
"He was trying to hit me."
She shrugged.

I went downstairs and could hear the buzzing before I made it to my seat. Within the first few hours I had taken thirty faxes up. Why don't they each have their own fax machine? Twenty-five secretaries and I had to run them all their faxes. Fucking machine! I was tired from barely sleeping the night before. I just wanted to sit down. It didn't help that the chair they had given me looked so comfortable. Every time I was about to test it out, the buzzing started and I was up again. I wanted to beat the shit out of the fax machine. Where was Dash? I thought. It had been his fight. He should be carrying half these damn faxes.

I took note of the soda machine that dispensed free cans of soda and Bud beer. That will be useful someday, I thought. It wasn't stealing if it was free. I went into one of the empty offices and stretched out on the floor for a short nap. Back to the job, a pile of faxes waited for me.

"Fucking fax machine," I said out loud.

"Hey man, you don't got to be running them up as they come out. Let them build up and run them all together," said one of the mailroom workers.

"My Dad gave me shit about getting the faxes to the lawyers fast." I carried them up. I dropped them off and walked into Father's office. The papers looked like they were taking over and were stacked high everywhere there was space. On his desk were photos of Sister and me taken at some point I didn't remember. We looked clean and nice. On the wall was a framed letter with a nickel taped to it:

> Rominski,
>
> Take the nickel, give it to Slippery Dick and have him fuck himself. He is a double no-count S.O.B.
>
> Jerry
>
> We have had enough of his garbage. He and you can go to hell.

"What's that?" I pointed at the framed note on the wall.

"When I started working on the Nixon case, some of the partners said I would never get a nickel. After the Times wrote about the case, I received this hate mail from a guy named Jerry in Texas." Father laughed. "I showed it to my partners and told them hey, I made a nickel."

It was August 25th and I was nineteen now.

"Dude, just buy me some records or something. Don't plan anything."

"No," said Baxter. "This year your birthday's gonna be great!"

The year before we had spent the night driving around in a search for acid that never materialized. Lars and Dash had begun arguing and I had gone home.

"No, no, this year is gonna be different," he declared, almost pleading.

Some kids from Georgetown Day School were having a party. In a townhouse with a long wooden deck that wrapped around its front, they had booze and that's all I cared about. It was my birthday and I'd survived another year, which was something to be proud of. Pierre, Lars, Ukala and Baxter packed into the minivan and we rolled up to the house. The climate changed dramatically when we made our entrance. Joyous banter turned to hushes and whispers, smiling faces transformed into frowns, and what had been confidence evaporated into fear. I recognized some of the faces. They were friends with Ted, my old neighbor. I saw a kid who had called me a retard when I had waited for the school bus. There was a girl I had once thought was cute who had told me to fuck off. The ones I didn't know were just like the type of kids who had tormented me. It occurred to me that the roles had switched. I could get revenge if I wanted to. The preppy kids were terrified and I couldn't blame them.

How many times had we gotten into fights at their parties? The GDS students deemed us as the bad kids from the other side of the tracks, even though some of us were their neighbors and classmates.

I was thinking about Stephanie. I couldn't stop imagining her under Rev. Maybe this is better, I thought. At least it's clear she's off limits now. Dash should've been here but he was with Rev too. I wouldn't let myself get mad at Rev, just thinking it might get me beat up. I walked over to the friends I had left. Ukala stood off to the corner of the deck listening to Lars speak in his own drunken dialect.

"You can't let her sit on your mouth. It's too much all at once. Let her put her toe in your mouth and let the pee roll down her leg. She's standing over you, so you can see it going down her leg. You have to be careful. Don't drink it if it's black."

"Black pee? Why not?" Ukala mumbled, then chuckled.

"'Coz if her piss is black, it's poison." Lars' words drifted to the party's hostess, a young debutante.

Ukala nodded in agreement.

The debutante broke off her conversation and whispered to her boyfriend as his gaze moved vertically from the floor to Ukala and Lars. Ukala looked like a giant standing next to Lars. Lars had recently dyed his mohawk black. Some of the dye was dripping down the side of his face like the black poison he had been talking about.

Lars had started dating Edgea. Baxter pretended he didn't care, but I knew he did. He had really liked Edgea at one point. Edgea split off from the group and went upstairs. She was in one of the bedrooms, searching through the parents' dresser for jewelry to steal. I saw her on my way to the bathroom. When I got back downstairs, I noticed the girl who was throwing the party walking into the kitchen where she saw Ukala's head in the freezer.

"Can I help you?" she said. And Ukala retracted his head to face her. One of his zits had become infected after he had tried popping it. It was puffy, red and a bit bloody, and he looked like he was dying. His hair hadn't been washed in weeks and he smelled like a dog. She took a step back.

"Wart dar beer," he said. She couldn't understand what he had just said. He looked over her shoulder and saw the keg outside on the deck. He moved past her to get to the beer.

"So what high school do you go to?" a guy asked Pierre.

"I don't go to school. I just got out of Juvie," he said. Normally he didn't bring that up, but sometimes he did it just to get a reaction.

"That's cool," said the boy and then he went back to his friends to make his report. A group of them were talking, and I knew they were going to ask us to leave. The girl who lived there was about to cry. The boyfriend walked over to us with an uneasy expression.

"Do you guys know anyone here?" he asked.

"No," Lars replied with a look of indignation.

"Well, the party's over," he went on, "so if you don't know anyone, you have to go."

"We'll go when all the beer is gone," said Ukala, but it sounded more like "Werel grawl whent there breer isn guner"

The boyfriend retreated in the direction of his friends without another word.

In the corner, three big guys with varsity jackets were looking at something. They blocked my view so I walked over and peered over their shoulders. Charlie and his oversized head was cornered and looked scared. One of the jocks shoved him hard.

"Is there a problem?" I asked the biggest guy, peering into his eyes to see if he wanted to fight. "You guys want something?"

Ukala and Lars read my posture and moved in behind me.

"No man. There's no problem here," the biggest jock said before all three turned and faded into the house.

Paul showed up. I had given him directions earlier in the day. Paul gave me a show, flashing all his new tattoos: "Void" across his chest, skulls down his forearm, and a crucified skinhead draped in a D.C. flag on his ribs. He was covered in tattoos. It looked like a skin-tight suit. I wondered what his rabbi thought, or his mother. She probably wanted me dead for telling him to get them. Over Paul's shoulders I could see the hostess watching Paul with a disgusted look. No doubt she had never seen anyone with as many tattoos. Paul drank a beer and disappeared to use the bathroom. He was going to piss in the hand soap, shit in the bathtub and a variety of horrible things, like sticking a toothbrush up his ass.

The preppies gathered, huddling into a formation to elect a spokesperson to negotiate a bargain with Baxter. Baxter was the liaison between the two worlds of Dupont's Punks and GDS preppies; after all, he had once gone there and he understood them.

"Hey, Baxter, can you take your friends someplace else?" a kid said. I overheard the whole thing.

"No," Baxter said, acting offended. Tall and thin, Baxter looked down on the other kid like he was passing judgment.

"Her parents are out of town. We don't want anything to happen to the house. It was just supposed to be close friends."

Baxter gave the guy a blank expression in response.

"Look, why don't you just take the beer and go," offered the spokesman.

As Ukala loaded the keg into Baxter's minivan and closed the door, one of the skater's pulled up in a car, followed by six others. He rolled down the window.

"Is this where the party is?"

"Sure is," said Baxter. "Don't use the bathroom; someone shit on everything." As we drove away with the last of the beer, the skater and his friends invaded the house.

We went to Glover Park, just above Georgetown, and dragged the keg into a field bordered by trees. We had the park to ourselves. Ukala sat at the picnic bench, hunched over. He had the posture of an old man, even in his late 20's. Dash showed up and, since we had no more cups, he pumped the beer directly into his mouth. I started to get buzzed. Ukala suggested that we take the keg back to his house.

"No, cause that would mean I'd have to drive it there," said Baxter. "We are leaving it here."

"If we leave it here, someone's going to call the cops."

Baxter and Ukala started arguing over the keg. Raised voices escalated to shouting. I was under the impression that the spat would gradually burn itself out as so many of the others had. Baxter and Ukala were competitive and would make it a point constantly to test each other. Baxter, the intellectual, versus Ukala, the intellectually stunted. But on this night, the two started pushing and shoving each other as I tallied off another birthday ruined by my friends. *Why can't these asshole remember it's my birthday? Friends? They don't give a fuck about me; all they want to do is party.* I flew into a rage and threw myself between them as they readied to fight. I broadsided Baxter and kicked Ukala in the chest. Ukala went flying backwards.

"Fuck you assholes!" I screamed, picked up the almost empty keg and threw it deep into the woods. After hollering my last "Fuck yous", I stormed off in the general direction of Mother's house.

I was back at work for my last day of debt. My suit was wrinkled and my tie had never been tied correctly. The faxes were coming and I carried them with little care, seeing the end in sight.

"You sure you don't want to finish out your summer here?" said the office manger.

"I can't. I hate this job and I want to have a few days of fun before school starts again."

"Well, you have done a very good job. Most of the lawyers' kids who get jobs here are lazy and spend their time avoiding the work."

"I didn't know that was an option."

She laughed and I picked up my last paycheck and signed it over to Father. All that work and I was still broke. I went downstairs to the kitchen and filled my backpack with free beers from the vending machine and walked home.

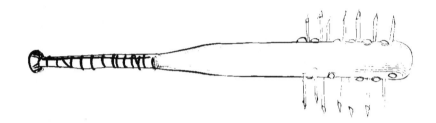

Seeing Red

THE SPECIALS
"Concrete Jungle"
Concrete Jungle, animals are after me
Concrete jungle, it ain't safe on the streets
Concrete jungle, glad I got my mates with me

"Tae Kwon Do is the only martial art as far as the scene is concerned and the only dojo to go to is Master Woo's," said Dash. He was talking to me but looking over my shoulder, keeping an eye on the movement of the people in the room. We were at a party in a run down townhouse in Northeast. After starting classes at Woo's, Dash was never comfortable and acted as if someone was sneaking up on him all the time. Maybe it had to do with Paul shooting him or the fight he got into at G.W. where I got arrested.

He went on, "In Korea, the Master fought in the streets to perfect his skills. During the time he spent in jail, guards both feared and respected him, bringing him hookers and wine. The jail became his home and the guards just houseboys. For a time he taught the South Korean Army and he realized he could make good money teaching. When the Master immigrated to America, he opened a school of his own in D.C., above Tenley

Circle. Another story I heard was that a drunk Redskin football player came into the dojo and tried to pick a fight with Master Woo. Master Woo didn't want to fight him, but in the end he had no choice and sent the guy to the hospital bleeding out of every orifice. Then when the guy got better, he came back and took his classes. That's what I heard."

"I don't know about that, but it's possible," I said. It was like Dash had become a cult member. "Who is the top student?"

"Rev. He has a natural talent… " As Dash said Rev's name, Rev came in the room and we dropped the conversation.

"What's up, fellows?" he said. His voice almost squeaked. With black hair and brown, cold eyes, he stood about five and a half feet. He had recently given up the traditional skinhead style of a shaved head, bomber jacket and boots, now blending in with the rest of the D.C. population. I wondered if he thought the whole skinhead thing was stupid now or maybe he just thought he could get away with more if he didn't stand out. It wasn't my place to ask, so I didn't. We exchanged a few words with Rev but when he saw a guy talking to Stephanie, he left us to stand next to her.

Dash picked up the conversation where we had dropped it.

"Rev is a third-degree black belt. He is the best fighter I have ever seen."

Stephanie was drunk. When Rev and she started to fight, they left and the party ended. Dash drove me back to Mother's. I thought of Rev and the power he held over the scene. Rev got his respect, gave respect, and took it away by taking down giants with their private beanstalks. He was educated and from a good home. He was the alpha male of the pack.

With every fight, Rev's legend grew and so did the number of scenesters who joined the dojo. By joining, you instantly had bragging rights, laced with the threat of violence and backed up by Rev. The students were called the Woo Boys. They wore running suits and Adidas Sambas, black indoor soccer shoes with white stripes - which made them easy to identify. I never studied with Woo, but by wearing the Sambas and the running suit, I never had to. I knew most of the students and now I began to dress like them. People just assumed I was one of them, even if I still had blond-white hair and wore my leather jacket.

Out front of the 9:30 Club, a crowd had encircled two men who were slugging it out. I stood next to Dash, watching. It made me feel a bit sick. I couldn't help but picture myself in the fight. Winner or loser, it didn't matter either way; someone was getting hurt. Blitz was tearing apart his opponent. He sat atop him, punching in furious downward motions. It didn't matter who had started it or what it was about; it never did. Rev watched, chuckling to himself. Overhearing him, Big Steve said, "What are you laughing at, faggot?"

Big Steve stood well over six feet. His race was mixed, giving him skin a few shades darker than white. With a voice that resonated with a buzz, Steve was an imposing figure. A menacing giant, he had been in and out of prisons most of his life. He was crazy and not in the funny way; he was completely nuts, especially when he smoked boat or crack. The drugs were what made him violent and the violence is what put him in jail.

A few years before, Steve had been sent to Riker's Island on charges of aggravated assault in both New Jersey and D.C. In New Jersey, he had beaten a kid into a coma with a baseball bat. Steve had been caught at the Holland Tunnel after breaking a cab driver's jaw.

I remembered my phone ringing. I'd picked it up, hoping it might be a girl.

"You have a collect call from Riker's Island from Steve."

He would have heard if I had refused the call and I hadn't wanted to be on his bad side.

"Yes, I'll take it. What's up, man? How are things?"

"They fuck with me 'cause I'm a skin. So you know what I did?" Big Steve had yelled into the plastic receiver.

"No, what?"

"Do you know what I did?" he'd repeated.

"No, how the hell would I know what you did?"

"I tattooed *skinhead* across my forehead. That'll show 'em. Yeah, then they transferred me into the psychiatric ward. It's great! I'm the biggest guy in here. I run the place."

Mother had put a block on the phone so that Pierre couldn't make sex calls, so I didn't worry about receiving collect calls anymore.

Outside the 9:30 Club, Steve was high on crack and his eyes were wide open like white plates with small black cakes sitting in the middle.

"Little man, what are you laughing at?" Steve reaffirmed his challenge.

Rev didn't bite the bait and walked away, carrying a blank expression. The fight was over. Blitz had won and everyone moved inside to see the headlining band, the Cro-Mags. John Joseph, the frontman, sang "Hard Times," as the crowd danced a mosh. Steve walked past the mini-hurricane of bodies and went downstairs to the bathroom so he could take a drag of the pipe. Just inside the door, someone tapped him on the shoulder from behind. He turned and looked down to see Rev.

"Remember me?" asked Rev.

Steve didn't have a chance to reply before Rev kicked him in the face with a jumping roundhouse. Steve, dazed, was grabbed by his neck and slammed face-first into a porcelain sink. He blacked out. I used the bathroom moments later and saw him bleeding on the floor. I got the bouncer and they took him outside, but he didn't want to go to the hospital.

A few days later I saw Steve. His eyes were bruised, his face swollen, and his nose looked like a rotten potato. He kept wiping the blood with a dirty bandana.

"Maybe you should go to the hospital," I suggested.

"Nah, I'll be fine," he said.

I didn't think I should ask him what had happened, but I couldn't help myself. He seemed eager to tell me about the fight with Rev.

Even losing a fight to Rev gained some level of street credit.

Men who talk about fighting constantly, those who are braggarts, are most often the docile ones when it really comes down to it. To identify a real threat takes skill and patience. No matter what a person's facade told, their eyes always gave them away. Rev's eyes were stone cold and would stare straight past you, even while peering at you. Of all the stories I heard about Rev, not one of them came from him directly. The stories were a part of Washington Mythology. From Massachusetts on down to Florida, the scenes had their own stories of Rev.

Rev perfected his skills and made a cult out of a martial arts studio. As his reputation grew, the kids whispered about him at the shows. The bands, bouncers and bartenders all recognized him. He was as famous as a movie star. The fiercest of fighters curtsied as he passed.

The small clubs, half bar, half venue, were all the same. A bar off to the side, a small stage only a foot or two off the ground with a dance floor in front of it, tiny bathrooms covered in graffiti and stickers. If you were lucky, you might find one of the toilet seats with a lid and seat still attached. Behind the stage was a room for the bands with a case of beer.

I was at a show buying a shirt when I heard another story.

"You from Virginia?" asked the guy. He worked for a band from New Jersey.

"No. I'm from D.C."

"Oh, yeah? You know a guy named Rev?" he asked.

"Yes. I know who he is."

"I once watched him kick the shit out of these guys." He looked around the room to see who else might overhear, then went on to tell me the story.

"New Jersey was the stomping ground of a skinhead gang called the Family. Blitz knocked out one of the gang members with a kick. I was standing outside when the club doors opened and a flood of bodies, all with shaven heads appeared. When they saw their local hero lying face down in a pile of garbage, they got mad pissed. Rev and Blitz ran with sixteen after them. They escaped." When he finished, I noticed that the guy telling me the story looked like a skinhead and I wondered if he was a member of the Family.

I told the Family story to Dash and Baxter as we drove in search of that night's party. Eight cars followed our lead. They hadn't heard the story and to get gossip, you had to give some.

"I have a story about Rev. I was there for this one and it was kinda my fault," said Dash as he popped his head over the back seat.

"Well, go on, then tell us," I said.

"We were at a Caps game." Dash had season tickets and never missed a game. I stopped going with him after he almost got us into a fight with the opposing fans.

"They were playing the Rangers and so I was cheering for the Caps."

"You mean yelling 'Rangers suck my balls!'" said Baxter.

"Yeah, I did some of that, too. So there are these guys in front of us; I mean Rev and me. I brought him to the game. And these guys keep turning around, telling me to shut the fuck up and yelling fucking this and fucking that. They were from New York and came down for the game. So whatever, I keep yelling until the game is over."

"Who won?" I cut Dash off.

"The Rangers, three to zero, but that's not the point. So we walk out to the parking lot and everyone moves out of the stadium together. These Ranger fans are in front of us, yelling 'Let's go Rangers', so I cupped my hands around my mouth like a megaphone and yelled 'Rangers Suck!' The three guys in front of us got mad and turned around and one of them hit me. I fell down fast, I mean really fast. Then right away, Rev started fighting. The first guy was the biggest and had a mullet and was wearing Terminator sunglasses. Rev chopped him across the nose, breaking the shades and his nose. Then Rev side-kicked the guy to his right, who hunched over, and Rev dropped an ax kick on him. His heel landed on top of the guy's head. He beat the crap out of all of them, helped me up and we walked back to the car. He didn't talk about the fight on the way home or nothing. He just said thanks for taking him to the game... It was crazy, like something out of a movie, man."

Baxter was not interested in Dash's story and must have heard it before over and over.

"So what's up? I know you got a story about Rev," I said, looking at Baxter as he drove.

"I got a little something I heard once, but you don't want to hear it," he said looking in the rearview mirror to see if Dash was buying his bullshit, since he had waited through two boring stories just to tell his.

"Just tell the fucking story," said Dash

"Rev had started at Whitman, then transferred to BCC."

"Whitman?" I said.

Baxter went on.

"Montgomery County has two large public schools: BCC and Whitman. With rival football teams, the same kind of kids and the same kind of everything, of course they are enemies. Tom was then the new bully at Whitman. After Rev left, he told everyone outside of school that he was tougher than Rev. When Rev first heard the rumor, he didn't seem to care. But when he heard that Tom had said he was going to kick his ass, everyone knew Rev was going to do something about it, everyone except Tom. In the middle of a regular school day, Rev paid a visit to his old school and called Tom out of his classroom." Baxter took a long pause, then grabbed the wheel with one hand and patted his jean jacket for a cigarette with the other. Finding his pack, he pulled one out and stuck it in his mouth.

"Light me," he said. I pushed in the lighter. When Baxter told a story he needed to have a cigarette.

Dash popped his head over the back seat.

"Go on, tell him what happened to Tom."

"A good story isn't rushed," Baxter said as the car lighter pushed out with a popping sound that delighted Baxter.

"Best music in the world," he said. I pulled it out and carefully pressed it against his cigarette. He sucked in air and the tip glowed.

"Okay, so it was Tom, right?" Baxter liked to pretend he was lost in his own story just to see if we were paying attention.

"Yes," Dash and I said in unison.

"Tom obliged Rev, and met him in the hallway. Without saying a word, Rev kicked him three times in his face, leaving the impressions of tennis shoe treads across his forehead. From that day on, Tom never mentioned Rev again. Tom's nickname became Tread Head or just T.H. for short."

"That story wasn't so good," I said, just to knock Baxter a bit.

The most personal thing I knew about Rev I'd heard from Stephanie.

I was like an obsessed groupie wanting to know everything, but I never asked. That would have been too strange. "He loves his dog, his little sister and his mother. Everyone is scared of him but to me he is just a good guy if you give him a chance. A lot of people who have never even talked to him just think he is stupid. He gets good grades and is planning to go to law school," she said. Stephanie and Rev had started dating. I didn't like it, but there was nothing I could do about it since Rev could kill me and I had ditched Stephanie in Boston. Besides, in a way it made things clear for me. Stephanie was out of the picture, so now there was only Maggie. But then again Maggie was out of the picture too, because of Baxter.

It was the next day and I was driving Stephanie and Kim, Rev's little sister to Rev's house. Stephanie had become good friends with Kim. Stephanie looked good. I should have dated her, I thought. But now she was ruined. Who would want to date her after Rev? I glanced over at Kim. She was cute, too, but you would have had to be nuts to date her, as well. We pulled up in front of Rev's house.

"Are you sure it's okay for us to just go in there?" I asked.

"Stop being a pussy," Stephanie said. I dropped the subject since I didn't like being called a pussy.

Rev's home was a small townhouse in Bethesda, a few blocks from Wisconsin Avenue. I walked up to the door, but wasn't going to be the first to walk in, just in case he was there. This way I might have a chance to run. The neighborhood was quiet. Cars were parked in front of every house. I could hear the trees rustling. I was lost in thought for a moment, but it abruptly ended when I heard the rage of a dog on the other side of the door. Jolted, I grabbed the car keys in my pocket. The girls didn't notice.

"I should stay out here."

"No. We're going to be awhile," said Stephanie.

Kim stuck her hand through the mail slot opening to let Luger have a sniff and confirm her identity. Luger stood guard. We walked in, and the girls abandoned me. I sat on the couch. Luger stared at me, not moving, but baring his teeth.

"Great," I said, and the dog started to growl. He smelled of musk and old chewed wool. Rev's dog was a one hundred fifty pound Rottweiler, named after the German-made pistol favored by the Nazis during World War II. Luger had bad hips, common for large breeds and especially for Rottweilers. He walked bow-legged, like an experienced cowboy. Rev shared the same strut and they complemented each other when they walked, paralleling each other's personality. Guests had to be especially careful when approaching any of the women of the house. *This dog wants to kill someone.*

On the couch, I sat patiently and avoided eye contact. I waited until Stephanie came back.

"Leave him alone, you stupid dog," she said and dragged him by his collar into another room and locked the door.

I felt inspired to get my own Rottweiler.

The next time I saw Rev was at Fort Reno. He stood in the sun, a bit bored. When he looked in my direction, he nodded hello, so I walked over to him. It was like he was the king and he had granted me a moment of his time.

"Hey, Rev, I was thinking of getting a Rottweiler. Do you have any tips?" I tried to keep eye contact, but he made me nervous. I kept looking at my shoes for the better part of our conversation.

"The first thing is to make sure they have papers. You want to know that they have good hips. So ask about papers for the parents, and grandparents, too. There are ads in the Post. When you call, look for a guy who's a professional breeder and not someone who's just took two Rotties and bred them to make a fast buck. A well-bred dog will cost a lot more than a hundred. When you go to check out the dogs, get in the pen with the puppies and pick the one that plays with you. Ones that are squeamish aren't good for you. Out of the playful ones, don't pick the one that's too big or too small. Luger was the biggest of the litter and he's got bad hips." As he was talking, I wondered if he knew I had been at his house, and that's what had sparked my interest to get a dog. Rev went on about the best way to pick a puppy until his sister walked by with a boy neither of us had seen before. Rev's attention shifted.

Even the toughest guys have their weaknesses: girlfriends, sisters, mothers and dogs. Kim was every bit a little sister, tough because she'd learned to fight from her brother, yet beautiful and buxom. With long brown hair and the curves of a woman, she was plenty of trouble for an older brother to deal with. Most of the boys had a crush on Kim and most of them had the same reaction when they found out she was Rev's younger sister: they vanished. At sixteen, Kim wanted to date boys, but her brother's reputation was omnipresent.

"So what's up with Kim?" asked Baxter. Great, I thought. Just what I need. If Baxter tries anything with Kim, Rev will kill him. We were in Baxter's room. The rest of the house was quiet. It was late.

"Listen, you don't want to deal with this," I started. "It will bring you a ton of trouble."

He was flipping through his record collection and was only half listening to my story.

"Kim and her mother were driving down Wisconsin Avenue when two guys from Gonzaga High School drove past and flipped them the bird. When Rev heard that someone had disrespect his mother and sister, he got pissed. He took Kim and went looking for the guys. Bethesda is small, with only a few main roads. It's easy to find people. The guys pulled up to the stoplight in the lane next to Rev's. 'Oh, oh! That's the guy!' screamed Kim. Rev hopped out of his car with a baseball bat. He bashed in the headlights, smashed in the side window and pulled the driver through, then kicked his ass. When Rev felt satisfied, he strolled over to the passenger's side and gestured for the other kid to roll down his window. The kid slowly rolled it down and Rev punched him in the face, walked back to his car and sped off." When I was finished, I searched Baxter's face for any signs of fear, but he didn't seem to care. I'm sure in Baxter's mind he thought Rev would understand, but I knew Rev wouldn't like it.

"I don't think you could beat me up," I said to Stephanie. "Girls are the weaker sex and if I really wanted to, I could beat your ass."

We were at Dash's house in the back yard. The ramp he used to skate was now rotting wood. Charlie and Dash were passing a joint back and forth. I thought September meant it would be cold, but it was still warm. Stephanie circled around to my side.

"You had better watch it or I'll show you," she warned. She was small but tough.

"Come on then, show me," I said. She kicked me in the stomach. I hunched over, the wind knocked out of me. It was obvious that Rev had been teaching her. Whenever Stephanie was around me, my head felt funny like I wasn't sure what was going to happen, but I had to remember she was dating Rev.

"I told you," she said shifting her weight to her back leg. Standing over me she looked like she was posing for the cover of some B movie poster from the 70's. Her long hair covering most of her face and her hand rested on the curve of her hip. She had on white jeans and a skin tight t-shirt that said Slayer. It was torn at the neck revealing plenty of cleavage.

"It didn't hurt at all. A matter of fact, I think it was kind of soft."

She kicked me hard in the shin and I rubbed the spot. It turned me on but I didn't let on.

"Okay, okay, I'm just messing with you. Take it easy." I could barely speak.

Between my beatings from Stephanie, I noticed that Baxter and Kim were taking longer and longer cigarette breaks. At first everything was innocent with Baxter and Kim, but after dropping Baxter off one night, I heard the girls talking.

"Baxter is cute," Kim was saying. I knew it would be trouble from then on.

Baxter and Edgea had broken up over her cheating. Baxter was looking for the next thing. Since Edgea had started dating Lars, Baxter didn't want to be the one alone.

Baxter and Kim casually dated. Their relationship hadn't lasted for even a month, but that didn't matter to Rev. The uneasy feeling of violence simmered. Rev's anger was egged on by Blitz, who'd had his own feelings for Kim or so Dash warned me. I passed it on to Baxter, who shrugged it off. Nothing had happened so he was under the impression that it never would. School had started again and everything in the scene had slowed down during the days we had to be in class. When we had breaks, everything happened fast since there was no school work to distract anyone. I knew something was brewing with Rev and Blitz; I just wasn't sure when it would happen.

I walked over to Baxter's house. We picked up Ukala and drove out to the Yesterday and Today record store in Rockville. In the van, Baxter popped in a tape of Public Enemy. "Terminator X" came on and the build-up to the song started with the sounds of a live show.

Baxter cleared his throat, then said;

"I've been getting prank calls, someone saying they're going to kick my ass, then hanging up. Are you guys fucking around?"

"That's probably Rev getting ready to get your ass," said Ukala. I kicked the back of Ukala's seat so he would shut up.

Baxter noticed. "What's going on?" he said.

"Nothing."

"Is Rev after me?"

"Dude, I warned you… And yes, he's after you. Even Dash told you."

"Rev's prank calling me?"

"No. That's Blitz. Rev wouldn't bother."

"Why didn't you tell me?"

"I did. Besides, I'm at risk just for being your friend. If you get beat up, I'm sure I will too. I'll be standing right next to you and I'll get fifty percent of whatever you get."

Now suddenly Baxter was nervous. Maybe it was the direct contact from the prank calls. Baxter did his best to hide it as he flipped through the record bins. I was nervous for him. With Rev, there would be no opportunity of fighting back and no point. It was best just to take his blows and think about what kind of food was being served at the hospital.

I had no luck finding the Green S.O.A. 7", but I did find a first pressing of an Iron Cross 7" and took it up to the cashier.

"This is a great find. How come it's so cheap?"

"Wendell Blow brings in a box whenever he's low on money so we have lots of them," said the cashier.

Back in the minivan I told Baxter what the cashier had said and asked; "Who is Wendell Blow?"

"He's one of the guys in Iron Cross. Look on the back of your record." I thought of Pierre, since he was the one who had gotten me into Iron Cross.

"I haven't seen Pierre around."

"He's in jail," said Ukala in his way.

"Jail!"

"He turned himself in," said Baxter.

"Why?"

"He said it was going to get cold soon and he needed a break from all the partying. They never would have caught him." That was the funny thing about the scene. You could get wrapped up in your little world and miss what was going on right next to you. Relationships shifted. You could be best friends with a guy and the next week barely hang out, then a month after be best friends again. Give it a month or two and he'll contact me, I thought. What else had I missed? Charlie had left for college. We hadn't had a party or anything for him. I hadn't asked if he'd wanted one, but he'd said he would be back soon. Pierre was in his own style of college, Lorton prison. *He had graduated to the real deal.* I had thought I'd known everything, but apparently I had been wrong. *Sister might be going to college soon too.* I wasn't sure how I felt about that. After Dash and she had dated, I had stopped hanging out with her when my friends were around. I liked keeping her separate.

"Baxter better watch his ass," said Dash. It was a Monday morning in November just before the first bell rang. "Rev and Blitz were waiting outside Baxter's place, holding baseball bats with nails driven through them."

"What happened?"

"Nothing. Some guy came out from the neighbor's house with a gun and chased them off." The body guard for the lady who owns the Washington Post no doubt.

Later that night I called Baxter. "Did you know they were outside?"

"Maggie said they were outside and wanted to talk to me," he said. "I had my twenty-two rifle and stayed in." As if in a Western, Baxter was at the homestead, encircled by howling Indians. The night ended peacefully and the subject seemed forgotten, since a month went by and nothing happened. Rev wasn't seen anywhere. He just vanished, but Baxter was still nervous.

Pierre remained in Lorton Prison. He told me this story in a letter:

Most of the time I spend watching life pass me by in the yard. Whites are the minority. My friend Cross is here. He got busted for armed robbery. One day, Rev walked into the gym. I was surprised to see him there. He seemed like the kind that didn't end up in jail. He took a slow stroll around the gym. Right away Cross sees him and wants to fuck with him. I told him you don't want to be messing with him. Cross said, fuck him. The next morning Cross saw Rev again. Rev was in the weight room. Cross was about to do something. Other guys were waiting to see what happened. Rev stretched out, kicking his leg upwards until it grazed his own face. Then he wandered over to the punching bag and kicked it with such force that its seams ripped and stuffing came out. Cross lost interest and everybody left him alone. But if it was any other guy, his ass would have been fucked.

New Year's Eve

1989 FUGAZI
"Waiting Room"
I am a patient boy
I wait I wait I wait I wait
My time's like water down a drain
Everybody's moving everybody's moving
everybody moving moving moving moving
Please don't leave me to remain

It had been more than a month when the rumors stirred about Rev's absence.

"I heard that Rev beat the hell out of a big time lawyer's son and got caught," said Dash. His teeth were so white; Dash could be a toothpaste model, I thought, as he talked. "You should ask your father."

"My father wouldn't tell me shit if it violated attorney-client confidentiality," I said.

"But it's not his client."

"Wouldn't matter."

"At Woo's, I overheard Blitz talking to the Master, and he said that Rev worked out a deal and served a month to avoid any serious marks on his record. He's been in a million fights and got one month for just one."

"This is like when Tiny got busted and then no one cared who she was in the scene."

"This is totally different. Everyone respects him more. Think about it, man." Dash leaned in. "He went to jail and they didn't fuck with him there. It's just like the stories of Master Woo when he was in jail. Rev's a real legend." From Dash's expression I could tell he idolized Rev; I did too. "Rev will be here later. He got out a few days ago. I saw him at the dojo."

Dash's eyes followed a girl as she walked into the room carrying a cup filled with foam and some beer. He grabbed my hat and threw it at her. It bounced off her back. She stopped and turned around to see who had thrown it. I wondered if this was the kind of stunt he'd pulled on Sister.

"Sorry about my friend," Dash said to the girl. Then he looked back at me with a smile that said, "Don't be a dick, man!" He walked over to the girl, picking up the baseball cap with the Cro-Mags patch on the front. He put it on his own head and turned it to one side. The girl smiled and they started talking. It was New Year's Eve and I wasn't close to being drunk.

"Whose house is this?" I asked Stephanie. She had brought me.

"Two rich Iraqi girls," she said. The house was large and far out in Potomac, Maryland. It was an odd assortment of mods, punks, skins and rockers. Everyone important in the scene was supposed to be there. Even Fiona had shown up. She had pestered me about where everyone was going, so I'd invited her. Then Rev, Blitz and some of the other students from Woo's showed up. They had been drinking sake with Master Woo. Last I had known, Rev had had a problem with Baxter and Paul. They were both there at the party. If they'd wanted to, Rev and Blitz could have settled all of it that night.

When I knew for sure they were coming, I told Baxter.

"I can't hide forever," he said.

"I'm not saying hide forever, just until things calm down."

Anywhere I stood, I was within a few feet of someone Rev wanted to kick in the face. Baxter kept gravitating to me. Maybe he was unsure, too. I wanted to stay away from him. I moved a few feet over. Paul was busy playing a game of pool with a cluster of new skins from Maryland. I overheard a friend of Paul's ask him if he knew Rev.

"Yeah, I know him," said Paul in a low voice.

Holding his cue stick, Paul puffed out his chest a bit as he steered the conversation to anything other than Rev, hoping to avoid a problem. Rev staggered up to the table, drunk on sake, and slapped down a hundred dollar bill over the corner pocket. I moved away from Paul. Paul's gang of young skins watched Rev, sneaking side-glances, and talking in whispers. It was like they were little girls eyeing a cute boy. Paul's expression became serious. Rev moved behind Paul and leaned down to line up his eye with the stick and ball Paul had made ready for a shot at the corner pocket.

Rev leaned over the edge of the table. "It's yours if you make the shot, or..." he said, pulling out a boot knife, "Miss and I cut your throat." Rev's words were slow and sloppy.

Paul swallowed hard, drew back his arm, taking his time to carefully line up the stick with the cue ball, guessed the best angle to hit the solid 7 and deflect it into the corner pocket. His head hovered over the table and the stick. His arm, stretched across the green felt, was covered in a tangle of lines revealing skulls morphing into roses as they reached his wrist. The other skins, standing around the table, were quiet. Paul closed his eyes and then took a deep breath. Opening them, he quickly took his shot and missed. It wasn't like Paul couldn't take the beating - his head was rock hard - but if Rev kicked his ass, Paul's reputation within the skin scene would be done.

"Sorry." Paul stood up and looked at Rev for what was to come.

"Next time." Rev snatched up his money and staggered away.

The shortest of the new skins nudged Paul in the ribs.

"That was fucking cool," he said.

"Shut up, asshole... Let's go!" said Paul and he left, trailed by his gang.

Continuing his strut around the room, Rev stopped when he saw Baxter. I happened to be talking with Baxter, and again I backed up a few feet. Nothing had been resolved between them. Stephanie went over to Rev. "Please don't hurt him. He's a nice guy and nothing really happened between your sister and him." If Rev was too drunk to remember, Stephanie had just reminded him. Stephanie always had had a big mouth. Rev seemed unaffected by her. Baxter didn't run, Rev made his way over, then stopped in front of him. Rev lifted his eyes up to meet Baxter's, who was five inches taller than Rev.

"I know you fucked my sister." Rev was holding the knife in his hand. Baxter hadn't had sex with Kim, but pleading that case was pointless. So he didn't bother denying it.

I was watching them from a few feet away and was picturing the outcome: Rev kicking Baxter in the face or a back flip and a karate chop to Baxter's throat. Baxter falling over dead.

"I was going to kill you, but now I think you're alright," said Rev. He slapped Baxter on the back and then put his arm around Baxter's shoulder.

Baxter relaxed and prepared for a long and boring talk with a drunk.

"Three, two, one! Happy New Year!" the crowd screamed and I stole as many kisses as I could from all the cute girls, even the ones who had boyfriends, like Maggie. But the only one there I wanted to kiss was Stephanie, and for a moment I caught a glimpse of her looking over at me. I wondered if she was thinking the same thing. Rev made his way over to her and tried to kiss her on the mouth, but she turned her cheek away from him.

At 1:30 in the morning, Edgea kicked in a window of the garage. Paul had smeared dog shit on the door handle of Dash's car before he left with his gang. Fifteen minutes later, at 1:45 am, Lars and Edgea broke into the car of the girl who was having the party and took her backpack. She wouldn't find out until the next day. At 2:15, Rev started fighting with Stephanie. He seemed helpless against her anger. Rev was trying to get her to make out with him. She wouldn't. She asked me to escort her to her car. She never gave me a chance to say no, she took me by the arm and led me out.

"We just broke up," she said.

"Just now?"

She nodded. But she didn't seem upset. In fact she seemed happy.

At her car she stopped and peered into my eyes, reading me. I reverberated with a kind of calm. She hugged me, trying to force her way deeper into my embrace. Then suddenly, lines of worry creased her face as she peered over my shoulder.

"I think I saw something moving in the bushes," she said. I didn't see anything, but I had a creepy feeling like we were being watched. Something shifted in her; she distanced herself from me, then got in her car and left. As I headed back to the party, Rev emerged from the shrubbery where he had been hiding since following us out to Stephanie's car.

"Come here!" I heard him whisper.

A moment of panic swept over me as I was dragged into the bushes.

"We'll jump the next guy who passes by," he said as we huddled in the dark. I could smell the sake on his breath. It seemed like a long time, even though I knew it wasn't.

Charlie's oversized head rounded the corner. He was home from college for the holidays. Charlie had a magical ability to put himself in the wrong place at the wrong time. He still hadn't recovered emotionally from the beating Tiny had given him. *Why did I let him join my gang?*, I was asking myself when Rev started to shift his footing.

"No, he's my friend!" I let out. Charlie heard us, stopped and tried to see who was behind the bushes.

"Hello?" He said somewhat timidly, glancing around nervously the whole time.

Rev, though very drunk, nodded in understanding, to my relief. Usually he didn't beat people up without having a reason. Rev had to be pushed into violence. At least with Rev, anyone had a slight chance of applying rational thinking.

We came from behind the bushes. Charlie was surprised.

"What are you guys doing back there?" Charlie was smiling, implying it was something gay.

"Nothing. Let's go back inside." I was looking at Charlie; he was still smiling. Maybe I should've let Rev kick the shit out of him.

"You want a beer?" I asked Charlie.

He shook his head in an exaggerated gesture.

"No, I'm not drinking anymore. I'm Straight Edge."

"Why? All those guys who become Straight Edge, I just don't trust them. As soon as they stop drinking and doing the drugs, it's like they fill the void with talking shit."

"I'm not like that."

"We will see." I drank my beer and looked around the room to spy on Fiona, who was talking with Rev and Baxter. She probably wanted to date Rev. At least that way the scene might respect her. She needed to be the center of attention. Even from where I was standing, I could smell her overpowering perfume and see her heavily mascara'd eyes fluttering at Rev. Rev seemed uninterested or drunk.

"I just heard a good story about Rev... Come on, man, tell me what you guys were doing?" He barely spoke above a whisper.

"Nothing."

If I told Charlie the truth, he wouldn't drop it. At some point, he would bring it up to Rev, who wouldn't remember anything. Rev would ask, who said he wanted to beat up Charlie and Charlie would tell him I said so. Then there would be trouble for me.

"I heard he bricked some redneck last week," said Charlie.

"Oh yeah, what happened?"

Charlie looked around, just to make sure Rev wasn't standing right behind him and then told me the story.

"Rev and Eric, the singer for Stilz, were talking on a corner when a pick-up truck drove past carrying two mullet-styled rednecks from Virginia. One of them yelled, 'Fuck you, nigger!' from the truck as they turned the corner. You know Eric is a black guy. Eric was angry, though not worked-up enough to do anything about it. But Rev was pissed. Later they drove past a gas station where the same pick-up sat. The two rednecks stood next to their truck, pumping gas. Rev and Eric parked around the corner and walked over to them, and then one of the country boys turned and recognized them. "Hey!" was all he could blurt out before Rev smashed his face in with a brick." Charlie pretended he was throwing a brick at the back of the head of the kid standing near us. "Man, that's got to hurt," he said, spilling it all out in one breath. "I have another one–"

"I think I've had enough stories for one night." I suddenly came to the realization that it wasn't cool. It was like I had overdosed on the Rev myth. I looked around the room. Everyone either respected or feared him. For what? I thought. Dash wanted to be him. I looked down at my shoes. I had the same ones as Rev. I wanted to put my old boots back on. I had lost myself in Rev's world. What had he done, other than beat up people? I looked at Rev. He was just like Sermon or Highwater, just another bully. I knew it was easier to get along with him, but from that day on I didn't care about the stories. "How's that college thing going for you?"

"It's great, man," he said. "There are so many hot girls. You should go."

"Are any of them fooling around with you?"

"No."

Bang!

SHAM 69
"Hey Little Rich Boy"
Hey little rich boy
Take a good look at me

"Hold this." Dash lit a pack of firecrackers and handed them to me. "God damn it!" I threw them out the window and they exploded under the car behind us. Dash and Baxter laughed. The caravan of six cars behind us swerved to avoid the last few crackers.

"Whose party is this?" I asked.

"It's a Dischord party behind the National Zoo," said Baxter. Dischord was the record label in Washington that catered to Emo bands, a spin-off of the Punk Movement. The Dischord shows were peaceful, with a hippy-dippy theme of pious protests, fundraising and boycotts. They held their events at small churches or community centers, in basements under dimly lit blue fluorescent lights. The kids who went to the shows, played in the bands or worked for the record label were called the Dischords. The Dischords were already a shade of pasty white, but the fluorescent lights turned them a sickly green. I had never been to one of their parties and was curious. Outside the minivan the street was painted yellow by the lamps overhead. It was cold out and the pedestrians wore thick winter coats. It was the end of January. They looked like beetles scurrying along.

"Slow down," said Dash. I looked up the road and saw a little old lady walking her small dog. Dash pulled a pack of a hundred crackers from his bag and lit them.

"Dude! Don't!" As I was yelling, he threw the pack out the window and they landed a few feet behind her. The old lady dove into the bushes and her dog ran away as the rattling of deafening pops went off all around her. I watched from the back seat and followed her as we drove on, pushing my face up against the rear windshield, but I could only see her feet and sock garters sticking out from the ivy.

Dash pulled out the next pack of a hundred firecrackers, pulling the wick out at the bottom and lighting it. A spark shot off and he tried to toss it faster than he was ready to. Instead of going out the window, it bounced off the top of the door and landed in his lap.

"Oh fuck! Fuck! FUCK!" said Dash, and Baxter joined in when the crackers fell all over him. It was like someone was shooting off a machine gun inside the minivan. It filled with smoke and the smell of gunpowder. "Oh, it fucking burns!" screamed Dash. The minivan crossed the double line and I started yelling, "Watch the road!" Baxter pulled the wheel sharply and we avoided the car in the other lane.

We pulled up to the townhouse. The music inside rolled out and down the slope of the grass. An orange glow pulsated from the windows and underneath the front door. The surrounding street was oddly quiet. Pierre's mother's house was down the block. His image lingered in my thoughts for a moment. Dash stood next to the minivan, brushing the bits of paper off of him and looking at the back of his shirt, where he had char marks.

"The inside is covered in burns," said Baxter.

Walking in the door, I saw Blitz standing at the end of the room like a bodyguard. Rev sat on the couch, watching Fiona, his new girlfriend, dance with another man. The cars following Baxter found their parking spaces and the rest of our friends walked in, doubling the size of the party.

"Hey, check this out!" Dash unlatched his belt, wrenched it from its loops and gripped it by the buckle.

It whipped, snapping around my mid-section. His belt was typical of the uniforms of boy scouts and military personnel. It was simple in design, made from a strap of heavy canvas attached through a buckle and loop made of metal. Crack! He did it again.

"Fuck, man, what did you do that for?" I yelped.

"Today's lesson," said Dash proudly.

One of Woo's theories was that everything had the potential to be a weapon: a piece of glass, a belt or even a brick. Survival in the streets was the focus of every lesson. Master Woo taught street fighting, to fight dirty and brutal. Woo believed that nature was a murderous place. To survive, you had to attack first.

Ian, singer for Nation, was dancing with Fiona. Watching her, I knew she hadn't changed. She was incoherently drunk and hanging onto Ian to keep herself from falling, and at the same time doing her best to come onto him. It was sad and pathetic. She was a bad drunk. Dischords chatted, smoked and drank in the corners of the run-down townhouse. The wooden floor creaked as Ian spun Fiona. She took a low dip; he barely kept from dropping her. Dash went into the kitchen to search for leftover beer. The party had reached its peak long before we had shown up. Rev sat by the window, quietly brooding.

"Hey Rev, what's up?" I asked. He looked like he needed a friend and I felt bad for him. I knew what it was like to date Fiona.

"Nothing. Can you give me a ride?" he asked.

"If Baxter lets me borrow the minivan."

"Hey Baxter, can he borrow your van?" Rev said to Baxter. Baxter threw me his keys.

The party was over and I had nowhere else to go. Besides, I was too afraid to say no and Baxter didn't mind waiting. As a matter of fact, it would give him a reason to stay longer. Rev walked over to the dancing couple, now buried in each other's arms, and took Fiona by the hand to tear her away.

"Why are you always ruining my fun?" Her words slurred and slipped into a low mumble.

Rev, Fiona and I all climbed into Baxter's minivan and headed to Bethesda. I was surprised Rev hadn't beaten Ian, but then again, Fiona had an ability to weaken us men. She was beautiful and buxom, but slowly decaying. Her arms had become fatter and I knew the rest would follow soon. She wanted to wield her body as a weapon against us for as long as she could. I rolled down the window a bit. Her perfume was making me sick. The ride dragged. She tugged at the bra strap under her tight t-shirt. Rev was blindly staring out the window. Fiona saw me watching her in the rearview and smiled at me. My face wilted.

"Why did we leave?" Fiona whined. "I wanted to stay. Where's Ian? This car smells like someone's been shooting off fireworks."

Rev didn't say a word. When we got to Rev's house, he carried Fiona out of the minivan without forgetting to say "thanks" and shut the door.

A few days later, my phone rang.

"It's Dash. We're going for a ride. Do you want to come?"

I was debating what to do that night. There weren't any shows, no parties. I was thinking it might be nice just to stay in and beat off or listen to some new records or both.

"Who is we?" I needed to know before I would commit to anything. I had had plenty of nights with Rev and wasn't in a rush to have another.

"Blitz and me," he said. Rev's sidekick.

I didn't like the picture in my head, where I was sitting next to Blitz in the back seat of Dash's car and at the end of the night Blitz would want to stay at my place. Maybe that's why Dash wanted me to come.

"No, I'm staying in waiting for some girl to call," I said. There wasn't a girl, unless Maggie or Stephanie called out of the blue.

A few days later Dash would tell me this story. It was the last time we would speak. From time to time I think about it like this: Dash was hunched over the wheel, searching the street that crossed before them, but his concern didn't lie with traffic. "Over there. There's one," he said. He turned the car in the direction of a bum who was bent over a trashcan, picking through its contents at the bottom.

"Slow down," said Blitz, as he pointed the barrel of a paint gun. Pop, pop. A hollow sound of air banged through the metal tube and bounced off the inside of the car. The first shot hit the outside of the trashcan. As the bum pulled his head out to see what was happening, he was hit by the second shot in the ass. He fell over onto his side, not sure what had just happened. Laughter erupted from inside the car as they pulled away. They drove down Connecticut Avenue and turned left into Adams Morgan, driving past a gay bar. Pulling over to the curb, they came to a stop.

"Hey, how do I get to Dupont Circle?" yelled Dash.

A man walked over to the car, rested his hand on the door and leaned towards the window. Blitz raised the barrel of the gun parallel to the man's eye and squeezed the trigger. Gas filled the tube behind the neon green ball of hardened wax. The ball whipped through the air, striking the man in the bottom half of his left eye. Green paint marked the spot and began filling his eyeball as he dropped to his knees. Watching as the man curled up on the sidewalk and thinking it was a real gun, witnesses called the cops. The man was permanently blinded in his left eye.

Dash and Blitz were cruising the gay bar scene and had shot two other men before blinding the last. The Woo Boys thought the cops would consider it nothing more than a prank gone wrong and they'd get probation. It was Dash's first arrest. But the District Attorney pushed to prosecute the case as a hate crime. Blitz and Dash were looking at jail time ranging from thirty-five to forty years.

A month passed. In the basement of Father's house, the phone rang. I picked it up and heard Baxter's voice on the other end of the receiver.

"Turn on the TV to Channel Four," Baxter's tone was flat, his words precise. "Dash is on the news." *What kind of foolish thing could he have done to be on the news?*

Images of Dash's house, photos of him, and his neighborhood had been assembled into a montage.

"He was a nice, quiet young fellow," commented one neighbor. It was obvious they didn't know him.

The broadcast generically summed up his life; a yearbook photo portraying a plastic existence in which he looked particularly wholesome. There were photos of him from when we'd first met, chubby, with curly blond hair and a pair of thick black rimmed glasses. In under a minute, it was over. "His body was found in the late afternoon," said the reporter.

I sat on the floor, still watching the TV, but not seeing anything at all. I felt detached. It was like having someone drive you around. I was watching the world pass by outside the passenger window and wasn't a part of it. Then the car stopped and I was forced out into the cold rain, a hard rain that whipped through the air and stung my face. I was sitting in the living room. Something inside me crumbled. A cold shiver went up my spine. I felt desolate loneliness.

The awful truth began to sink in. The same thoughts pinballed through my mind, an endless game without a high score, just tilting and starting over. He was lost. "Lights out. It's all over. There is nothing after death," is what Mother had said, and I hoped she had been wrong. *It wasn't fair. He had his whole life in front of him. Who had done this, and why?* I couldn't clear my head. It was full of questions that wouldn't be answered. *Had he been murdered by someone he'd known?* I felt sick.

"What's the matter, son?" Father was trying to see my face and I was doing my best to hide it from him. I told him about Dash's murder and he had seen it on the news, too.

"I'm sorry, son. You're at an age when these things happen. You can't stop it, and no one deserves it, but sometimes bad things happen. I feel sorry for his family, but I'm glad it wasn't you." He gave me a hug and told me if I needed to talk, to come upstairs, and then he disappeared. I didn't talk about things like that with my family; I just kept it to myself. I ate it, and it became a part of me.

I went upstairs and told Sister. She was the reason we were at Father's house. She thought we should both go over to make sure Father was taking care of himself, buying food, paying his bills and the other things he sometimes forgot. As I stumbled through what I knew about Dash, I choked on the words. She sat on her floor looking up at me. She didn't say anything even when I asked her if she was okay. Her moon didn't come out. Her eyes were calm and steady on me. She didn't like to show emotion before, but after Dash's death, her reserve was even more extreme. I never heard her sobbing or crying. She wouldn't talk about Dash. She shut down and stayed in her room. I could tell she was deeply affected. It would be later that I noticed the change in her. It was subtle at first, a determined expression, a snide comment regarding political correctness, politics, or human rights, race, gender or class. If you argued the point, she would shake her head dismissively. It was as if she wanted to save the world, because she had lost one friend. As she grew older, her beliefs became hardened and she detached from the rest of the family, withdrawing into her extreme liberal existence.

The next day, Charlie called and filled me in on the details of Dash's death. Out on bail, Dash had let the killer into his home, feeling comfortable enough to turn his back on him. Wearing socks and a running suit, Dash ascended the stairs and was shot several times from behind.

Turning to face his killer, he raised his hand, trying to block his head. The last shot went through his hand and hit him above his eye. His killer took his time, carefully locking the door behind him.

Charlie then said, "I heard Dash pleaded guilty and was going to testify in front of the Grand Jury. He would have gotten a reduced sentence of eleven years."

Rumors swarmed. Woo's students imparted to detectives that shortly before Dash's death, he had witnessed a large-scale drug deal at the hotel where he had been working. These accounts pointed fingers in every direction except at the most likely suspects: Dash's own friends at the dojo. I kept going over everything. Charlie had said Dash had let the killer in and had turned his back on him. It had to have been someone he knew. Someone at Master Woo's?

Without Dash's testimony, the District Attorney had no case against Blitz for the hate crime and all charges were dropped. A thick curtain of silence fell around Master Woo's. The subjects of Blitz or Dash were off limits.

Stephanie and Dash had been close since she had dated Rev and she took his death the hardest, but made it a point of never publicly showing it. When questioned by the detectives, Stephanie gave them her true opinion: that Blitz and Rev were somehow responsible for Dash's murder. Ever since we had been kids, Stephanie had never hesitated to speak her mind. I was proud of her. The Woo Boys closed her out of their circle. But that was okay with her; she didn't want to be around them anyway.

"I left my bag at Rev's house," said Stephanie. She had just showed up at my backdoor at two in the morning. I was in my boxer shorts. She didn't seem to notice. What was left of the moon hung in the sky as our only witness, and its light made her features softer and more beautiful. I wanted to take her in my arms, lead her into my room and lay with her under the covers. But it was clear she needed her distance.

"Do you need it, the bag?"

"No, but I don't want them to think I'm scared," she said.

"You should be."

"I'm going."

"I'll go with you." I wasn't scared for myself. "Do you want to come in?"

"No."

"Do you want to talk?"

"Don't you want to talk?"

"About Dash?.. No. I can't." I said. *Not yet. It hurts too much.* I didn't want to start crying again, not in front of her. I had to be strong.

The next day, we drove over to Rev's. I sat in the car. The sun glowed behind a bank of clouds. His place seemed evil now. Stephanie got out. Inside I could see the jerking of a window curtain as if someone had been watching us drive up.

Then Fiona darted outside.

"What do you want, traitor?" she said, looking at Stephanie. Fiona's nostrils flared and her brow sloped. *Why had I ever thought that this person was attractive?* I had the feeling this had more to do with Stephanie telling me that Fiona had cheated when I had been at boarding school than anything to do with Dash. Or maybe because Stephanie had become everyone's darling on the scene and Fiona didn't like her getting all the attention. Fiona just didn't care unless it had to do with her.

"Dash was your friend, too," Stephanie pleaded. "Why are you doing this?"

"Dash sold Blitz out for a shorter sentence." She wiped away the mustache of perspiration above her lip. "He deserved what he got."

"How can you say that?" she said softly. "I just want my stuff, then I'll be going." There was an almost palpable sense of sadness from Stephanie

"No one has your shit, bitch! You better get the fuck outta here if you know what's good for you!" Fiona hollered.

At Rev's door, Blitz came out and stood watching. He gave me a menacing stare and folded his arms across his chest. I could make out Rev's profile watching from the shadows of the window.

"Let's just get out of here." I said, and got out of the car and took Stephanie by her arm, leading her back to the car.

Fiona followed as we pulled out onto the road.

"We know everything you said, you bitch!" she yelled as they drove off.

Stephanie's body shuddered, then she started to cry. I had never seen her cry.

"Its going to be okay," I said.

"Isn't that what you're supposed to say? I haven't had to deal with this before. I don't know what to do. I want to stop hurting. I don't want you to cry, but I don't know how to stop it."

She leaned on my arm and wept.

"How did they know what you said to the cops?" I asked. "Isn't that stuff confidential?"

"I know who told them. Rev's friend, Sermon."

"I knew a Sermon." I was surprised to hear his name. "There was a Sermon who used to throw my bag out the window at the Lab School when I was seven. Did he used to go to the Lab School?"

"Yeah, it's the same guy. I remember him too."

"He's a cop?"

"Yes, and he used to be a skinhead. He's a good friend of Rev's."

"You better stay away from these guys."

"I'm fine," she said. *How could she be so adult? When did she become a woman? She is so strong. I want to be strong like her.*

Sermon

"Come on, man. Get out of your bed," said Baxter. "Who let you in here?" I wasn't sleeping but didn't feel like moving either.

"Your sister let me in." I pulled the sheet back and sat up on the edge of the mattress. I had clothes on but since I had been lying on my stomach and face most of the afternoon, the wrinkles made it look like I had been asleep. Sister was worried about me. I suspected that she had called Baxter and had him come over to check on me.

"I'm sorry about Dash. Come on. Get your shit on and let's get out of here," he said and was done with the subject. Baxter wasn't fond of expressing emotions and when he did, we both felt uncomfortable. Emotionally we were still boys and didn't know how to talk about serious things without feeling uncomfortable. I wouldn't see a therapist; that had been tainted. I saw it as punishment because of the times when the court had sent me to a therapist after the break-in and when my parents had gotten divorced. I looked at my floor at the bits of scrap paper. Q- o- T- s- L. Individual letters cut out of magazines and silhouettes left from photos. I had removed the images. The scissors lay open next to the glue. I had been making my own flyers of fake bands. Sometimes I would go to Baxter's and use his copy machine. Then Baxter drove me around the city so I could staple them up.

Fits of Rage
Bloodwiser
Gang of One
At D.C. Space
Saturday Night, October 29th
Doors open at 8 p.m.
All Ages

I didn't want to play in a band; I just liked making them up. Charlie had once showed me one of the flyers I had put up, saying, "Check these guys out. I hear they're really great." He hadn't noticed the photo of Baxter, Ukala and me. I walked into the bathroom with scraps of paper sticking to the bottom of my feet. Sitting on the toilet, I pulled the scraps off. I had started the new flyer before Dash's murder and didn't feel like finishing it. I showered and met Baxter outside.

Driving down to the 9:30 Club, I didn't talk and watched the city move around me. We drove down M Street. Dash and I had walked that same street dozens of times. I could imagine Dash's gangly strut and him spinning around to catch a look at the back side of a beautiful girl we had just passed. Dash could be so cocky when it came to girls. *I wish he was here.* Baxter glanced at me, noting my change in clothes. I was wearing my leather jacket and Doc Martin boots. I didn't want to look like a Woo Boy anymore, so I'd left the running suit and Samba shoes at home. We passed the White House, then turned right, passing the Treasury Building. Secret Service cars were parked on every corner. The men inside looked bored. Parking down the street from the club gave me a few moments to gather myself before seeing everyone else. I was nervous on the way. I got that way before a show, as if I were going to perform. People stood outside of the club. We stopped at the doors and I looked around for friends or enemies. I didn't see any of the Woo Boys and relaxed a bit.

Monday after school, Edgea picked up Baxter and me and we drove out to the airport, past the Pentagon. There was a field at the edge of the runway. It was dusk and unseasonably warm for March. I had on my leather jacket and baseball cap. A few others were parked there, doing whatever they did in parks at night.

"Come over here." Edgea limped ahead. "It's great."

We walked up to the chain link fence and lay down in the grass, looking up. It was a clear night and the lights from the city were far enough away not to be a distraction.

"This is where I go whenever I feel like I just can't take it anymore," Edgea said, turning to look at the sky for a plane. "The trick is, how do you push out everything you can't stop thinking about?" She stopped and the rumbling of the jet grew.

"Here it comes," she said, then laid back down. "Just keep looking up." The noise was deafening and I started yelling just because I could and no one would know what I was saying.

"FUCK YOU! YOU CHEAP FUCKING WHORE! YOU FUCKING BASTARD! FUCK BLITZ! FUCK REV! FUCK DASH! FUCK OFF!" I tilted my head up and the world was upside down. The belly of the plane looked full and ready to set down on us. It moved close and I felt its weight. The DC-10 floated by and landed a few hundred yards from us with a skidding sound. We drove back to the city. It was quiet until Edgea spoke.

"I'm sorry about your friend Dash."

I felt sad but I smiled instead.

"Have you talked with his mother?"

I shook my head.

"It must be hard for her."

I shrugged. I couldn't go to the funeral. I didn't want to see his casket.

"Where to next?" asked Baxter. He was trying to protect me by changing the subject to anything other than Dash. I just wasn't ready to talk about him, maybe I never would be.

Stephanie sat behind the counter in a blazer and a respectable skirt that didn't flatter her at all. It was Tuesday after school. She didn't look right, like a beautiful bird trapped in an ugly cage. I wanted to set her free. Lars was ambling down the aisle looking at the plates. His mohawk stood up for once. We were at the Georgetown mall on the top floor in a little glass boutique where Stephanie worked. Plates lined the shelves and walls. They were garish and hideous at the same time.

"I wish I'd never dated Rev," she said, looking down at the glass plate she was cleaning.

"I feel the same way about Fiona," I said and then wished I hadn't, knowing it would bring up memories of Stephanie telling me the same thing. The truth was that Dash's death had changed the relationship between Stephanie and me and now it was filled with sadness. She reminded me of his murder and I wanted to forget. But then again, everything reminded me.

She closed the shop and we went down to Dupont Circle. I thought of Edgea being raped here and tried to put it out of my mind, but things like that seemed to linger in my thoughts. Stephanie noticed I was quiet and asked if I was okay. I said nothing.

It was Thursday morning and I had been sent to another school again for one of those tests the city made me take every three years or so. The public high school was in the roughest part of the city, Southeast. Walking down the hall, I saw that the lockers were warped, as if someone had taken a sledgehammer and beaten them. Yet the floors were mopped and the walls were free of graffiti. In the office I waited for the security guard to take me to some small room, away from the student body.

The test began with the same psychobabble bullshit I had heard as a kid. Word association, where I was shown cards and had to describe their meanings.

Understanding the dynamics of the test was simple. If there was a picture of a man sitting at a desk and I said, "It looks like a man waiting for a fax, as his life slowly drains away," it was scratched off the list. Next he placed a board in front of me with levers, bolts and other physical labor-type stuff. I pretended to be slow or not to understand the way to unscrew a bolt. Construction and jobs that required physical labor were scratched off the list. This test was different than the ones I had done before. Why were they centered around subjects that related to work?

It was lunch when the guard walked me back to the office. I hadn't seen any other students. I hadn't heard them anywhere in the building.

"Here are your choices, son," said the lady behind the counter. The guard had a gun on his hip and wore army greens. "You can eat your lunch with the rest of the students or you can eat it here in the office. It's safer here and we would rather you stay here, but it's up to you."

"I'll eat here." I took out my peanut butter and jelly sandwich. The white bread had flattened out and the jelly had leaked through. It was going to look the same in my belly, so I ate it.

"What is this test for?" I asked the lady behind the desk.

"It's an aptitude test."

"What is that?"

"It figures out what kind of work you would be good at."

I didn't know what I wanted to do.

"If you want to go to college you can, or you can stay here and get a job." Mother's words rang in my ear. It was almost a threat: Go to school or go to work! A job? Hell no! But college! Would that be any better?

When lunch was over I went back to the test. The photos were flipped and I deciphered them.

"A man touching other people's crap and breaking his back, while the people in the house watch him throw their garbage into the back of the truck. The people in the house are laughing."

Flip.

"A crazy man who becomes a psychiatrist so he can work through his own problems."

Flip.

"A man who spends his life training for the big battle and when it comes, he's the first one killed by a sniper's bullet."

Flip.

This picture was different. The man was smiling, holding a magic wand and with a rabbit popping its head out of a top hat. I looked up at the guy giving me the test and he looked a bit frustrated. I wondered what had happened when he'd taken this test. Had he seen a picture of a man giving a test? I turned my attention back to the picture he was holding up.

"He looks likes he's having a grand old time and he loves his work," I said, and it brought a smile to the tester's face.

"The artist," he said. I hadn't thought about it until he said it like that. "Entertainment or the arts," I said driving home, and it felt good. The test wasn't for them to find out something about me. I'd had it backwards. It was for me to find out what I wanted, and I felt good. I had spent my whole life thinking about the things I couldn't do, acting like the retard they wanted me to be. Then I had gotten into punk rock and it had been the only thing that mattered. Then Dash had been killed and I'd come up for air. There was a world out there that I hadn't seen and suddenly I had sight. But what did I want? What could I do? What could I get away with doing and be successful at the same time? I had liked the art class at boarding school. I liked to make fake band flyers, too. Making art meant I didn't need to read and write. I would have to think more. There wasn't an easy answer, but I knew the direction - art.

Marginal Man played Friday night. I had a few of their singles, but it was the first time I had seen them. The amphitheater on George Washington University's campus was the wrong space for a punk concert. The seats were bolted to the floor. During the show, most of the punks stood on their chairs or crowded the small space between the stage and the rows. I shouldn't have been there. I was banned from the campus after having been arrested with Dash for the fight. But I went because I knew Dash would have wanted me to go. It was like giving a giant middle finger to G.W. I kept an eye out for any of the chubby campus security guards who had caught me the first time, but none of them were there. After the show, I went out front for a few rounds of chit chat to make my presence known on the scene.

There was a city cop staring at me and I wondered if I had been spotted by someone from the university.

"You went to the Lab School, right?" he said. He was a barrel-chested man with short cropped hair in a military style cut.

"Yeah." Shit, did I have a warrant?

"Sermon," he said. I gave back the expression of a question mark. But I knew exactly who he was. He was the one who had told Rev everything Stephanie had said to the detectives. I got a bad feeling but shook it off. He was an asshole and had always been an asshole, I thought. But he was a cop and it was better to be friendly since he had the power.

"I was a few years older than you. I took your book bag and threw it out the front window onto the steps. You know, the Lab School."

"Yeah, I remember. You're not going to throw my stuff out a window now are you?"

"Do you have anything for me to throw?"

"No."

"Next time, then."

Ukala looked at Sermon and me and wondered what was going on.

I looked over at Sermon's patrol car and noticed he didn't have a partner. I asked him why.

He said, "It's about presence. The city wants it to look like there are a lot of cops without having to pay a lot of cops."

The crowd outside of the venue dissipated.

"Hey, do you think you can arrest me and throw me in the back of your car?" I asked. "Maybe drive me around the corner and let me out? It will freak out my friends." Ukala was still watching me from a distance, too afraid to come over.

"I might beat you over the head with my night stick and throw you in the trunk."

"Nah, forget it." We shook hands and Sermon got in his car and left.

"Whoert dert that?" said Ukala.

"Some cop who just asked me a whole lot of questions about you. Don't worry man, I told him that you are a drug dealer, and probably have a lot of acid on you."

Ukala took out his tabs of acid and ate them.

A week had passed, and I was at a show after school on Monday night. It was Gray Matter and a few of the Dischord bands. They were playing at a church just off of 16th Street. It was a show to protest apartheid in South Africa. When I went outside I saw Sermon again. He waved me over.

"What's happening man?" he said. Not shitbag, but man now. I guess I had moved up in the world.

Out of the corner of my eye I thought I saw Paul walking hand in hand with Stephanie. I turned and could see the back of a couple. It could have been them but I wasn't sure. No, I thought. She would never date Paul. I turned back to Sermon. He was looking over my shoulder for hot young punk chicks. "Did you know Dash?" I asked. But of course he did, he had thrown his books out the window for years.

His look said it all. He didn't expect to hear that name from me. Then it came to him. Dash and I were friends.

"I'm sorry about what happened to your friend. I got to get back to work." He held his hand out for me to shake. I didn't. I left and went home.

Mother came down to my floor and knocked at the door. She was carrying pamphlets and a sandwich to distract me. I took the sandwich and pretended not to see the pamphlets.

"Here are a few colleges to think about. School of Visual Arts is in New York City. They have film, fine arts, photography and graphic design. Rhode Island School of Design has a similar program and that's right near my sister's and parents' so I could come up all the time. NYU has a good film and acting program. And the last one is a culinary school with a hotel course where they run a real hotel." They were all out of town. Maybe Mother wanted me to get away from D.C. Getting away sounded good.

"I was thinking of taking some courses here at the Corcoran School, to see what I like and build up a portfolio."

"I think that's a great idea."

Mother smiled at me. I took a bite of her sandwich and smiled back.

"Okay kiddo," she said and went upstairs. I turned on the TV. The news was on and since I didn't have a remote, I left the channel where it was. Television had been my babysitter ever since I could remember. When my parents had been married, they would drop Sister and me in front of it and leave us to play or fight. I had put it on and not watched it most times. I'd just liked the noise. The voice of the broadcaster had made it feel like there was someone in the room. I hadn't liked being by myself.

"A mini-mart robbery gone wrong when a police officer walked in on the crime as it was happening." I flipped through the SVA pamphlet. On the television screen was a mug shot. The face looked familiar but at the time I didn't recognize that it was Cross. I put away the pamphlets and walked to Smash. Paul was standing out front smoking a cigarette and looking around like he had done something bad, or maybe was waiting for someone. His head was clean-shaven and the acne stood out.

"What's up, man?" I said and we knocked fists.

"Dude, did you hear about Sermon?" he said. He followed me inside.

"Yeah, I just saw him." I picked up a test pressing of Bad Brains and flipped it over. There was nothing on the back. "He's a cop."

"No. He just killed some dude!"

"No shit." I put the record back in the bin and turned to Paul. Blitz, Rev, who?

"No shit. It's all over the news."

"When I heard he was a cop, I wondered if he did it just so he could harass more people. Being a cop is the bully's dream."

"But wasn't he a skinhead?" said Paul.

"It's the same fucking thing. Being a skin works like prep school for the military or police department. They dress in uniform: bomber jacket, jeans, combat boots, heads shaved, and they have an attitude for the fight." I was pointing at each item Paul had on as I talked. "Skins are organized into gangs with a hierarchy that trains them to take orders." After I had finished, I noticed my statement had bummed Paul out so I softened it a bit. "But you're not like that at all, man. You're alright." I lied. It was the same for all skinheads.

I walked back up the hill towards Mother's house and thought about Sermon. The Woo Boys were the mini-Mafia of the scene and Sermon was their police informant. I called Stephanie's house. Her mother said she was in Georgetown meeting a friend. I thought that was funny since I was her only friend who lived here. Why wouldn't she have called me? Later that night she called me back. I told her I had run into Sermon and about the shooting.

"Internal Affairs found out about him telling Rev and Blitz about Dash and warned him," she said. "He took the warning seriously and tapered down his association with Rev."

"How do you know?"

"I still have a few friends at Woo's."

A week later, walking into Poser's, I showed the doorman the driver's license that I had re-stenciled and re-laminated. He let me in. At the bar, Sermon sat nursing a beer. He wasn't in uniform and I didn't recognize him until he waved me over.

"Yeah, it's a good day for down time," he said and I sat next to him. We went a few rounds of the boring talk, but I knew he had more to tell me so I didn't ask any of the obvious questions. I let him get to it when he was ready. He wanted a friend and I just wanted to be witness to his pain. I didn't need more friends, not after Dash.

"You know I killed a man?" he said without looking at me.

"Yeah," I said and then he told me his story.

"I went to the mini-mart to pick up a sandwich. I didn't lock my patrol car. I remember thinking, 'Who would steal a cruiser?' I smiled at a kid on a bike. The kid smiled back. That felt good. Most of the black kids just run from me."

As he spoke, I pictured it. I saw the sun beating down on his face just before he opened the door and the street and surrounding houses. It was as if I were there, watching like a surveillance camera.

Cross saw Sermon coming into the mini-mart in his cop uniform. Without warning, Cross fired the first shot and it hit above the door. The sound was loud, like a sledgehammer hitting a sheet of metal a few inches from your ear.

"I fell behind a row of bread, not hit but also not sure what had just happened. The second shot blew through the bread and passed out the front window, shattering the glass," he said.

"Motherfucker, I'm a fucking cop!"

"Why you think I'm shooting at you, man," Cross yelled back.

Sermon looked around the store and saw the drawer from the cash register on the floor. The customers were already down with their heads covered. He pulled his gun and crawled around the back of the aisle. Cross was still aiming at the spot where he thought Sermon was. The clerk looked over and saw Sermon's feet and butt sticking out from behind the rack of magazines.

"Hey!" shouted Sermon.

Cross turned and fired. Sermon fired back, emptying his gun. Cross was dead. Sermon sat on the floor and waited for the clerk to call the cops. Detectives working the scene took Sermon's gun, noting the clip was empty. "It wasn't like on TV," said Sermon. "I was a mess. Food and crap all over me. I was drenched in sweat and light-headed, my ears were ringing. I still hadn't eaten but was sick to my stomach. The last thing I wanted to do was talk about it. I just wanted to go home and get real drunk and pass out."

As Sermon talked, I thought about Cross. I wanted to tell Sermon I had met Cross and that Cross was a piece of shit who deserved what he got. But I didn't want to interrupt and perhaps it would have just made him sadder.

"I'm suspended with pay while they investigate the case, but that is common with shootings involving the police. The only question that needs to be resolved is how many shots I think I fired versus how many shots were actually fired." He finished. I noticed he hadn't been drinking any of his beer.

I would later find out from Stephanie and her friends at Woo's that at the close of the investigation, he was cleared and returned to active duty. But Sermon lost his heart for the job and quit the department to become a private detective. He spent his time in bars, drunk on his own sorrows. I would always be nice to him, but secretly I was glad he was suffering. He was upset about killing a man, but did he once think about Dash? What was the difference between a man he never knew and Dash?

The Beach

Baxter, the self-styled adventurer, would often surrender to the call of his restless spirit, and the result was always a spontaneous road trip. Destinations were decided hours before our departures, but sometimes changed mid-trip. Baxter was always the driver. After all, he had the perfect Punk Rock vehicle: the minivan. At that time, minivans were an oddity. They never became the "cool" ride they'd been advertised to be. An all-American family was expected to pop out of one, but instead degenerates exited. The tips of Baxter's long blond liberty spikes spread out from his head and brushed against the inside of the door. Pierre slid the side door back; his shiny clean-shaven black head looked like a buffed eight ball. He had just gotten out of prison. Ukala climbed out after Pierre. Ukala stood erect, towering over us, his face covered in bad acne even though he was much older than any of us. I stepped out of the shotgun seat; my orange hair was so bright it might've been on fire.

Before we embarked on the road trip, our first stop was Dupont Circle to pick up acid and beer. Apparently they always got their acid at the Circle.

"You sure you want to do this?" asked Baxter. He usually hid his drug use from me but now I wanted to try acid too.

"Yeah, I want to."

"Okay. You can always change your mind." Baxter's task was to get the acid while Ukala, being the only one of legal age, collected the beer from Habib's deli. It was a few blocks from the Circle and a few steps below street level.

I thought about the acid sitting in my pocket as we drove. Something needed to change. *Trying acid was new, at least.* I didn't think it would make me happy, but it might change something. I didn't know what. Maybe I felt a little self destructive? I was dealing with pressure from Mother about college, Dash's death, girls I wanted to kiss, and I was lonely. I wanted to date Stephanie, but knew I had blown that years ago. She had called me that afternoon and left a message for me to call her back, but I hadn't. What was the point? She wouldn't date me.

We took Route 50, which beelines straight from D.C. to Ocean City, Maryland, and headed onto the Chesapeake Bay Bridge. Pierre put Screwdriver into the tape deck.

"Nigger, nigger, get out of here! Nigger, nigger swim!"

It boggled my mind that Pierre, a black skinhead, loved Screwdriver, a Neo-Nazi White Supremacist Oi band from England.

Snickering, he said, "No one cares what they say. The music's good. Besides, for a fat white guy, he sure sounds like a black soul singer."

"Should you even be going to the beach?" I asked, "Doesn't your mother want to see you?" After all, he had just gotten out of jail again.

"She came to see me inside. Where were you?"

"Sorry. I had a few things on my mind."

"That's fine. Hand me a beer."

As we started our ascent on the bridge, Baxter demanded that everyone down a six-pack before reaching its end, so we would have a proper buzz on before we reached Ocean City. The alcohol content of Milwaukee's Best gauged in at slightly above that of water. Chesapeake Bay Bridge is long; it takes over 10 minutes to cross it at normal speeds and 45 minutes if there is traffic. At nineteen years old, I had been training for challenges exactly like this one every weekend in my backyard with a beer bong. One of us would clutch the bong high in the air while pouring a beer or two into a funnel connected to plastic tubing that would cause the beer to travel into your mouth. Gravity did its work. Onlookers envied those who could master a six-pack in one go. I managed to accomplish this once, only to puke most of it up a moment later.

In a moving vehicle on an upward slope of a bridge, beer bongs are inappropriate and difficult to handle, so I resorted to shot-gunning four cans. It didn't bother me to drink as long as Baxter was driving and right now I wanted to forget everything, especially Dash.

"Did you hear that Paul and Stephanie have been hooking up?" said Baxter.

"Der hot Girl?" asked Ukala.

"Yup," said Baxter.

"Bullshit," I said.

"He must have drugged her, or maybe he's paying her," said Pierre. "There is no way she would go along. He plays with his shit!"

"I'm just telling you," said Baxter.

What the fuck, I thought. She knew I liked her. Maybe this was her way of getting even with me for not dating her when we were kids. I looked out the window down from the bridge at the naval base and the battle ships far below. I can't do a thing about it now, I thought. I grabbed another beer.

"You know who asked about you?" said Baxter.

"Who?"

"Maggie."

"Your sister?" Her image floated before me. Black hair with bangs cut like Betty Page, but she was younger and hotter. Her skin porcelain white, with features perfectly arranged. She smelled of cotton candy. I thought of her nuzzling me in the minivan on Saint Patrick's Day. I was suffused with joy for a moment.

"Yeah, you should take her out."

"What are you, fucking nuts?"

"You don't think she's hot?"

"I do, but you're her brother."

"So? That stuff never bothered me. In fact I think it always bothered you a little too much. I trust you and I know you will watch out for her. What would be better? Her dating some asshole or having you over all the time?" Maybe he was trying to make me feel better. It was working.

"I'll have to think about it." I needed to change the subject. "I had a strange dream last night," I said. They were listening, so I continued. "It wasn't like a cartoon. Everything looked real. It was an old zoo. But there weren't any people, just animals. It was a prison for animals that were criminally insane. All the guards were hundred-year-old, vegetarian tortoises. They were very smart but slow. When they wanted to move a prisoner, they had to put on shackles that were chained to the turtles' backs. If the prisoner didn't want to put them on, the tortoises would just wait and slowly say over and over, 'put them on.' It would drive the animals nuts, but after a week or so, they would just do it to shut the tortoises up. The prisoners were mostly meat eaters but there were a few elephants. The rule was: it was okay to kill animals for food, territory or mating, but not for pleasure."

"How do you remember all of that?" said Baxter.

"I don't know. I just do. So let me finish. So there was this one bear. He was big, not as big as the grizzly, but still big. He was gnarled and missing hair. One of his eyes was bigger than the other and he was lumpy and misshapen from muscles that were in places they shouldn't be."

"It's standing up?" asked Pierre.

"Yeah, it is. All the animals take on this human-like thing. So this bear was playing basketball with a bunch of the prisoners. A cobra, grizzly bear, black bear, mountain lion, gorilla and so on. All different kinda tough animals. But this fucked up bear got the cobra all upset. The cobra was ready to bite when the bear blasted the snake in the face with the ball, killing it."

"I like that," said Pierre.

"This bear was smart and dangerous. And somehow it escaped."

"How?" said Baxter.

"I don't know, but it just did. It's not important. Anyway it was riding in a yellow pinto like the one my parents had when I was a kid. This smaller, normal bear was driving and as they talked, the smaller bear realized he'd just picked up a scary fucking dude. That's it. That's all I can remember."

"Where is the ending?" said Baxter.

"I dream in stories but they are never complete."

"It would make a good cartoon," said Pierre.

"Maybe... all the animals had strange shapes. They had small heads, big muscles and were mean-looking. And I could tell that there was going to be a hero who tracked this bear down. But I didn't get that far."

"You should write them down," said Baxter.

"When I was like, eight, I would tell them on the school bus."

"That's one fucked up story," mumbled Ukala and then I realized he looked like the psycho bear from my dream. "Maybe you need a shrink." He started to chuckle to himself. I punched him hard on the arm.

It was sunset when we arrived at the beach. Darkness was already starting to settle. I carefully placed the small square of paper on the back of my tongue, and moments later tasted the acrid chemical in the back of my throat. *Maybe I shouldn't do this. What if I freak out? You can't start thinking like this or you will have a bad trip for sure. Baxter said stay positive and everything will be okay. Besides, it's too late now.* We finished the last of the beers.

I turned to Pierre and said, "Do you really think it's a good idea to take the acid when you just got back out?"

"Yeah, sure. They would have to test my hair for that and I really got none." As he spoke, he made a pass with his hand over his clean head.

Ocean City was made up of bikers, rednecks, homeboys and all around derelicts of varying degrees. The boardwalk was jam-packed with gift shops, arcades, bars and joints selling funnel cake, cotton candy, hot dogs and soft ice cream, with names such as "Rusty Jack's," or "The One-Eyed Clam Bar." Rebel Flag towels and Budweiser inflatable rafts swung in the breeze in front of the surf shops. The boardwalk stretched out along the beach for ten miles and we sauntered to its very end.

"Do you feel anything? I don't feel anything." Baxter updated me every few minutes. I felt normal, maybe a little drunk.

"I have to piss. I'll be right back," I said and walked to the bathroom with Baxter shouting at me, "Don't split up the group man." The neon sign outside of the arcade looked alive as my eyes licked its edge and followed the line in the letters to its end. I didn't feel a thing and I thought I was ripped off on the acid. My stomach felt a bit off and I let out a rather long fart. The bathroom was made of cinder blocks and painted an institutional lime green. A young boy sat outside with an odd grin, the corners of his mouth spread almost to his ears. I was a bit frightened but still needed to piss. The boy nodded at me and I realized I had a large smile on my face that I just couldn't shake. I walked in and a big man with bad posture vanished into the supply closet. *Fuck. Have I walked into a dungeon or a torture chamber? Or was it the acid?* I felt like I was in my dream at the zoo for criminally insane animals. I stood at the urinal and had no problem pissing. The mouth of the urinal hung open without a tongue. I stepped back, fearing it might swallow me. I finished my piss with a high arch that reached the edge of the urinal. The room was empty and the stalls looked like cells. I tried not to look at them but I couldn't help myself. *Fuck. Just act normal and walk out. Could I just walk out?* I wasn't sure anymore. The walls pushed in and the exit shrank. I wanted to head for the door but stopped at the sink to wash my hands and calm down. *Would the kid outside let me just walk away?* Looking in the mirror, my reflection looked back at me and said, "You're okay man. You can leave." I smiled and felt better but wondered if I was talking out loud. I found the group and told Baxter not to use the bathroom.

"Do you feel anything?" he said.

"Yeah. Things are getting a bit strange."

"My stomach is bothering me. So I know it's working."

Pierre and Ukala sat on a low wall and, after a few attempts to move them, I gave up.

"Look at the colors," said Baxter.

"Hey what's that?" I pointed at one of the games inside the arcade that had spinning wheels where you tried to get your quarter to knock more quarters off a shelf. Baxter followed me into the arcade. Reds appeared more vibrant. His pupils dilated to the size of planets. I could make out everything, even in the shadowy depths. Each pixel of the video game bounced around with its own life. Baxter's gestures became freakishly animated. Everything was still based in reality, but fun and alive.

"Don't you feel a connection with the people who have tripped around the world in the past and future, like the Indians using peyote, like the tribesman in South America and Africa? We are connected to writers like Hunter S. Thompson. It's different yet the same. We are experiencing the same feeling at the same moment as thousands of others are around the world. Can you feel it?" I looked at Baxter and realized I may have been talking non-stop for twenty minutes.

"Dude, I'm tripping my balls off," he said and I knew he had heard little of what I had said.

Ocean City is a legendary hick town. Hicks were everywhere, moving about me, ghosts with dumbfounded expressions lacking any sense of style, wearing t-shirts that read, "I'm the beer patrol - Stand still as you watch me drink your beer", or, on the back, "If you can read this, then the bitch fell off the bike." They must have bought their clothes from a Salvation Army's bargain bin. Sunburned and fat, their breed had always fascinated me. I noticed a redneck giving me hard looks. I couldn't decide this for certain. I was out of my mind at that point. I was also in the middle of an intense game of Whack-a-Mole, my favorite beach game. Moles popped out of wooden holes and as they appeared, you had to smite them down with a mighty hammer (which was actually nothing more than a club with a tightly sewn pillow for a head). Whack-a-Mole allowed me to be the God Thor. I wasn't a punk or a dyslexic, I was a master at Whack-a-Mole.

"Hey Mister, if I pay for your game, do you think you'd play for my kid? All he wants is the stuffed lemur," asked a sunburned woman a foot shorter than me, but twice as wide. I turned to her; my eyes were black and sucking in the light as I swung my face down to hers, letting out a loud, satisfying fart.

"Sure." The lady looked scared of me and took a step back but still reached up to the kid towering over the Whack-a-Mole and handed him the dollar for two games.

Her son got his lemur, three times larger than the one he'd initially wanted. Still transfixed by the game, I continued playing, convinced a stuffed purple grape was whispering my name. But it was just Baxter having a joke on me.

The redneck with a staring problem was now wearing my patience thin. I couldn't focus on the game. I felt his stare on my back. I waited impatiently for him to provoke me in any way. But instead, he pretended not to see me when I was looking right at him. I trailed him around the arcade for a bit, making eye contact the whole time.

I was accustomed to getting harassed for the way I dressed. Walking the streets of Northwest Washington, Metro buses would pass me by and kids would scream "Nice hair, freak!" from the window. If a car drove by with an entire family, they'd turn to gawk. For the most part, I embraced this negative attention and often sought it out. Growing up in Chevy Chase, I had spent enough time as a faceless, bored kid waiting for something exciting to happen.

I looked for the redneck but he was gone. People just disappear when you're on acid.

Outside, I walked over to a bench which had a backrest you could pull forward or backwards, depending on the view you wanted. I pushed the back toward the ocean so I could watch the boardwalk, and sat down. Baxter joined me, sitting high with his ass on the backrest and putting his boots down where you were supposed to sit.

"It's sandy," he said as we watched people walking by, families, dudes looking for dates, high school kids, college kids and troublemakers. I only wanted to see hot young redneck girls who dressed trashy. But when we tried talking to them, it hurt our brains listening to them. "Y'all from dar city, aren't ya?" a fifteen year-old asked me. She was half dressed, but I only noticed her bare parts. Her friends, two girls with teased and frizzy hair pulled back in scrunchies, started calling her and she ran off.

"Let's walk down some. Go see the beach," I said and stood up. We walked down the boardwalk and I heard a rumbling behind me, but was afraid to look.

"Maybe we should find Pierre and Ukala? The people here are fucking weirdos." I turned to see if Baxter was listening and instead of Baxter, there was a man pulling his kid in a beat-up wagon. Behind him trailed a fat wife and behind her were two more kids. The man looked beaten by life and walked by like a zombie without noticing me. They looked more like the crazy bear from my dream, slowly lumbering along. The wheels of the wagon rolled across the boards, making a creepy sound. I walked back and found Baxter staring at a machine with a giant claw that was lowered by a crane and grabbed at the tops of stuffed animals.

"Dude, I just saw a little girl win a bear bigger than she was. Is this thing real or in my head?" he said.

"I think it's real. You want to try it?"

"Hell, no." There was a pay phone nearby and I had an urge to call Stephanie. But what would I say? I had no claim on her and I wasn't going to badmouth Paul. He didn't deserve that. In fact, he should have a good girl, I thought, just not her. *Fuck, I'd probably introduced them when we were kids.* I had a faint memory of them shaking hands and Paul acting oddly polite. Ronnie Motherfucking Collins would have said, *"Don't worry about that motherfucker."* Dash would have said I should tell her that I liked her, at least. Maybe I should go to college and get away from everything, I thought.

Eventually the crowds dissipated. The buzzing hum of fluorescent lights died as they blinked out. Gates rolled down with a crash. Only the dregs still staggered on the boards. After the arcades had all closed, we journeyed down to the beach, where I found entertainment dodging the waves, sprinting back and forth, letting them just get close enough to lick my boots.

"Hey, watch out!" Baxter yelled out.

"I'm okay," I muttered, mesmerized by the beauty of the moonlight shimmering off the ocean. Caught in a trance, an enormous wave I had been watching, yet whose path I'd forgotten I was standing in, hit me.

When it receded, I was left soaked from the waist down. Filled with sand, my boxer shorts transformed into sandpaper that wore away at my ball sack. "I'm done with the beach." I walked back to the boardwalk.

It was still dark. We walked around for a few more hours. Cops walked past us looking for someone who would give them a reason to be pricks, but we knew how to avoid them: just keep walking like you're going back to a hotel, not Baxter's minivan. The sky began to show light blue at the edges of the horizon. It was our warning to go back. Walking back to the parking lot at the end of the boardwalk, I saw the back of Pierre's perfectly egg-shaped head. He was sitting with Ukala, whose posture was so bad that when he sat he seemed folded in the middle. It made him appear shorter than the rest of us. They were on a cement wall next to the beach.

"Where the hell have you guys been?" said Baxter.

Ukala turned around first, still drunk, and mumbled in his own language.

"I don't know where the hell we are now. How am I supposed to know where I have been?"

"I'm still feeling the acid," Pierre chuckled to himself and fell off the wall. I looked at the storefronts and realized it was the same spot where we had left them. Baxter grabbed Pierre by the arm and helped him to his feet. In the minivan, the dashboard clock read 5:37.

I was crashed out, lying in the back seat. I couldn't force my eyes closed; it must have been the acid. At least that's what Baxter thought when he said he also couldn't sleep. Baxter drove around through the beach's residential neighborhoods looking for the quickest spot to park as the seagulls screeches mocked my sleepless night. Damn them, if only I could wipe out those flying vermin, I thought, night would reign forever. The last effects of the acid presented an epiphany and I thought of the reality of my life divided between day and night. There was a whole world that thrived under the sun. I had a great disdain for the sun and the well-rested, happy families with their children making the racket one hears, standing outside of a playground. *Those damn kids are worse than the birds.* But was I missing out? Soon I would be out of school and would have to be up early, unless I took night classes or found a night job. The strange creatures, those day people, walked by the minivan on their hikes to the beach and caught a glimpse of the carnage that marked the end of our road trip.

"It's safe in the minivan," Baxter said, trying to get comfortable in the driver's seat, then dozing off to sleep. As I drifted off, I wondered what Dash would have thought of me dating Maggie. Then I imagined Maggie next to me, smiling. It was comforting.

Maggie

THE REPLY
"Wake Up (socialism in E minor)"
Who can we turn to now
they've got us where they want us
wedged underneath the bow
of a ship made of brick
beached up on the shore

"It's after five and you're still in bed?" Mother said from my doorway. After school I had come home and taken a nap. "I signed you up for a printing class on Thursday nights and a beginners drawing class on Saturday mornings."

"Saturdays. Why Saturdays?" I had planned on calling Maggie and was thinking of asking her to hang out Saturday.

"Because it was the only day available." She walked down the hall, carrying laundry. Rolling onto my back, I stared up at the ceiling wondering if art was worth giving up Saturdays for. Sticking my finger in my ear, I found sand from the beach.

Corcoran School of Art had its main building downtown, with a few other classrooms around the city. The print class was at night. I did my time in high school, went home for a few hours to eat and then went to my night class. The teacher ran us through the basics of a few forms of printmaking. I focused on silk screening. After taking an image and making it into a transparency, I placed it on the screen. The screen was covered in an emulsion that was sensitive to bright lights. Placing the screen on the light table with the transparency between the light and the silk, I flipped on the switch. Air was pumped out and once the motor cut off, I knew there was a tight seal. I set the time and pushed the button. It sparked and made a crackling sound. The light came on after a few failed attempts. Spots not covered by the rubber allowed rays of light to escape. It seemed close to the sun in its intensity, but tinted a light blue. The buzzing and the light died when the timer ran out. Carrying the screen, I leaned it on the back of the large sink and picked up a hose with a nozzle on its end that forced the water into a powerful spray.

"It's very strong and can cut you, so be careful with that," said the teacher, who then made his way to the next student. I didn't believe him, or I just wanted to see for myself, so I put the tip of my finger in the way of the spray. It felt like a knife. Examining the tip, I noticed tiny cuts from the water. Water turned into a knife, I thought. That would be a strange weapon. I aimed the water gun at the screen and washed away the emulsion that had not been cooked by the light. The image appeared of a soldier carrying a baby. I had taken the photo from a Time Life book. I sprayed the rest of the screen, which revealed the other elements of a graveyard and a background that I had designed to be in different colors.

I built up the image into something new. The soldier was carrying a longhaired child through the graveyard with a sky of reds, oranges and yellows. I numbered each print, starting with the best one of 50, and signed my name in pencil. I kept a few prints and gave away the rest to friends and family. When I first finished that print, I was happy with it. But after a short time, I noticed the imperfections and started thinking of something new.

I called Maggie on Sunday. I tried on Saturday but Baxter answered. I felt weird asking for his sister, so I went record shopping with him. Plus Lars had said to me, "Wouldn't that be like dating Baxter? It would be like you were fucking Baxter, you fucking sicko!" Would it?, I thought. They had the same eyes, but other than that, they didn't look alike. He was skinny and tall, with naturally blond hair, and she was shorter than me, beautiful, with dark hair, almost black.

"I'll get Baxter for you," she said when I finally got her on the phone.

"No, wait a minute." I choked, a frog in my throat. "I'm calling for you."

I could hear her pulling the phone from her ear, then my words stopped her. Her voice came back to the receiver.

"You are?"

"We should hang out." Hanging out was the same thing as a date, but without the pressure. I had just bought a used maroon P200E Vespa scooter. There was no parking downtown where I was taking class at the Corcoran. I convinced Mother that I wouldn't get killed. She agreed, as long as I wore the helmet she had gotten me. The scooter had cost $300; the helmet had cost $350. It matched my scooter. I rode it over to Maggie's house and parked in front. I looked up at the box shaped building. White clouds looked as if they had been pulled across the sky by invisible giant hands. I rang her doorbell, hoping Baxter wasn't there. I could feel my heart beating up in my neck. *What if their mother opens the door? She probably won't let her come out with me. Maybe this is a mistake? But what am I going to do, sit home and think about these girls? Why are you being such a pussy? Man up and be cool. All the times you thought about her naked and now you might have a chance, don't blow it.*

I could hear the lock rolling over. The knob turned. I knew Baxter wanted me to take her out, but what if it didn't work out with Maggie? She opened the door, looked past me to where my scooter stood and then back to my face. She smiled. I hadn't noticed before the freckles that bridged cheek to cheek across her nose. They invited a kiss for each one, but I resisted the urge. I climbed on the scooter; she got on the back. I started the bike and it stalled. She giggled. On the second try, we were off, speeding down R Street toward M street. She was holding on tightly. It was a good day, warm for that time of year, but going fast kept us cool. We were headed towards the Potomac. I wanted to cruise next to the river, and turned down Wisconsin Avenue, below Georgetown. I stopped at the light on M Street and thought about the day I'd bought the scooter. I had been told that the back brakes needed to be replaced, but since I mostly used the front brakes, I'd put that chore on my mental list of things that would never get done.

The light turned green. I let the clutch out. I hardly ever stalled at that point and my confidence had grown. The engine roared out of its putt-putt to a mean hum and we moved forward. I always looked both ways, even down passing side streets. Mother had said, "Assume you're the best driver in the world. You still have to watch out for everyone else." That's when I noticed a car moving where I didn't think it should be. A woman failed to stop at her stop sign. We were going to collide. I added new brakes to my 'Get Done Now" list.

The accident was exactly how people always describe one: everything moved in slow motion. The woman's car pulled out into the intersection and directly into our path. Knowing one set of brakes wasn't going to be enough to stop us, I made a quick decision. I could slide into the car, taking the impact to the left side, which would send Maggie crashing headlong into the car. Or I could keep my path and slam directly into the car and act as a cushion for her, but I wasn't sure how I might fare. It didn't look good for me. I would rather have been crippled than have her harmed at all. Slamming on the brakes, the back of my scooter lost contact with the street and shifted itself into a front-end wheelie. Maggie pressed into me and I slammed into the car, my head bouncing off its roof and my knees colliding with the leg guards of the Vespa. It was over. Dazed, I picked myself up. *This is what it was like for my parents when they got hit by the drunk driver.*

"Is she okay?" I just kept repeating myself until someone led me over to the steel supports of the highway overhead. I sat down. He was a man only a few years older than me.

"She's fine, but you look like you're in a bad shape. You slammed into the car. You're very lucky that you had that helmet on," he said, and I thought of Mother. I hadn't even wanted the helmet. Thank God for Mother, I thought. She'd saved my life, but I needed to see if Maggie was alright. Maggie ran over to my side. She was fine and so was I, with the exception of my knees, which were bleeding into my white socks. I didn't care about the socks, or the blood; I just wanted Maggie to be okay.

"You should go to the hospital," said the man.

"No, I'm fine, just cut up a bit. I just want to go home."

The witnesses on the scene had pointed out that the woman had failed to stop. Lucky for me, no one noticed that I had no real brakes. The woman ended up paying for all the damages, including my new set of brakes. Sometimes it's good to be a lawyer's son. We left the scooter to be picked up by a tow truck and I took a cab back to Mother's house. The sky surrendered it's blue to dark, gray clouds. Maggie followed me into Mother's. We stayed in my room until it was late.

"Maybe you should call your mother or Baxter?" I said.

"It's okay. Baxter knows I'm with you."

I saw flashes of lightning outside and heard the thunder that followed. The rain came down and it was warm and cozy inside. The storm and the accident gave me reasons to hold her tight. I felt at ease. Her mouth pressed against mine. Her lips parted slowly, methodically. We rolled our tongues over each other's. I could feel the heat of her breath brush my upper lip. Our hands discovered each other's bodies over our clothes. She trembled under my touch. *All the times I had seen her making out with other boys and now I'm doing it. Don't blow it. Don't tell her how beautiful she is or how long you liked her. Remember what Ronnie Motherfucking Collins had said.* "The trick to getting some hot motherfucking chick to like you, motherfucker is not to let that motherfucker know. It's like they smell motherfucking fear and eat that shit. Treat her with respect motherfucker, but don't be no motherfucking sucker either."

"Did you just say something?" she asked.

"No."

"It sounded like you said motherfucker?"

"No sorry I was–" She shut me up by sticking her tongue in my mouth. I was pinned against the wall. My hand moved up to the side of her face. Her cheeks were flushed and her lips swollen from being kissed non-stop for the better part of two hours. Her eyes darted between mine. She undid the buckle of my pants and then tugged them down part way. I took them off, then undid her slacks and helped her pull them off. I had learned things from Fiona and Sally. I shouldn't have been nervous, but I was. She touched my erection and everything I was thinking slipped away.

"You're so beautiful," I murmured, practically unaware.

"I know," she said. She was tugging softly and pulling my hips closer. I reached behind the mattress where I had a secret stash of condoms and fumbled to get one on, hoping she wouldn't change her mind. Then quickly I was inside. She arched her back as if she was making room inside herself or was adjusting to the new feeling. I peeked at her and she made a face I had seen Baxter make. It freaked me out a little so I kept my eyes closed. It wasn't like the other times. It wasn't dirty like it had been with Fiona.

The next day I hobbled out of my bathroom and found a package on my bed with a label from the School of Visual Arts. It was Monday morning and I was already late for school. I didn't care. Nothing could put me in a bad mood. Maggie's lingering cotton candy smell hung in the air. I picked the package up and felt its weight. It was more than the paper inside. It was a choice that might affect everything. I opened it and read the acceptance letter. I still wasn't sure if I wanted to go.

Details of My Misspent Youth

I locked Maggie out of my house in an attempt to give her a moment to calm down from the hysterical state she was in. It was two weeks later. Our relationship had gone through the gamut of emotions so quickly that I was baffled when it came to dealing with her. I was nineteen. She was seventeen. Looking back on it, I now realize that teenage girls have the same chemical imbalances that teenage boys do. Her emotions were so tangled that at one point she started crying, yelling, and then threw things around my backyard.

Her eyes were fixed on mine through the window. She couldn't articulate what was wrong. It started when I forgot to call her after school. I was so used to coming home and taking a nap, I just forgot. Dating isn't just sex; you had to learn how to share everything, especially your time. I was woken up by her pounding on the back door. I knew I was in trouble and I detected bitterness in her voice when she asked, "Why didn't you call me?" *I had talked to her twice a day, everyday, since we hooked up, I forgot last night before I took a nap. Ronnie said I shouldn't act like I liked her too much. Maybe I should have listened? I didn't want her to break up with me.* The temperature outside had dropped suddenly. Fallen leaves swirled on the pavement behind her. The scene looked tranquil, but, I could see her anger building.

"Open this fucking door right now!" I clung stubbornly, refusing to detach myself from the blanket I was wrapped in. Where Pierre had his magic for money, I had magic for making my girlfriends crazy. Maggie's involuntary periods of screaming, crying and laughing were scaring me. I stepped out back.

"Why are you making me stand out in the cold?" she barked at me.

"You're freaking me out." I could feel a chasm opening between us. The sun was now hidden from view. A brisk air stung my ears.

She looked at me in dismay. No doubt she was wondering if she had made a mistake.

"Why are you being such an asshole?"

"I'm not trying to be." I said in a calm voice, but the more calm I was, the more agitated she became.

"You're just like every other guy! You're all nice until you get what you want and then you don't care!"

"That's not true, but I'm human and I make mistakes."

"If we hadn't had sex, you wouldn't have forgotten to call me!"

She was right, but that didn't mean I didn't like her. I liked her a lot.

Then suddenly, she rushed at me and I braced for the blows. When she bumped into me and stumbled, I took my chance. Grabbing Maggie by her shoulders, I pushed her back onto the patio and locked the door behind me. She looked possessed. Instead of calming down, she started pounding the glass doors with such force that her Swatch watch shattered, cutting her. It looked bad. She needed more than a bandage. She started to panic, but she wasn't going to hit me now so I opened the door and led her into the bathroom.

"This is all your fault!"

"I didn't tell you to bang on the door."

"You were being such an asshole I didn't know what to do!"

"I don't understand why you are so upset."

"Don't you know a thing about girls? You have a mother and a sister, for Christ sakes!"

And then it struck me. I had seen this before when Mother and Sister had been premenstrual. Why hadn't Maggie just said that? I would have just said yes to whatever she'd wanted. I took her wrist and washed it out. Blood kept pouring out. It didn't look good. I called Mother. When she showed up, she gave Maggie a warm and tender look, as if she understood what she was going through. Somehow I had become the enemy.

Mother wrapped up her bleeding wrist and escorted her to Georgetown Hospital's Emergency Room, which happened to be right around the corner. In the waiting room, Maggie was glum. Mother turned to her and uttered her golden advice, words she made sure Sister knew, too:

"No man is worth this. Not even my own son."

Later that day, I said to Mother in a sarcastic tone;

"Thanks for telling her to dump me."

She rebutted with, "I did you both a favor."

"She's crazy, what can I tell you," said Baxter when I called him. "She's in her room crying." The image of her crying didn't make me feel better. I was soon to discover that we would break up often around the time she became premenstrual, only to get back together the next week. By June I had become used to her mood swings.

On Monday a memo had been read before all the classes. "Any student who has an A average will be allowed to leave school a week early." I had made honor roll every semester since I had been there, so I was sure I was going to get the extra week. I double-checked with the principal and he said I could go. Maybe he felt a little guilty for asking me to take a piss test that time. That night I brought it up with Father and suggested that we take our family vacation that week. The family vacations happened once a year after many hours of negotiations between the two lawyer parents. It was agreed that they would split the trip between them; Father took the first half, then traded off to Mother. They split everything between Sister and me, including the vacations. Sister would be out by then, and since she had been accepted to Cornell, it was going to be her last summer before college, too.

"You need to stay at my house before the trip," said Father.

"Why? I've got my own car so what's the difference?"

"We have to go over a few things."

"Like what?" He was just trying to trick me into spending more time at his place.

"Directions, and how and where to pick up the keys if you arrive before me, and I need to give you a little spending cash."

The money sounded good. I needed cash to buy beer so later that night I drove over to Father's house.

I grabbed a pile of clean band t-shirts and threw them into the trunk, opened a can of Coke, and climbed into the driver's seat of the Oldsmobile. I drove over to Chevy Chase from Georgetown. It was past 3 am and Father was in a deep sleep. I watched a few talk shows on his old Sony TV and fell asleep dreaming of Maggie in a bikini.

The next morning, stepping out the door, I was enveloped in the humidity. Inside Father's house the air conditioning was on full blast and I needed a blanket just to watch TV. Outside I surrendered my senses to the heat and settled into a dull haze that would last for the duration of the summer. Before there were comforts such as air conditioning, Washington's elite retreated to the countryside each summer to avoid the swampy, sweltering air. By nightfall, I would be at the beach. On the table, Father left an envelope with $100 in it and directions on a legal pad. His handwriting was hard to read. The lines bounced outside of their intended path. If he had just slowed down, his hand wouldn't have been so shaky. At the top of the page it read, "Directions to beach house in Rehoboth Beach Delaware," and at the end it said, "Love Dad." Years later, I found out Father had Parkinson's disease and his shaky handwriting was the first sign.

We rented a house no more than a block or two from the beach and boardwalk. The richest families rented houses on the beach and there was status in being close to the rich. The Parents let us bring friends, knowing that they would keep us entertained. Sister had brought Nicole along with her. I asked Maggie. She said no. We were still fighting, or she was still fighting. I was waiting for her to get over it. Since Maggie wouldn't come, I brought Pierre and Ukala. Before heading down to Rehoboth Beach, I stopped off at Habib's on M Street. It was prearranged between Sister and me that I would be the one getting the beer. After all, I was carting Ukala along and his old age was good for something.

Taking Route 50, we passed farms and small towns. Pierre stretched out on the back seat with his shades on and his pork pie hat covering his face. Ukala opened his window and let the air hit his face, like a dog would. He smiled as the wind whipped his greasy hair.

"What are you going to do with your life?" I asked Ukala. I wanted to compare my options with his.

"Derrr, un, don't know." His demeanor and manner of speech were surprisingly gentle. I translated in my head as he spoke. "I like to cook. Maybe cooking school. Someday I could be a chef." He was the physical embodiment of my dyslexia and he didn't seem scared of the future, so why was I? Maybe that's why I needed him around. *If I went to art school how much writing would they expect? I mean most of my grades would be based on the art I made.* And I also didn't want to stay at home or get a job. If I got a job it would be like starting my adult life before I knew what I wanted to do. I glanced at Ukala and simultaneously pictured his future. *He might become a cook at a diner or some other small restaurant, but then what? Find a wife, have a kid, then the wife and kid leave him. He would grow to be an old man who did drugs and drank too much. That wasn't going to happen to me.* Ukala sat slouched in his seat, then turned from the open window to me. *I shouldn't judge him; he had always been kind to me.* I focused back on the road. The tolls and gas ate away at the last of my money until we pulled onto Rehoboth Avenue.

Arriving at the beach house before Father, we had enough time to find an appropriate hiding place for all the beer. At the foot of the closet in my room was the only hiding place I had ever used whenever I'd traveled. Sister joined the daisy chain while Nicole kept an eye on the traffic in anticipation of Father's arrival. The last case had just slipped through the doorway when Father pulled up in his Turbo Saab. I loved that car. Sometimes I would take it out for a spin, testing how fast I could go down Nebraska Avenue. It went from zero to a hundred miles per hour in under a minute.

Father had driven down from the city by himself that day. I helped him carry his bags into the beach house like a good son should. Once he was settled in, he took out his recorder and paced the living room. I brought beer and he brought Nixon.

"Hey man, your dad is talking to himself," said Pierre.

"It's how he prepares for a case. He rehearses speeches before a trial. The best is when you see him preparing for arguments; he plays both people in the conversation. It's totally fucking insane." I told him.

"You know, you do the same thing, but you chew your tongue when you do it," said Sister, scratching her nose. She wore a *No Nukes* shirt and had a variety of colored bands on her wrist that represented her various causes: AIDS awareness, Save the Whales, and Meat is Murder. Glancing at them I couldn't remember which was which.

"Bullshit."

"No, she's right," said Pierre. "You chew your tongue a lot."

Maybe I was insane like Father. Maybe I was going to be a workaholic.

Father worked nonstop and because of it, my parents had gotten a divorce. The work is what drove him nuts. Maybe I shouldn't go to college, I thought. It would just lead me to the same place he is now. A slave to a job. I respected Father. He was a good man. I knew he loved us, but he had also neglected us.

The next day he found the stack of warm beer. When we were out at the beach and on the boardwalk, he threw it all out, all ten cases. Stepping into the empty closet, I realized the tragedy. Without the beer, I was no longer on vacation but in family therapy instead. And it was a session that my friends were about to witness.

"I had to throw it out, I'm an officer of the court," said Father. "I represent the law and I swore an oath to uphold it. I'm not going to have underage drinking going on in the house while I'm here." He never yelled and didn't seem to be angry, just concerned.

"Are you fucking crazy!" I yelled. "That was my beer! We're at the beach, away from your job. It's the whole reason for being here! I'm turning twenty in August!" I threw my best tantrum. But it failed to provoke the response I was looking for, the return of the beer, and I settled into a silent treatment.

"I had to throw it out. The closet was too warm. The beer was going bad and would have made you sick. And you are nineteen. The drinking age is twenty-one," said Father on the third day.

If only he'd known about how many other times I had drunk warm beer that was sitting under my bed. I still said nothing.

"Someday you will understand that I am trying to protect you and that I love you very much," said Father, and I pretended not to hear him.

"He's such an asshole," I said, and as I said it, I knew it wasn't true, but it felt good anyway at the moment.

"You can get more beer when you get back," said Maggie over the phone. She was still angry at me for leading her to break her own watch on my back window.

"That's not the point."

"Don't you steal beer from his office?"

"Yeah. So what?"

"Well, then it's like you owe it to him, anyway."

"Can you put your brother on the phone?"

I could hear the receiver dropping to the floor and her walking away.

"Hello," said Baxter.

"She's still mad at me."

"She'll get over it."

"Are you coming down?"

"I'm not sure yet. I hear you have no beer."

Mid-week the shift changed. Mother was our new warden. Her first official act was to buy a few cases of beer. That was the difference between Mother and Father. He was a constant worrier and when he started to stress about something, he didn't have the ability to let it go. Mother, on the other hand, made it a point to walk away from her work when she vacationed. Even though she wasn't much for letting me drink, her rules were scaled down for our time at the beach.

I filled the refrigerator with cold Miller High Life, which was much better than the cases of warm Milwaukee's Best we'd had.

"Rich boy cries for Momma," Pierre teased me with a smile.

I dropped the brat act and there was peace in the beach house for that last few days.

Baxter's minivan pulled up in front of the beach house. Sister and Nicole packed the last of their bags into my car and I handed my keys to Sister.

"Did you tell the Parents that you're staying?" she said.

"No, could you do that for me?" I asked, looking over my shoulder.

"Yeah, but you'd better call them yourself at some point."

"Thanks," I said and waved bye to Nicole. It was strange seeing my car driven away without me in it. But Baxter always said it's safe in the minivan. Sliding open the back door of the minivan, I hopped in. Ukala had already taken shotgun and was grinning at me. Pierre was sleeping in the far back and couldn't be seen. It smelled of spilled beer.

"Where to?" I said and opened a beer, taking a long drink.

We drove up to the next town, five minutes away, Dewey Beach, and stayed with friends of Baxter from Georgetown Day School. Their beach week had just started. Beach week was different for each school. The beach weeks spread throughout the summer, so at any given time you might find dozens of schools represented on the coast from Delaware to Maryland. At the house, I made up for the beers Father had thrown out. After four days in a drunken haze, Baxter asked the date.

"June 17th," said a kid.

"Fuck man, it's my birthday," said Baxter.

"Dude, I graduate on the 17th." I said.

"I have to get back to D.C. My dad's taking me out to dinner tonight," announced Baxter.

"I can't miss graduation," I added.

Ukala and Pierre stayed at the beach house and would get a ride back with one of the GDS kids. We climbed into the minivan and Baxter sped back to D.C. The clouds ahead darkened and I wondered if God was sending me a message. *Don't graduate, stay nineteen and live at home forever.* The rain came down and when it let up, I saw a tornado in a cornfield nearby. As other drivers pulled over under bridges or slowed to a safe speed, Baxter sped up.

"Hand me a beer," he said. I did, even though it broke some of my rules about driving. I was still drunk from the night before and when I felt the buzz slipping away, I opened a beer too. A little over three hours later, I was drunk but close to the auditorium where my fellow classmates were lined up and waiting to be called. Baxter let me out and yelled his congratulations as I stumbled around the parking lot looking for a way in.

They had called the first few names and Paul was crossing the stage. The teacher stopped him and put his yellow tassel on the other side of his cap, handing him some paper rolled up and tied with a bow. I searched the audience and found his parents clapping. Next to them was Stephanie; she spotted me and waved. I waved back, swaying a little. She gave me a suspicious look; no doubt she knew I was drunk. She was in a formal dress and looked beautiful. I thought about what it would be like to make out with her. Then I felt guilty and looked back at the stage. Paul and the teacher shook hands and Paul made his way back to his seat, leaving a faint scent of marijuana in his wake. I thought of Dash. *He should be up there too. He should have been at the beach with me and standing next to me right now. Maybe if I had gone out with him that night I could have stopped him from shooting people with the paint gun and then he wouldn't have been in trouble and then no one would have had to kill him.* But in my heart I knew that it would have ended the same for him somehow.

One of the teachers found me in the wings of the stage and threw a gown over my head, slammed a square cap on top of my head and pushed me into my spot in line. Other students were ahead of me and I noticed they all had yellow tassels and that mine was blue.

"What the fuck?" I said to the teacher. "Why can't I have a yellow tassel?"

"Yours is supposed to be blue."

"What the hell did I do?"

The line moved and the teacher disappeared. I opened the can of beer I had in my pocket and drank it down. I tossed the empty can into the base of an artificial plant, then walked up onto the stage. I stopped in front of the principal and he handed me the roll of paper. Some flashing went off and the audience cheered. Father, Mother and Sister were clapping and I was surprised they were all there. Then the ceremony was over and our families milled about, talking, shaking hands and taking more photos.

"There's nothing on here," said Paul as he unrolled the paper.

"They give you the diploma later, dear," said his mother.

Stephanie made her way over and gave me a hug, working her way into me until her mouth was by my ear.

"Congratulations, you smell like beer." She felt warm and safe. Then she pushed off of me and went to Paul, standing by his side.

Sister made her way to me before the Parents. She had replaced her *No Nukes* shirt with *C.I.A. Get Out of South America*. Her moon was orbiting.

"You dumb ass. You were supposed to call the Parents. When you didn't, Father started freaking out. So I told him you'd called and that I'd talked to you. I said you knew about the graduation and that you were going to be here on time. But I had no clue if you were going to show up." She socked me in the arm. "And you didn't even shave." She sniffed the air around me. "Are you drunk?"

Mother walked up and Father was close behind her.

"Congratulations," she said, echoed by Father.

"Why did they give me a blue tassel?"

"Because you graduated valedictorian," said Father.

"What's that?"

"You graduated with the highest grades in the school," said Mother. "Lucky for you, you didn't have to give a speech. I know you don't like reading in front of people. We figured that's why you didn't call." Sister put her face in her hands and shook her head, her moon was spinning faster than ever.

Lars' Way

It was a Friday night at the beginning of the summer. Edgea and I walked through the crowd of kids at Fort Reno. I had found that the more scenesters I knew, the more status I had. Two girls were watching me. I didn't want them to get the impression I was dating Edgea, so I broke off from her and sat down by Lars. He was leaning over to one side, too drunk to keep upright. His mohawk sat dead on top of his head like a drowned rat laying spread eagle. Looking to me, Lars' eyes were yellow and red.

"Art school, huh? You be getting gay soon, man."

"Fuck you," I said back.

A rank odor drifted from Lars as he lifted one cheek off the ground and let loose a slow fart that picked up volume at its end.

"You fuck! God, how old are you?" I shook my head and leaned to the side, trying to escape his poison. That was Lars' way. Living a nightmare of a wasted life, Lars embodied everything our parents had warned us about, a misspent youth.

Edgea came limping over with her one big shoe.

"What's going on tonight?"

"Lars' place," I said. I thought I would punish him by bringing the party to his place, but he seemed complacent.

I stepped into Lars' apartment, a dingy little place near Chevy Chase Circle. There were no curtains, plants or any other such accouterment. In fact the place was rather barren, except for an ornate sofa covered in a French floral print. Lars walked across the room in his boxer shorts. His mohawk was slicked back, his faded tattoos speckled his body. He was filthy but he didn't seem to mind sitting on the white and blue print couch next to Edgea. Her legs were crossed, making her orthopedic boot rest on top of her thigh. Smoke circled Edgea as she puffed on weed, then held it out for me to take.

"No, thanks." They were testing the waters. Periodically they would offer me weed. I had always said no.

"What? You did acid when you guys went to the beach!" she said.

"That was once."

"What's the difference? You'll be gone soon and you might as well have fun this summer."

"I don't know if I'm going. I haven't made up my mind. What would college do for me?"

You're too uptight not to go," said Lars.

"What the hell does that mean?"

"You're a little uptight. Everyone knows that about you," she said.

"Fuck all you guys." Father was uptight, not me. She was still holding the joint. I took it and pulled a drag off and coughed it up right away.

"You got to hold it in, man," said Lars. I already knew that from Dash and wanted to tell him, but was coughing too hard. Lars handed me his beer. I drank it to cool down my throat and remembered why I didn't share my beers with Lars. It tasted like him and the thought made me a bit sick. Lars held the joint at me.

"Have another hit. It'll feel better." I took the joint and had another pull, but smaller this time. I coughed but it wasn't as bad.

Lars and Edgea stared at me. *What was I supposed to feel? The joint made another round. I thought I felt a bit high. What is high? Is it a little happy? A little numb? A little hungry?* I felt all of those, but I also felt less alive. *Why would you want to feel that way? Why were my friends so infatuated with it?*

I had once watched Lars, Edgea and Victor shoot up and the experience had left me cold. They didn't share needles and they took the time to set up everything, but it was still grotesque. Lars had recently started smoking crack. He was the example of the depths of lowliness that drugs and drink could take a person to. For all his punk rock talk, he was nothing more than a bum, who had survived on his charms. He was quick with a joke or a funny face to keep us laughing. He never offended beyond what was accepted. Offending the wrong kid in the scene would make him an outcast. He was in a constant state of performing for us, his audience.

The Parents hated Lars, especially Mother. She had banned Ronnie Motherfucking Collins from our house and Lars had been next on her list. Ronnie hadn't been a problem. He was always so doped-up he couldn't remember where my house was. Lars, on the other hand, couldn't forget where I lived and whenever he was in our neighborhood, he would stop by.

"A kid with a funny haircut stopped by looking for you. He said his name was Lars and he just wanted to say hi." Mother relayed the message with a look of concern, which meant I was going to be nagged endlessly about it.

"Thanks, Mom," I said, trying to make a quick exit.

"I think he's on drugs." she said with a hint of questioning in her voice.

No shit, I thought, but why single him out? All of my friends were on drugs. Maybe it was so obvious because of his big blood-shot eyes, glazed and yellow. Or maybe it was because of his breath, which stank of cheap booze. It could've been that he hadn't showered in days and was wearing an old beaten-up band t-shirt I had thrown out.

"I'm sure it wasn't drugs or anything. He just doesn't sleep much." I was attempting to put her mind at ease, but it never worked.

"Yeah, well tell him not to come around here anymore." Her eyes were serious and fixed on me. Mother was afraid I was going to end up like Lars from hanging around him, but hanging around him was exactly what made me want to stay away from drugs and work hard.

Lars' apartment was transformed into that weekend's headquarters and the center of our social intercourse. On Saturday night, Ukala was searching the fridge for a hidden beer.

"Comrren on man, drive me to the market," he said from behind the door. "There's no beer here."

"Ukala, later. We just got here," I told him.

"Come on, it will only take a few minutes."

"Stop being an asshole."

"Fuck you, I'm not an asshole."

"Then drive yourself."

He kept talking but I ignored him. Baxter played DJ and made the selection on the stereo. Pierre napped in a corner, arms crossing his chest as if he were laying in a coffin. His porkpie hat rested on top of his head, and covered his eyes. Since he didn't have a place to stay, he had to take naps whenever he could. Maggie was there but she was still ignoring me. I caught her sneaking a glance at me. I couldn't recall why we were fighting. When we had first started dating, Maggie had said, "I'm not into games." But now I realized when girls say they aren't into games, that doesn't mean anything. There were a dozen other kids. Absent were Paul and Stephanie. I figured they were spending private time together. We were all waiting for Charlie to show up and lead us to tonight's party. He was back from college. Edgea and Lars were reclined on the sofa again, puffing away at a joint as its fumes spiraled into the untainted open air. I smelled the faint toxic odor of chemicals. Edgea passed the joint to me.

"Is that boat?" I questioned.

"No," replied Lars.

"I don't want any Loveboat." That was too far.

"It's not Loveboat." Edgea had lost the last shreds of her virginity with drugs and felt it was her duty to help bring the rest of us into her world. Misery loves company.

"It smells like a lab." I knew I was agitating them.

"It's not boat!" the pair screamed simultaneously.

I took a hit. It tasted synthetic.

"This is boat," I stated, exhaling, and had a coughing attack.

"You smoked boat!" chimed Edgea.

I felt it lightly creep in and began deciphering its effect. I didn't have super-human strength or the ability to lose all inhibition. I didn't feel aggressive enough to want to take on ten cops. I thought about how Lars and Blitz had kicked in some guy's head when they had smoked some boat once. It tilted me minimally from the norm, but it was nothing dramatic. After all, I had just taken one pull.

"You smoked boat!" they sang together as they made their way to the door locked arm in arm. Charlie had just shown up with a caravan of party cars.

"Who smoked boat?" he said at the door. The apartment cleared of the dozen or so people and as I left, Lars cornered me on the front lawn. Puffing out his cheeks and opening his eyes wide, he dropped down on all fours and began crawling and barking, keeping me at bay, maneuvering to block my escape. I watched him, confused, until I became fed up and pushed him to one side, making a run for the car.

En route to that night's entertainment, Lars was pleased with himself.

"Man, you really thought I was a dog! I bugged you out! You were freaked!" This was far from true. But that was Lars' way.

Edgea sat on the other side of me. I looked over at her. The next day she was going to be sent away by her father to a summer school for bad kids. It was meant to be some form of punishment, but Edgea didn't seem to care. When it came to her father, it was all punishment. He had raped her mind and body and she just didn't care anymore. And her not caring allowed her to win the battles against him, since torture only works when you feel pain.

Edgea turned to me and I looked down at my boots and hers. The sole of her one shoe was three inches thick. I wondered how it would feel to walk in her shoes. I was glad I had the parents I did. That was the funny thing about the scene. Other kids with money complained about their parents non-stop. I knew I was lucky, even if I was ignored.

"Hey, at this school they aren't going to let me call or write, but next Tuesday they'll have some kind of fair where anyone can come. They won't be able to stop you. Will you make sure they come?" She gestured to the rest of the boys in the car.

"Yeah, no problem."

"Man, that will piss off my dad," she said. She told me the directions but since I knew I wouldn't remember, I made her tell them over again to Baxter.

It was Tuesday and Baxter was driving, but this time in Edgea's gray Hyundai instead of the minivan. She had left it in his care for the month she was in exile. We jetted along the back roads of Maryland as if on a roller coaster, riding the ups and downs of the streets. It might have been fun if I could have ignored the fact that Baxter was a maniac behind the wheel and we were not at an amusement park. No one was safe, but I said nothing. It wasn't his first time driving, or even the first time he'd driven drunk. But the combination of drink and one-lane country roads made me nervous. I was the only one with my head in my lap, eyes closed, praying we would make it. Everyone else was only worried about how many cans of beer were left. Breaking the speed limit wasn't going to get us there any faster though because we stopped every twenty minutes or so, and half the car filed out and lined themselves up along the side of the road to water the lawns of unsuspecting homeowners. Another twenty minutes would tick by, and the other half of the car was begging to stop. Everyone on board kept up with the drinking and Baxter was fed up with making frequent stops.

"I's gotta motherfucking piss. Pull this bitch over man," said Lars. Baxter refused to stop.

"Let me out of this mother! I gotta piss!" Lars yelled, wiggling his body through the open window.

Standing on top of the seat and leaning out of the passenger window, Lars undid his fly. Making no attempt to aim, his prick flopped in the rushing wind. From inside the car, his big ass completely obscured any view; his cheeks were lightly covered with curly black hair. It was a sight of horror. He sprayed the side of the road, the car itself and a road construction crew that didn't seem to appreciate the shower one bit, judging from the obscenities and their shaking fists as we passed. One guy even flung his hard hat at the car, but missed. That was Lars' way.

Edgea limped out to meet us. I wondered if her orthopedic shoe fit her right or if that was just another cruel deed by her father. The school was made up of a few buildings and dorms, nothing special. It reminded me of my old boarding school. In the center of the campus were amusement park booths and small rides. Kids ran about with painted faces and balloons bent into hats. I found a balloon hat lying on the ground and stepped on it. The kids from the school stood in small groups or by themselves, slowly stewing. The families were having fun and they were the ones the event was truly for.

"Walk this way," said Edgea and I almost copied her limp, like I had seen in a Pink Panther movie. She wouldn't have thought it was funny so I didn't. We passed an older man who gave us an agitated stare. I stuck my tongue out at him with a half smile. We walked behind one of the dorms. Lars pulled out a joint from his dirty pants. As I watched, he rolled it between his fingers to put it back into shape. I thought of him pissing and not washing his hands. They lit up. It passed from Lars to Edgea to Ukala and came to me, and I thought of the piss on everyone's hands.

"No, thanks." Baxter took a hit and we walked back out to the fun. The angry man was staring at us again.

"Who's that asshole?" I said to Edgea.

"Oh, that's my dad," she said and made a smug face in his direction just to make sure he knew that his plan had failed.

"Where would I stay if I went to New York?" I asked Mother the next day. It was late afternoon. I had just woken up and she had just gotten back from work. She had on a gray blazer and black slacks. I had on my boxer shorts and an old Minor Threat t-shirt with the sleeve torn from wrestling with Dash once. The sunlight pooled on the table in the kitchen. It reflected back and lit Mother from below.

"Well, you *are* going and SVA has two floors at the YMCA."

"YMCA?... How would I get all my stuff up there?"

"We will ship most of it. Then you would take a train up."

"I don't think I want to go to school."

"You're going," she said in a stern voice.

"You can't make me!"

"I can kick you out!" She was bluffing.

"Do you really think I couldn't find somewhere to stay in D.C? I don't need you!"

"I know you don't understand right now. But it's a fact that the more education you have, the better your quality of life."

"I don't think you understand how hard it is for me to do school work! It takes me five times longer than everyone else to read one page. When I'm reading, my eyes and brain hurt, it's physically exhausting! I don't even understand most of it! And now you want me to spend four more years doing it! You'll be wasting your money. It's torture. Why don't you cut off my legs and ask me to run a marathon? You always make me do so many things: skating, swimming, ballet, and whatever crazy class you and Dad dream up! Did you ever think for once that I'm just stupid? That everyone else is right? I'm a fucking retard!"

"No, you're not! And I don't want you ever to say that about yourself again! Why would you listen to people who don't know you? I think I know you better than you know yourself! I know you're smart. I never needed a test to tell me that. You can do anything you put your mind to. I'm sure if you want to write a book or become a lawyer or a doctor, you will be great. But I don't care if you're a doctor. I just want you to be happy and if that means I make you do something you don't like at the moment, I'll do it for your future. I'm not your friend, I'm your mother, and that's the way it is."

That night, I told Baxter about the YMCA and going to art school.

"That's so gay," he said. He told everyone else.

"Art school's for girls," Lars declared. We were at a party at Edgea's house. She had lasted only days at the summer school before they had kicked her out. Her parents were out of town. Her father told her she couldn't have friends over so of course she had decided to have a big party. The townhouse was nice. The kitchen was renovated and there was a small yard filled with plants and ivy creeping over the fence. All summer, Edgea had been stealing jewelry, watches, cash and credit cards at the parties she attended. When I asked her if she was scared people might steal from her she said, "Why? I locked my room. If there is something you want, take it."

"If you're not a homo yet, you'll be one after four years of sucking cock," said Paul.

"Don't worry," said Ukala in his own language. "There are a lot of cool gay guys. Look at Boy George."

To my friends, the YMCA meant the Village People and gay housing.

When I walked into the party, "YMCA" blared from the stereo speakers. Whoops and hollers followed. Baxter had bought the record just to torment me. For the rest of the summer, they would play that song every chance they got.

Charlie showed up with six cars of college friends. By the end of the night the house would be strewn with empty beer cans, pictures knocked off walls, spilled booze on rugs and sofas, a table tipped over, and Edgea's father's Rolex stolen. No doubt she took the watch and pawned it.

A few days later, I said to Mother, "Mom, I'm afraid I'm going to go to art school and come back gay." She was reading the New York Times in the living room on the second floor of her townhouse. The large windows framed the blue sky. I wished it was dark already.

"I'm not worried about that," she smiled.

"Why?"

"Because I walked past your room last night and you were busy entertaining a female friend of yours," she said.

My face flushed. I thought we were being quiet. I had been having sex with Maggie. Maggie had come over late. We hadn't been getting along but somehow we had ended up in bed. Mother went upstairs to her room. After the embarrassment faded, I felt better. Mother always knew what to say to me. No matter how bad I thought something was or even if I just felt panicky, she would put things in perspective.

The soda machine at my father's law firm that spit out free beer to minors was better than the wheel, the light bulb, or anything else ever invented.

Walking down to M Street, Baxter and I met up with Ukala on the way.

"What's the backpack for?" asked Ukala, sounding a little more coherent than usual.

"Hiking in Rock Creek Park."

It was my weekly pilgrimage (or should I say pillage) to the machine. We made our entrance into the firm's lobby, and nothing struck me as odd. But a nudge in the ribs by Baxter made me fully appreciate the situation. Edgea was seated behind the reception desk. No one else was there and she had taken the liberty of propping her giant boot on the desk. Her hair was a mix of brass and black roots. Her face was hidden under a thick layer of foundation. Her attire was still punk, if you noticed the safety pins in the gray blazer. She was smiling away at me. Usually we would yield to the rounds of howdy-dos, which were meant to pacify any inquisitive receptionists who might bar our way to the Temple of Free Beer. But there was no point anymore. Edgea wouldn't stop us or anyone else for that matter. With bags full, we scurried off to our secret place of worship. Taking a trail adjacent to the building, we ventured into Rock

Creek Park and descended a dirt slope that supported one of the sides of the M Street Bridge.

"So, Edgea works at your dad's office. I didn't know you got along like that," Baxter grinned. "If your dad needs any secretaries, I know some crack whores. They don't type so well, but they suck your dick for practically nothin'."

I was agitated. I felt like Lars and Edgea were going to take advantage of Father. *Should I call the cops?* But I didn't know if they'd done anything yet. *They must have used my name. Why hadn't Father asked me about her?* Maybe I was the one who's fucked up? She was my friend. But I wasn't going to let her steal from Father. I decided I would say something later.

"Blitz and Rev are back out on the scene," said Baxter. I didn't want to see them since they just reminded me of what happened to Dash.

"Yeah, Blitz beat the hell out of some kid," said Ukala wiping spit from his mouth.

We sat there for an hour or so; legs locked under our butts to keep ourselves from sliding down the dirt hill. They kept on teasing me and I kept worrying about Father.

Even though I was robbing Father's office of its beer, I was still protective of him. Edgea was not allowed into Mother's house. I knew she would steal from me. Mother was right to ban her. I could imagine the variety of ways she would pilfer the law firm: getting high on the liquid paper, stealing bags or any cash left out, going out on errands but returning empty handed or worse, letting Lars in to steal furniture, computers, or whatever else he could carry off.

"We got robbed!" she'd say and would employ every tactic in the book. There was no security and she'd rob Father's office blind. Worse than that, what if she chummed up with Father and started coming over on holidays with Lars?

Later that night at Father's house, I had a chat with him. Walking from room to room, I noticed nothing had changed since Mother had left except there was a layer of dust on everything. Even the chair backs had dust. I sat in one and tried not to lean back so it didn't get on my shirt. Father had to suspect that something was up since I never went over to his house but, then again, if it wasn't about Nixon he was clueless. The table in the living room was rickety. Glancing around the room, I realized he had the same Salvation Army sofa from when we were little kids. Piles of dirty laundry sat around the room. The only clothes he cared about were his suits and they were dry cleaned. How did he function without Mother? How did he eat? His life was owned by Nixon now.

"I know your receptionist."

"She seems very nice," said Father, always kind to a fault. Without a doubt, he was the nicest person I had ever known. Always the optimist, Father was blind to the ugliest qualities of mankind. I, on the other hand, noticed every detail and hated people because of it. Maybe I learned that from Ronnie Motherfucking Collins.

"She had a good recommendation?" I asked, not to be deterred.

"She must have. Why?" asked Father.

Edgea's recommendations were falsified, I was sure, a trick mastered by Pierre.

"I would double-check them if I were you," I said. I felt justified in ratting her out.

"I'm sure they checked all her recommendations," he said.

"Here's my recommendation. She's a thieving addict who will rob you and has a bum of a boyfriend. So I doubt she'll be making employee of the month," I told him as I crossed my arms tightly around my chest. I felt my face on the verge of turning red. In my family, we held things in until we couldn't any longer, and then blurted them out.

"I don't have anything to do with the hiring or firing practices at the firm," he said.

"If that's true then how did I get those summer jobs? Did they hire me 'cause my resume was so good?" The only other job I had ever had was working as an usher at a movie theater.

"That's different. You're my son." He ended the conversation by walking into the dining room where he was working on Nixon. Papers were spread across the dining room table so you could never use it to eat on.

A few days later they fired her.

The phone rang. It was Charlie.

"What are you up to tonight?" I already knew it would be a party or a show.

"I can't believe I was fired like that!" Edgea complained in the background on Charlie's end.

"Who's with you?"
"Lars and Edgea."
"You let them in your house?"
"Yeah."
I couldn't help but chuckle.
"What's so funny?" asked Charlie.
"Nothing. What's up?"
"You know Mike?"
"No."
"Well, he's a friend of Baxter's and mine. He's having a party and wants someone to work security. I thought maybe you, Lars, and your friends could do it." Charlie sounded older on the phone.
"Is he going to pay us?"
"Well.... no," said Charlie, "but you can have all the free beer you can drink.

The party was the typical "parents out of town" scenario, with a neat crowd that organized themselves into lines to take turns tapping the keg and pumping out suds into their cups. Lars couldn't wait his turn and simply walked up to the keg and butted in line to fill his plastic pint-sized cup.

I was wrestling with Charlie. I thought I had a tight hold on him until he lifted his giant head. Colliding with my jaw, he chipped my tooth, just a bit off the corner. That big head of his was like a hammer.

"That's what you get for horsing around," came Mother's voice floating through my subconscious. I was tonguing the spot where my pearly white used to have its top when Charlie started apologizing.

"Sorry about that, I'm always breaking things. When I was young, like three or maybe four, I broke my playpen, I don't think you should even keep a kid that old in one of those things, but my family is strange like that, I never chipped a tooth but I'm sure I will some day, I know a kid's father who is a dentist, I could ask him if he could ask his dad to fix it, it's small so it shouldn't be that much trouble... ." Charlie was running with his words, ready to roll them until he fell off the edge of the world, and then he would keep talking as he fell through space. I had to speak up and slam my words into his stream of run-on sentences.

"That's all right. It gives me character."

"I think Lars and Edgea stole some of my mother's things, do you think you could ask for them back? I think you're good at these things."

"When did that happen?"

"They stopped by my place when I was at school. They asked if I was there, then Edgea asked to use the bathroom. I think she stole the stuff when she was supposed to be in the bathroom, but I don't have any proof." Charlie's over-sized head tilted forward. "That's why I asked them over today. To see if they might steal again." His breath reeked.

"You're on your own with that one," I said and Charlie went on talking. There was chatter as the partygoers focused their attention towards the front of the house. Some kid came over and said something in Charlie's ear, then went to tell some other kids. I asked Charlie what was going on.

"Harly's here and Mike went out there to tell him to leave. Harly's probably going to kick Mike's ass."

"Who is Harly?"

"Harly is the son of the Episcopal Bishop of Washington. You met him once."

"I did?"

"Yeah, he was giving me a hard time at a party and you made him leave me alone."

"Is that why you had me come to this party?"

"Maybe."

"So why would he want to fight?"

As Charlie told me the legend of Harly, I gathered a full picture. He attended Saint Albans, an all-boys school affiliated with the National Cathedral, not your typical host for thugs. Harly attacked GDS students. The rumors amongst the GDS students made him out to be a barbarian, although I hadn't heard of him until that night. Charlie described him as "One bad dude." It sounded like trouble, so I went looking for Mike with Charlie was trotting alongside.

I was rounding the corner. The perfect green lawn sloped around to the garage..

"That's Harly," Charlie pointed at a black kid standing next to a car.

"Get Lars," I ordered and with that, I was off to confront the Great Harly, the terror of GDS.

Mike's house was at the dead end of the street. Harly and Mike were talking just a few yards from Harly's Volvo. I could see from their postures that Harly didn't care for what Mike was saying and that Mike was afraid. The rest of the party was filling up the front lawn and street.

"You gotta get out of here," I demanded of Harly, stepping between the two of them. Mike's shoulders drooped and he let out a long sigh of relief. Harly's flat top haircut alluded to football player status, as did the varsity jacket he wore smugly.

"Whatcha say, motherfucker?" he huffed. Puffing out his chest, he played the role of an angry black man and fell into a threatening posture. With a few slow strides, he closed the distance between us, standing inches from my face.

"I'm gonna fuck you up, motherfucker," he breathed. At that point, he expected me to back down, but when he failed to hit me, I knew he was afraid. I wasn't going to fall for his bullshit.

Harly just stood there, waiting for me to react. I later found out that he had had an upbringing that paralleled my own.

"Look, motherfucker, you're asking for a world of hurt, white boy," Harly barked, but his words bounced off the top of my head and straight into outer space, never to be heard again.

His act wasn't convincing. I grabbed him around the neck and slammed him down on the hood of his car. Two sets of eyes, framed by faces of soft milky white skin, pushed out from the darkness inside his car. For a moment, they peered out from behind the windshield at Harly and me. I was caught in their gaze. Harly even gave up the fight to see what I was looking at. Both sides of the glass watched each other for what might happen next, until one of the girls in the car started to scream. I tightened my grip, lifted Harly a few inches off the hood, only to slam him back down hard. Caught in my clutch, he went on.

"You best let go right now, motherfucker."

"You're not going anywhere," I said, watching over my shoulder for Lars.

"Motherfucker, you're fucking dead!"

"Just calm down," I told him. He was doing his best to break free from my firm grasp. Lars finally appeared at my side. Harly blurted out more threats. Lars held a short club, half the size of a standard billy club, and brought it to bear on Harly's head.

"I'm going to fuck you up, nigger!" Harly was yelling at Lars, or so I assumed. Thud!

"You better stop it, man!"

Lars struck him again.

He hit Harly a few times. Harly cried out, "Stop, stop, stop!" in between blows. The terror of GDS started to cry like a girl. I let go and took a step back. The entire party had encircled the Volvo. Fear of Harly was replaced by jeers and laughter, mostly from the boys.

"Please stop!" he pleaded, now groveling for mercy. I pulled Lars back and grabbed Harly by his shoulders, pushing him into the driver's seat. The two girls in the car were still screaming hysterically. I just wanted them all to shut up.

"Just get outta here. I can't keep them from getting you," I told him, as if I were his Lord and Protector.

The party had pushed in closer, riled up by the violence. Lars walked around to the front of the car, bashed in the headlight, and went to work on the windshield, sending a crack down the middle. He was handy with that small bat. Lars, furiously silent, opened the driver's door, snatched Harly out and threw him down. Harly lay on the ground, wiggling his limbs in an attempt to catch the slightest foothold. Lars undid his pants and whipped out his prick, showering Harly in a urine bath. The crowd began laughing, but not me. It was too much. I felt bad for Harly, embarrassed and ashamed that I had helped put him in that spot.

"Lars, I got this. Go back inside." I pushed him back into the crowd. "Harly, just go home. It's over. And don't kill anyone when you drive out of here," I said to him. I couldn't tell if he was listening to me, since he wouldn't look me in the eyes. The girls were still screaming in the car. Harly jumped into his seat and sped off.

A few days later, a buzz reached my tender eardrums. Harly was spreading the news, telling everyone Lars and I were dead. Or in his words, "I'm going to kill those motherfuckers!"

Harly and his company were at the Burger King in Dupont Circle when Lars made his way to where they sat. Lars later told me that he had made himself look crazy.

"I rubbed dirt on my face and some grease from a spot in the parking lot. If he grabbed me, he wouldn't have been able to keep a hold of me. I also held my little bat in my hand, but made sure only he could see it.

My mohawk was in my eyes. Then I said, so I heard you're going to shoot me."

"I don't know what you're talking about," Harly replied, without looking Lars in the eyes.

"Here's your chance. You got all your boys. Shoot me." Lars stared directly at him.

"I don't have a problem with you," Harly countered. And that's the way he left things with Lars.

I had little faith that the incident had improved my own situation with Harly. Since I had heard it from Lars, I didn't even know if it was true. "Better be watching out for this motherfucker," Ronnie's voice played in my head. "Motherfuckers be getting shot for nothing in this motherfucking city and it don't matter how tough a motherfucker is, a motherfucking bullet will end a motherfucker for sure." Another week went by.

Edgea picked me up on the way to a party. She wasn't allowed in my house, but she didn't mind driving and, if I was going to drink, I wouldn't drive.

"By the way, how did you get out of that boarding school so fast?" I asked her.

"I came on to all the teachers."

"And they threw you out for that?"

"No. They threw me out for sleeping with them."

"How many did you sleep with?"

"As many as I could. And when it got back to my dad, he was so embarrassed that he pulled me out of the school."

"And that's why they fired all the teachers."

She nodded. "I hate school. I'm not going next year. Besides, no school wants me."

"So you are just going to live with Lars?"

She nodded.

"What about money?"

"We don't need much. Maybe we'll move to San Francisco."

"Why there?"

"Its not too hot and never gets too cold. There are lots of people on the streets and I hear it's easy to get by." I pictured myself on the streets.

I didn't like it. I needed a clean, comfortable bed and a TV. Pierre was on his way to being homeless.

We drove up to Baxter's giant house.

"But don't tell Baxter, okay?" She was dating Lars but still had a thing for Baxter. Baxter had taken her to the emergency room after she had overdosed. Lars might have left her to die. She had wanted to die, but she also knew Baxter was the better man.

"I won't," I said as Baxter walked up to the car door.

We met up with Charlie, the party ambassador, and we followed his caravan of cars.

> *VILLAGE PEOPLE*
> *"Y.M.C.A."*
>> *Young man, there's a place you can go*
>> *I said, young man, when you're short on your dough*
>> *You can stay there, and I'm sure you will find*
>> *Many ways to have a good time.*

Baxter popped in a tape and hit play. "You've got to stay at the YMCA," squawked through the speakers. Laughter erupted from the back seat. Ukala and Pierre were back there. Pierre looked fit. His clothes were clean and pressed. His boots were shiny. It was like it was his first day in school and he wanted to impress.

"Very funny," I said.

"I'm thinking of moving to California," said Baxter.

"Why in the hell would you want to do that?" We finally had our gang back together, with the exception of Dash, who was never coming back.

"I'm not doing anything here."

I didn't want him to move to the other coast. I liked the idea of him being close to New York City.

We pulled up in front of a large house in Chevy Chase without knowing any of the vital information: What school? Saint Albans. What kind of crowd was it? Jocks who hated us. A half an hour into it, I came to the realization that it was Harly's party. Charlie, Ukala, Pierre and the rest of the guys had already gone on to another party. Only Baxter and Edgea stayed with me and neither of them were the pugilistic sort. The faces at the party weren't friendly; these were the same guys who started fights with punks every weekend. And there I was, with my bright spiky hair and black leather jacket with pyramid studs on the lapel. I might as well have been the poster boy for punk rock... "Come, kick my face in," my outfit screamed. I had no desire to be victimized by them.

"Hey Baxter, give me your pocketknife," I demanded, holding my hand out until he complied.

I examined the knife. It had a folding blade which was encrusted with rust. The handle was manufactured of cheap brown plastic, and had no safety lock. I would get cut for sure if I used it. Maybe even end up at the hospital for a tetanus shot for the rust. But if they ganged up on me, I wouldn't go easy on them. I decided I would stab as many as I could. I thought of Dash. I wasn't going to go easily. I would fight to live. After Dash had died, I had become more acutely aware of my surroundings. Who was behind me, who was staring at me, who wanted to hurt me? If I ate out, I had to have my back against the wall and my eye on the door. I wouldn't run. I would fight to survive. But I also wouldn't start a fight for no reason.

Edgea was chatting it up with a group of Harly's friends from the Southeast. Real thugs. These friends bolstered Harly's tough image. I understood the benefits of having thugs as friends; they watched out for you. The only problem was that they expected you to back them up in return. Harly was a rich kid from a good family who had all his choices laid out before him. A good high school, college, graduate school, and beyond that, a job of his choosing. But for now, he wanted the thug image. I was just like him.

Harly's friends surrounded Edgea and Baxter. It looked like trouble at first, but once I stepped closer, I realized the thugs were just enjoying the freak show. Fascinated, they stared at Edgea as she and Baxter sat on the back of her Hyundai, Edgea with her fluorescent green mohawk. Most kids from the roughest neighborhoods were afraid of punk rockers.

"You is crazy," one kid said, shaking his head. He meant it.

They thought punks had escaped from an asylum, certifiably insane, as if we ran around waving our arms uncontrollably, spitting, cursing and mumbling unintelligible things. Baxter was a curiosity, as well, but there was something else about Edgea. Even though she was a freak, a punk, crazy, with one boot too large and ugly, there was a raw sexual animalistic appeal to her. But sex with her would be like tying bacon around your privates, then trying to make it with a hungry pit bull. One of the thugs was homing in on her dangerous sex appeal. The rest stood there, bearing witness as he did his best to flirt with her.

"You is tight, baby," he said.

"I could stab you in the face," she said then laughed as if it were a joke, but she wasn't joking.

A few football players from Saint Albans, wearing their blue and white letterman's jackets, slid past us into the house. I could simply have retreated and avoided conflict, but in a city of such restricted dimensions, it was useless to avoid Harly. On this day, the odds were in his favor. If he had a problem with me, I'd know about it. My palms moistened with sweat and my heart started to race. I had found that when I was scared, the best way to defy fear was to rush headlong into it. If I were about to receive a beating, it would be that day. It was like I was at war with myself and I was getting ready to charge the front line. I plodded into the house, drifted in and out of its rooms, my eyes meeting other people's and scouring them for a trace of recognition. All fights began with that angry, fixed stare. Harly was sitting amongst his friends, most of whom were large and menacing, yet I faced him directly. His gaze fixed upon me for a split second. I thought the fight was on. But he blinked and passed over me without a hint of identification. He knew who I was. I knew he did. There weren't many punks in that city with bright orange hair. I accepted his silence as an answer and knew then that I wouldn't hear a peep from him. Perhaps he wasn't inclined to relive the moment of being treated like a human urinal. Regardless, he submitted entirely. In the world of the Criminal Minded, subtleties of negotiations can be as simple as a blank expression. There is no such thing as forgive and forget. To forgive would reveal weakness and to forget would expose stupidity. Blanking out on someone puts the incident in a nowhere land, in an open void.

Even though I knew there wasn't going to be a fight, I didn't want to change his mind by continuing to stand in the doorway staring at him. I turned and walked down the hall, looking at the variety of photos on the wall, touching each one as I passed, leaving them slightly crooked. Winding down the stairs, I passed through the kitchen and out the back door.

In the backyard, I pulled on the keg and gulped down a cupful in relief.

Lars' way wasn't going to become my way. I realized then that I wanted to go to school, not get caught in the middle of someone else's problem. I drank my beer and counted how many days I had left before I went to New York City.

Gone

I was thinking about what I needed to bring to New York when Baxter knocked at the back door.

"I want to show you something" he said and I followed him outside. "Check out my new car. I mean, it's new to me. It's actually used."

The car was a Ford and the body sat like a low rider. Records, guitar, clothes and the giant American flag that he had rescued from the garbage after his mother threw it out, were all in the trunk, weighing it down.

"What? You're going right now?"

"Yeah, man. I got to. This place is killing me," he said and I felt sad.

"Why didn't you tell me it was going to be today?"

"I knew it would stress you out. I just wanted to stop by and say goodbye."

"This sucks. Why don't you wait until the end of August, then we can both leave at the same time?"

"You can always come out and see me."

"Yeah, I guess so…. Where will you be?"

"Santa Cruz."

"Why Santa Cruz?" I asked, as I leaned against his car. Who was I going to hang out with now? Paul was still around. Fucking hell, I thought. I don't want to sit around watching him kiss a girl that should be kissing me. But then again, at least I would be hanging out with Stephanie. When something bad happened she was always the first person I wanted to talk to. I couldn't call her now that she was dating Paul. Baxter ran his hand over his head. His hair was cut short, somewhat like a skinhead. I squinted, reading his new clothing. He was dressed like a mod.

"I read this book on the American Scooter scene, you know, mods and skins. One of the chapters was on Santa Cruz, and it had this photo of a scooter club. They're all standing next to their scooters, dressed sharp. It looked cool. I decided I wanted to move there." Baxter forced the corners of his mouth to curl into a half smile.

"Which way are you going?" I asked.

"Over the Key Bridge. Why?" he answered.

"Give me a ride to Smash. It can be your last official act as a Washingtonian."

Baxter's car pulled out onto 35th Street.

Scientists say that it takes seven years for every cell in your body to regenerate. That means that every seven years, you become a completely new person. Watching Baxter, I wondered if he might change his mind and go back to school.

"Listen to this," said Baxter as he popped a tape in the player. It slowly built up, with a melody that I enjoyed. The vocals were familiar but I didn't remember having heard the band before.

"Who is this?"

"It's me," said Baxter. "I have been working on it for years. I want the vocals to be perfect, so these aren't the lyrics that I'll use in the end. It's just something I put down for now."

"I didn't know you were working on music."

"I haven't played this for anyone."

"You should do something with this."

"I will. I just want it to be good, and I can't get the words right."

Even with the windows rolled down, it was too hot. Baxter's forearms were covered with new matching dueling pistols in an ornate design, reminiscent of Spain. Cars passing us in the opposite direction were few, but to the ones that did pass, we must have looked like two freaks. Him with his tattoos and me with my now white spiked hair.

"We look like criminals, like the Criminal Minded," I said.

Baxter's eyebrows lifted. "What? That crap Ronnie used to talk about?"

"It wasn't crap."

"Yes, it was crap. He would paint this picture like there was honor among the thugs and wannabe criminals. Well, there wasn't. They were just criminals and nothing more. There was no honor. Ronnie didn't even follow his own rules, so how can you respect that?"

"It helped me."

"No, it didn't." Dragging on his cigarette, smoke curled in hard puffs from his nostrils. "Your father and mother made you who you are, and if anyone should be looking up to someone, it should have been Ronnie looking up to you. He was smart and wasted it, chasing a high. You have been given a hard time your whole life for being stupid and then you're the valedictorian. Ronnie had it easy. You have it harder, so you will have to work twice as hard." He stubbed out his still burning cigarette in the already filled ashtray.

"I thought the Criminal Minded would help me survive."

"You survive because you're smart, not because you follow a set of rules made up by a dead junkie." Baxter changed the tape.

T.S.O.L
"Code Blue"
I wanna fuck I wanna fuck the dead

The scene was out to see Ignition at one of the church benefit shows put on by the Dischords in Adams Morgan. Paul's head was oddly shaped and his eyes were too big for his face. Pale, he looked as if he had spent his whole life stuck to the bottom of someone's shoe. He was ugly by every standard, but instead of being ashamed, he took pride in his appearance, and worked hard to be as ugly as possible. He decorated himself with gruesome tattoos. His arms and legs had been covered since he had first started getting into being a skinhead. Paul was wearing overalls without a shirt, and his tattooed skin could be seen at the sides. Even when he didn't wear a shirt, it looked like he had one on. He was standing by a table with an assortment of petitions and flyers for shows. Paul had a smile that never seemed to leave his face, a mischievous look.

"They want me to sign a petition banning hunting. What a bunch of fucking hippies," he said and then signed his name as *Arnold Schwarzenegger*; but when he thought he had spelled it wrong, he scratched that out and wrote underneath The Fox. Fox was one of the first three-letter words we had had to learn at the Lab School. It was also one of those words that had tripped me up in kindergarten. It was one of those words that had led me down this path to this very spot, and it was one of those words that had reappeared on every test the city had given me. Words like "fox" caused me plenty of grief in my life. No doubt it had had the same effect on Paul. With Baxter in California, there was no one left to hang out with so I had called Paul and asked if he wanted to go to the show.

Stephanie came over and whispered something in Paul's ear and he went outside.

I felt Stephanie watching me. I turned to her.

"What?"

"Nothing," she said.

"Where did you send Paul?"

"I heard the ice cream man and I want a cone. Why, don't you like just hanging out with me?"

"I do. I just don't want to get myself in trouble."

That made her smile.

"And what do you think?" I asked.

"Of what?"

"The Dischords?"

"They're a bunch of rich kids pretending to be poor, even if they are talented," Stephanie answered, and then smiled at me, knowing I was one of the rich kids. I pictured her doing the splits on the floor of her back porch at three in the morning when we had been younger. What had happened? She used to have a crush on me; now things had flipped. I wanted to kiss her, but I knew she would punch me in the face. Paul was still watching us. This city is too small, I thought. It was like my friends were threads of the same tapestry that wrapped around me. Their stories interconnected with the city, my dyslexia, and my family. I wanted to get away from all of them. I wanted to be normal. But the only time I felt normal was around Stephanie.

Paul pulled her towards him, ending our conversation.

Stephanie had grown into her nose, which had a slight bump midway down, giving her a slightly Roman aesthetic. Had she always looked good? Or was it that I couldn't remember the hair she used to have on her upper lip? Her dress had changed from the iron-on t-shirt and jellies to a blue bomber jacket with an American flag on one arm and red ox-blood Doc Martens. She was shorter than me. I imagined leaning down to kiss her.

Paul gave Stephanie's arm a squeeze, signaling that we should go outside. We walked over to Paul's car, which was mangled and probably had been stolen.

Paul was crazy. He would do anything that would get him noticed in the scene. But most of the scene just avoided him. He would piss his pants at hardcore shows, then leap upon the backs of the unsuspecting. His victims must have assumed it was sweat, but then they went home with the tainted smell of urine. If a show was over-packed, Paul would head-walk, an activity akin to crowd surfing, with the exception of using heads as stepping-stones and running as far as he could before falling. For a night out, he prepared well in advance, feasting on beans, rice and ketchup. It was a meal made with the sole purpose of running through one's intestinal tract with the utmost expedience. He was infamous in the scene as a fecalphile and prankster. Stephanie would watch from the back of the club as people watch monkeys at the zoo, but he treated her with the kind of respect given to a goddess or a mother.

Paul went off to the bathroom. A few minutes passed and then he returned. A few minutes after that, two Dischord kids came from the bathroom and I overheard them.

"Someone shit all over the place. I mean they covered the seat, the floor, the walls and even part of the ceiling. How did they get it up on the ceiling?"

Paul grinned. No doubt his dyslexia had a lot to do with his behavior.

I had a week left before I was going to New York. Ukala's head was buried in the fridge downstairs at Mother's, looking for a beer, but it was packed with cans of Coca Cola and a jar of strawberry jelly.

"You should take some photos with you," said Maggie. She was there to help, but just sat on the floor looking a my photo albums. She pulled a picture of herself out then skipped over three pages of Stephanie and pulled a few out of Dash, Ukala and Charlie.

The wall behind her used to be covered with old band flyers. I had packed them and now they were sitting in a box near the back door. The box was marked "Punk stuff." Some of my favorite records were packed, too. I opened the closet to make sure I wasn't forgetting anything. On the floor sat the half wheel that I used for exercise when I was younger. I remembered how I had had to hold it off of the bridge of my nose and move the pegs around to improve my hand eye coordination. I picked it up and threw it into a pile that was going to the trash. In the trash were two paper guns Dash and I had made when we were kids. I had thought about keeping them but they had started falling apart. On a hanger back in the corner was a Slap Shot shirt I had picked up at the shows in Boston. I threw it onto the pile of shirts I would bring with me. On the shelf were some VHS tapes. I had a collection of videos that I had copied from rentals. I put on "One Flew Over The Cuckoos' Nest." McMurphy had just stolen a fishing boat and was heading out to sea with a few patients from his ward. I sat on my bed. Maggie and Ukala on either side of me. The door was open, and at first I didn't see Sister, who had come to tell me that someone was on the phone for me. She had on a white shirt with red lettering that said, *You Have Been Warned*. I kept my ringer turned off so no one could wake me. I had seen the movie many times and could leave without losing my place, so I picked up the phone in the corner near the backdoor. Stephanie's mother was on the line and before she spoke, I knew something wasn't right. She had never called me before.

"I'm sorry to bother you. I found your number in Stephanie's phone book. She had written a heart and *xoxoxox* next to your name." Her voice sounded weak. I had to press the receiver to my ear. "You're the first one I've called. I'm not sure how to put this." She spoke awkwardly, slowly. "Something has happened." Flat monotone, each word puncturing my eardrum and registering. "Late last night, Stephanie's aunt found her..." The hairs on the back of my arms jumping to attention. "Stephanie passed away last night."

"I don't understand." I had seen her a few days ago. As a matter of fact, she and Paul were supposed to show up soon to watch the movie. I had started it without them since I had known they were just coming to say goodbye to me. I looked out the backdoor to see if she was there. But the backyard was empty.

"They found her body late last night."

"I don't understand."

"She was driving to her aunt's house and something happened."

"What happened?"

"I don't know yet." I could hear talking in the background. "I'm sorry, I have to go."

"Does Paul know?"

"He's been out looking for her. I'm calling him next."

She hung up.

I stood there holding the phone. It was the same feeling as when I had been a kid, held under my arms over the pool of water and then dropped in, breaking the surface and sinking to the bottom.

"Are you okay?" asked Maggie.

Ukala was chuckling at Miss Ratchet.

I walked back to the bed and took my seat between them and said nothing, watching the video. It was like melting an ice cube on a hot skillet. The bottom melts right away but it takes a few moments before it reaches the top. The water pools, then quickly boils. I wanted to squeeze my own neck, cutting off pain, before my brain pooled and boiled like the ice cube.

The hardest thing to do is not to cry when your heart is saying you will. Like holding your breath, preventing a sneeze from escaping or a cough when you're choking. A sullen silence and then the tears that poured down my face gave me away.

"Are you okay?" Maggie asked again. I didn't answer. Ukala noticed and stepped out quietly. Maggie tried to stay, but when I finally said something, it was to ask her to leave. After Dash had died I had heard everyone say what they could to try and make me feel better, but when it happens to you, you quickly realize nothing they can say will take the pain away. The only thing that will make you feel better is time, but when it happens, time ticks by very slowly. I just wanted to sleep, turn off, disappear until the bad feeling went way. After Dash had died, I knew more of my friends would die. But not Stephanie. She was supposed to be there for me.

Stephanie had been driving from her mother's house to her aunt's house, a fifteen-mile journey. She'd never made it. A few hours had passed since her disappearance. Her mother and her aunt had made calls to the police department. Arlington detectives had considered her a runaway for the first twenty-four hours and hadn't looked for her. Stephanie's aunt had known something was wrong and hadn't been willing to wait until the next day. The aunt searched numerous times between her and her sister's house, until she had finally come across the abandoned car. Police had now started looking at Stephanie's disappearance as serious. The aunt obsessed, had traveled the back roads by car and foot. Late that night, she had found Stephanie's body.

I wouldn't hear the whole story for months. Her car had broken down. "Four white adult males had stopped to give her assistance," as described by an eyewitness driving past the car parked on the shoulder of the road. There had been no evidence of a struggle at her abandoned car. She had willingly left with them in their car and had been taken to a second location. At the second location there were drag marks. Two of them had dragged her out of the car. She had struggled, but there had been too many of them. They had gang raped and strangled her. They had concealed Stephanie's body under loose brush and debris.

I had two days left. I couldn't stop thinking of Stephanie. I needed to get away. The moon wasn't far enough. An American flag on the sleeve of a jacket, a middle eastern girl with a slight break in her nose, her old house and my old neighborhood and a thousand minute details reminded me of her. Even my sleep was stolen. If I did sleep I had recurring nightmares. When I awoke, I felt nothing but sadness and anger. Walking down M Street, I thought the fronts of the buildings looked like a movie set, fake and flimsy, lacking heart or substance. I had always thought that one day Stephanie and I would end up together, or at least be close friends.

Maggie tapped at my bedroom window, sometime after three in the afternoon. I pulled back the curtain next to my bed and glanced at her through the window and then I noticed that she resembled Stephanie. Maybe that was part of the attraction? Maybe I couldn't see it before when Stephanie was alive? Maggie knocked again. I got up just to stop the knocking. Half dead, I unlocked the door and crawled back under the sheets. Maggie opened the door and a blast of warm air rushed in. I kept Mother's basement very cold, liking the brisk breeze hitting my face as I lay under the warm sheets. The hotter and more humid outside, the more I liked being inside.

A caffeine junkie, she ran over to my bed and jumped on me, bouncing up and down. She was on a mission to cheer me up. I would miss her when I left. She was the only thing I really wanted to take with me.

"Wake up! Wake up!" she yelled.

"Let me sleep." There were dark circles under my eyes. My body ached.

There was another tapping at my window. It was Paul. Since Stephanie's death, I had not expected Paul to stop by. Perfect time for a ride, I thought. His driving like a maniac might make me forget, at least for a moment. I opened the door. Paul looked glum. He had a new tattoo. It stretched across the front of his neck, starting at the scar on the left side and ending on the right side. In thick black gothic lettering it said *Stephanie*. He looked insane. Maybe he was contemplating suicide and this was some kind of note? I let him inside. I didn't know what to say. Sorry just wouldn't cover it. So I stared at him without expression, hoping the words would come to me. His face drooped and his eyes were red and puffy, as if he had been crying for a long time.

"Come on, let's do this thing," he said.

"Sure, sure." I wanted things to be normal, but nothing was. I was becoming a stranger in the city where I had grown up. Stephanie's death had severed a part of my childhood and the happy memories of Glover Park and her back porch, crushes on girls that I would never kiss. No one would kiss her again.

Paul went outside to wait for us.

"I don't think we should go," said Maggie.

"I think right now he needs a friend. What would Stephanie want us to do?"

She couldn't argue with that. Maggie and I climbed into the back seat and found ourselves sitting on the gas tank. Paul hit the pedal hard and the car jumped forward. He started relating to me what had transpired the previous night, and the renovation of his car. Paul had parked in Georgetown on K Street, below the aqueduct, and it had been broken into. They had stolen an AM radio that hadn't worked. He didn't say so, but I pictured him sitting next to the back tire and crying. If there had been any other cars parked there, he would have bashed in their windows. If anybody else had been there, he would have killed them. If he had had the means, he would have killed himself. Instead, he had lit the inside of his car on fire and stood aside, watching it burn. When the flames had died out, he had gutted it with his bare hands and then drove home. There, he had blow-torched the top off, turning it into a car for the Devil. Paul gripped the steering wheel so tight that his knuckles looked like they might rip through his skin. The car sped along, obeying traffic rules that existed only in his mind. He sped up for stop signs, didn't seem to notice any red lights and only used the brakes to keep the automobile from rolling over and hitting scattered parked cars.

"Let me out of this fucking car right now, you fucking maniac!" screamed Maggie. Sensing any plea might foster more anger in Paul, I kept quiet. Suddenly, we hit a sand-filled construction barrier, which exploded over the street. The joyride ended abruptly as the car stalled and Maggie started screaming again. "Let me the fuck out of this car right now!"

I pushed Paul's seat forward, making him kiss the dashboard. He gave no resistance. I opened his door and let her out. I saw that it was my last chance as well and bolted. The car started, backed up, then drove on down the street, cutting across the corner and running over a trashcan before disappearing behind a building. Looking around, I realized it was K Street, the same intersection where I had first taken Maggie out and we had gotten hit by the car. It seemed like a long time ago, but it really wasn't. I didn't mention it. Maybe I should have. Maggie was in a bad mood. At the moment I really didn't care. I walked her back to her house and I went home.

A Bad Brains vinyl was on my record player. I placed the needle on the track and put the volume down low. I laid down on my bed. My boots were still on. I didn't bother getting under the covers since I hadn't slept in the days ever since Stephanie had died. I wanted to stop thinking. I did my best to follow the lyrics of the song; concentrating on anything else was a task. By the middle of the record, my eyes shut. I couldn't have kept them open if I had wanted. I drifted between sleep and listening to the music. Then I fell into a deep sleep, dreaming I was in Baxter's minivan. I heard Baxter's voice saying it's safe in the minivan. I was floating above the road looking down on it. The minivan was the needle and the road became green vinyl. The land began to rotate. Every record marked a chapter in my life, every girl linked to a song. Punk rock had saved my life, but it had killed my friends. Suddenly I was sitting in the backseat of the minivan. Dash was sitting next to me, Stephanie was in the front passenger seat just out of reach. No one was driving. There was no sound other than a soft static that you might hear at the end of a record and the occasional pop as the needle bounces over the last groove.

I knew Dash and Stephanie were dead, but it seemed normal. Dash's bright and beautiful eyes fell on me. Outside the window, I recognized the landscape of downtown D.C. We were driving to the 9:30 Club. He clutched under his arm the green vinyl S.O.A. 7" I had been searching for. He handed it over to me. I let the record slip out of its sleeve and into my hand. It was three times thicker than other 7"s. My eyes swept over the grooves. They were free of scratches. I knew it had never been played.

"You can keep it if you want," said Dash.

"I can't take your copy."

"I don't care, but if you take it your search will be over."

His words struck a chord. I took the record. It took me a moment to untangle the meaning of what he was saying. It wasn't really about the record. It was about the search. I pondered that for a while. What was I searching for?

ACKNOWLEDGEMENTS

One night, while I was working at the bar, a lady said, "You know if you wrote a book I could get it published." I had been writing a fanzine since 1988 and had been handing it out since then. She went on: "I mean, your writing is good, but you need to do something bigger than the fanzine. It can only bring you so far." I hadn't thought about a book until then. But what to write about? A dyslexic writing a book is like a blind man painting. At first I was afraid I'd be laughed at, but then I thought being laughed at might be just what I needed.

Cynthia Collins, Christine Holt, Mystie Chamberlin, Jennifer Liang, Caitlin, Un Lee, Colin Clarke, Mandy Rice, Marissa Bea, Charlotte Eerie, Ben P, Tanya Monroe, Judith McCaffrey, Jina Lee, Jessen Jurado, Margery Passett and others read my drafts back to me, fixing misspellings and grammatical errors. Imagine writing the details of losing your virginity, then having your mother reading them back to you over and over. Making this book wasn't easy and I couldn't do it without help. Thank you.

Additional support provided by Hyon Lee Troutman.

CREDITS

Grateful acknowledgement is made to the following for permission to reprint their lyrics:

"BUILDING", by Embrace, reprinted courtesy of Embrace and Dischord Records, Music Publisher.

"SCREAMING AT A WALL" by Minor Threat, reprinted courtesy of Minor Threat and Dischord Records, Music Publisher.

"CAN I SAY" by Dag Nasty, reprinted courtesy of Dag Nasty and Dischord Records, Music Publisher.

"SONIC REDUCER", written by Eugene Richard O'Connor and David Lynn Thomas, reprinted courtesy of Scion Three Music LLC and Larry Spier Music LLC, New York, NY.

"BACK ON THE MAP" by written by Jack Kelly, Jonathan Anastas, Steve Risteen and Mark McKay, reprinted courtesy of Jack Kelly, Jonathan Anastas, Steve Risteen and Mark McKay and Century Media Records, Music Publisher.

"ADD IT UP" Written by Gordon Gano © 1980, Gorno Music (ASCAP) Used with the permission of Gorno Music (administered by Alan N. Skiena, Esq.).

"ALL THIS AND MORE" reprinted courtesy of Larry Spier Music LLC, New York, NY.

"BURN NO BRIDGES" by Gray Matter, reprinted courtesy of Gray Matter and Dischord Records, Music Publisher.

"DRAW BLANK" by SOA, reprinted courtesy of SOA and Dischord Records, Music Publisher.

"GIRL PROBLEMS" by SOA, reprinted courtesy of SOA and Dischord Records, Music Publisher.

"WON'T BREATHE FOR YOU" by SWIZ, reprinted courtesy of SWIZ.

"WHO ARE YOU?" by Void, reprinted courtesy of Void and Dischord Records, Music Publisher.

"BABY" by Soul Side, reprinted courtesy of Soul Side, Bobby Sullivan and Dischord Records, Music Publisher.

"BREAK DOWN THE WALLS", written by Ray Cappo, reprinted courtesy of Ray Cappo.

"ONE SIDED" by Ignition, reprinted courtesy of Ignition and Dischord Records, Music Publisher.

"PATIENCE" by Rites of Spring, reprinted courtesy of Rites of Spring and Dischord Records, Music Publisher.

"TEENAGER IN A BOX" by John Stabb of Government Issue, reprinted courtesy of John Stabb, Government Issue and Dischord Records, Music Publisher.

"CRUCIFIED FOR YOUR SINS" by Iron Cross, reprinted courtesy of Iron Cross and Dischord Records, Music Publisher.

"1 DOWN 3 TO GO" by Tesco Vee of The Meatmen, reprinted courtesy of Tesco Vee and The Meatmen.

"HARD TIMES" by the Cro-Mags, reprinted courtesy of the Cro-Mags.

Lyric extract from the song: "WHERE ARE THEY NOW?" (words & music by Steve Bruce/Steve Burgess/Colin McFaull/Michael Beaufoy), reproduced by permission of Orange Songs Ltd.

CONCRETE JUNGLE (BYERS) © 1979 Plangent Visions Music, Inc./Plangent Visions Music Limited

"WAITING ROOM" by Fugazi, reprinted courtesy of Fugazi and Dischord Records, Music Publisher.

"HEY LITTLE RICH BOY" written by David R Parsons & James T Pursey. Published by Maxwood Music Limited. Used by kind permission.

"WAKE UP (socialism in E minor)" by Ted Riederer of The Reply, reprinted courtesy of Ted Riederer and The Reply.

"Y.M.C.A." written by H. Belolo, J. Morali and V. Willis ©1978 Can't Stop Music used by permission

"CODE BLUE" by written by Todd Barnes, Ronald Lewis Emory, Jack Loyd Grisham and Michael Paul Roche, reprinted courtesy of Todd Barnes, Ronald Lewis Emory, Jack Loyd Grisham and Michael Paul Roche and Bug Music and American Lesion Music, Music Publishers.

To learn more about Dischord Records and the Dischord bands featured in this book visit: http://www.dischord.com/

If you enjoyed Rich Boy Cries for Momma, Ethan H. Minsker's second book, Barstool Prophets, is available for purchase online in both paper back and e-book formats.

Barstool Prophets is not just the coming-of-age story of a young writer working in a bar in New York's East Village, but also the chronicle of an iconic neighborhood and its wild spectrum of characters. From a love-addled bartender to a suicidal doorman to the junkies in Tompkins Square Park, they are a family, of sorts. In many cases, this is only family some of them have, complete with all the joys and dysfunctions. The nameless narrator guides himself, the reader and, in some ways, the entire neighborhood through the highs and lows of the past and into the present.

In addition to his writing
Ethan H. Minsker has films now on DVD

AVAILABLE ONLINE